# BLACK
# OPS

# BLACK OPS

## THE LIFE OF A
## CIA SHADOW WARRIOR

### RIC
### PRADO

ST. MARTIN'S PRESS
NEW YORK

First published in the United States by St. Martin's Press, an imprint of St. Martin's Publishing Group

BLACK OPS. Copyright © 2022 by Enrique Prado. All rights reserved. Printed in the United States of America. For information, address St. Martin's Publishing Group, 120 Broadway, New York, NY 10271.

www.stmartins.com

Designed by Omar Chapa

All photos courtesy of author's private collection.

Library of Congress Cataloging-in-Publication Data

Names: Prado, Ric, author.
Title: Black ops : the life of a CIA shadow warrior / Ric Prado.
Description: First edition. | New York : St. Martin's Press, [2022] |
    Includes index.
Identifiers: LCCN 2021046532 | ISBN 9781250271846 (hardcover) |
    ISBN 9781250271853 (ebook)
Subjects: LCSH: Prado, Ric. | United States. Central Intelligence
    Agency—Officials and employees—Biography. | Refugees—Cuba—
    Biography. | Special operations (Military science)—United States. |
    War on Terrorism, 2001-2009—Personal narratives, American. | Cold
    War—Personal narratives, American.
Classification: LCC JK468.I6 A3 2022 | DDC 327.12730092 [B]—dc23/
    eng/20211026
LC record available at https://lccn.loc.gov/2021046532

Our books may be purchased in bulk for promotional, educational, or business use. Please contact your local bookseller or the Macmillan Corporate and Premium Sales Department at 1-800-221-7945, extension 5442, or by email at MacmillanSpecialMarkets@macmillan.com.

First Edition: 2022

10  9  8  7  6  5  4  3  2  1

I dedicate this book to my family, past and present.

From my Abuelo Emilin's constant example of stoic calm in times of tension, to my courageous mom and dad who put me on a plane, solo, to escape communism at the mature age of ten.

In the present, I would not have been successful in my vocation without the unwavering support of my loving wife, Carmen. In the same category, I enjoy the blessing of three wonderful "kids," all successful and contributing adults, and my beloved grandson, Christopher. I am also blessed with four wonderful godsons and goddaughters: Betty, Michael David, Vicky, and Marc.

My career was focused on making the world a better place to live for my family, for my God, and for my Country: the United States of America. Long may our flag wave.

# CONTENTS

# PREFACE

Until I began my own journey through the Agency, I had no idea what it took to protect the United States from dangerous forces and people bent on inflicting Americans harm. I was a street kid from Miami with a past, seeking adventure with a purpose and a way to strike back at the revolutionaries who stole my roots. I longed to wear "the white hat"!

My family had once lived in middle-class comfort in small-town Cuba. We owned a television and a beautiful 1957 Pontiac that was my father's pride and joy. Then the Castro revolution dumped our world upside down. We lost everything and everyone we loved in a bid to escape and have a chance to live in freedom once again. In desperation, my father got me out first, and I spent my first eight months in the U.S. in a Catholic orphanage in Pueblo, Colorado. America offered that freedom, but those first years in Florida were hardscrabble ones indeed. My father worked two jobs and dragged me with him to work on Saturdays. My mother labored away in a sweatshop making shirts. We lived in tiny, run-down apartments and learned to get by on a fraction of what we once enjoyed in pre-Castro Cuba.

We fought our way back to prosperity, chasing our version of the

American dream. The path was rocky, and more than once I strayed from it as a kid. I learned to fight, I learned to hustle. I also learned that loyalty is the greatest gift you can share or receive, while betrayal inflicts the brutal wounds to the heart.

The U.S. Air Force gave me purpose and discipline. I became a Pararescueman in 1972, just missing the tail end of the Vietnam War. My path to the Agency was as atypical as the rest of my life in America. Call it fate, call it God's will, when you find your calling, the tumblers in your heart click into place and suddenly the future makes sense. For me, that moment came as I walked past the Memorial Wall at Langley and realized the depth of my love and appreciation for America. Where else could a Cuban-born, once-orphaned boy go from Miami's back-alley brawls to the heart of the nation's first line of defense?

Those fledgling days in the Agency opened the door to a world I did not know existed. Sure, I avidly read Ian Fleming's James Bond books, but 007's spy universe bore no resemblance to the full-contact, dark world that became my life for the next few decades. Bond had his Goldfingers and Dr. Nos, but in the shadows we operated in, we faced no such cartoonish villains. Instead, we battled caudillos in communist guise, anarchist insurgencies, narco-terrorist groups, proliferators of weapons of mass destruction, traffickers of people, drugs, and illegal weapons.

I'd seen my family's life in Cuba destroyed by such people. Now, the Central Intelligence Agency gave me a chance to strike back at them. I started that new life in the jungles of northern Nicaragua, working closely with the Nicaraguan Contras—men and women vilified by the American press, yet who I knew to be true patriots wanting to liberate their country from the depredations of a carbon copy of Castro's regime. With them, I saw firsthand how the Sandinistas marauded through the Nicaraguan countryside, plundering from the already impoverished, inflicting starvation upon a long-suffering population. I saw how their vicious tactics drove desperate, traumatized people into the ranks of the Contras, where they were willing to live in the most primitive conditions imaginable, armed with ancient weapons cast off by the Israeli army. They faced every manner of jungle disease, privation, and sudden death. They did it with virtually no pay, armed only with the resolve that the Sandinista reign of terror had to be stopped if Nicaragua was to ever be free.

For three years, I helped fight the covert war against the communist Ortega regime. I emerged from the jungle, hardened to the realities of the dark world. I'd become a blunt instrument, at ease with a weapon in hand and a target to take out. That Cuban kid who lost his native country to revolutionaries now helped cut off some of the communist tentacles that threatened to engulf Latin America.

Ultimately, our Contra program was a definitively successful black op carried out solely by key personnel from the CIA.

But under legendary Bill Casey and Dewey Clarridge (the latter a beloved mentor of mine), this program grew a hundredfold, and our collective effort with the Contras resuscitated the post-Vietnam, decimated CIA back to relevance.

In 1984, the Agency ordered me from the Honduran jungles and sent me to the Farm to learn to be more than a paramilitary operator. I was trained on dead drops, running agents, conducting surveillance, and evading enemy tails. This was another new universe for me, one of finesse in the shadows of everyday life. It stood in stark contrast to the years I spent being at the pointy end of the spear. Yet it was a new way of standing on our nation's ramparts that appealed to me. The men and women I met at the Farm were not the Jason Bournes and Ethan Hunts of the silver screen. They were men and women devoted to one cause: keeping our country and our people safe from those who intend to do us harm. Sometimes we succeeded, sometimes we failed, but that was always our mission, our calling. Our life's purpose. The same courage, conviction, and guile that it took to operate in the jungles applied to how my colleagues and I operated in a much more complex and more traitorous jungle. A jungle of criminality, corruption, betrayals, and atrocious human rights abuses we were determined to help eradicate.

In the back alleys of the world, I saw how we fought back against these forces, and how sometimes our own sense of right and wrong undermined our ability to stop a foe that behaved with absolutely no scruples or humanity.

From the point of the spear to the velvet fist of the shadow world, my career took me through a full spectrum of how the Agency defends America. When the wall fell, I joined the counterterrorism fight. Like for most of us, 9/11 was a life-changing event for me. I owned the best job in the CIA at the time—Chief of Operations with the Counterterrorist Center. But the truth is, that role behind the front lines in the fight against al-Qaeda wasn't my course. Every time I've strayed from the path set forth for me, I've felt an unease that resonates through my spirit. In this dark hour of our nation's history, I knew headquarters was not the place for me.

From Bill Casey's "man in the Contra camps," to plank owner of the Bin Laden task force, to SIS-2 as Chief of the Koreas in 1998, to Chief of Operations at the CIA's Counterterrorist Center (CTC) on September 11, 2001, I found myself always in the right place at the right time. Always unplanned, always by fate. I followed where it took me and learned vital lessons on each point of this journey.

There is a war that goes on in broad daylight, in the everyday streets of cities around the world. It has its own rules, its own foot soldiers and leaders, and it is invisible to those simply wanting to live their lives in peace. Like a universal police officer walking a global beat of international crime and intrigue, you'll never look at everyday American life the same. You'll see that danger lurks from seemingly innocuous sources. You'll find Hezbollah sleeper cells in your own town, North Korean agents sneaking across our borders. Terrorists lurking and lying in wait. It is a thankless, anonymous task stopping these forces, but my colleagues do so not for accolades and fame; they seek only to preserve the lives of strangers in the nation they love.

It is for them that I write this book. This is the story of the men and women I worked with who dared to go through a dark, ominous portal, to see the clandestine world others cannot. They are warriors whose courage and selfless devotion have been ignored or disparaged by our own media for decades. All too often, the Agency is painted as evil, rogue, filled with crazed drug-smuggling killers or "enhanced" super-killers like Jason Bourne. The reality could not be more different from these portrayals.

Imagine an American family sitting around a dinner table, and a young son or daughter announces they want to join the FBI when they grow up. What's the immediate response? Pride, excitement? That child seeks purpose, wants to be a protector.

Now, what would be the typical first reaction if that kid said they want to join the CIA when they grow up? After all the decades of Hollywood portrayals, my guess is the average American parent would be appalled and might even drag their child to therapy to make sure they hadn't raised a sociopath.

This book is my attempt to correct the misperceptions that make the Agency one of the least understood and most mistrusted institutions in America today. The reality we faced on the ground in places from Muslim Africa to East Asia, to our own streets here at home, is one of persistent threats that must be countered to keep our people safe. Those who shoulder this responsibility are rugged, intelligent, capable. They understand the stakes. They understand that if they miss one crucial piece of the intel puzzle, our folks at home in our cities and suburbs will experience tragedy.

To this day, I pinch myself as I review my life, amazed at how many wonderful people were placed in my path to help correct my weaknesses and nurture my strengths. My pops, a simple carpenter with the heart of a lion who risked all to ensure I would live in freedom. My first sensei, Jim Alfano, a tough Marine and Vietnam Vet who immersed me in the martial arts. Or Pararescue legend Chief Master Sergeant Wayne Fisk, who befriended me as a young and raw PJ student. CIA legend and mentor Dewey Clarridge, who introduced me to our greatest DCI, Bill Casey. Last, but not least, legendary Special Forces Sergeant Major Billy Waugh, who till this day is a role model. Few men can count on this kind of backup in life's firefight.

The path set before me in the late 1970s opened the door to a world few see and even fewer know exists. It gave me a compass and course that tempered my vain adventurism into a life of dedicated service to a higher cause.

The words penned in the following pages are my way of passing the torch to our next generation, to show the mettle of the Agency and the quality people who are drawn to it. They are, as Paulo Coelho calls them, the Warriors of Light. It is time America knows of these protectors. So come with me, the portal's open. The shadow world awaits.

# PART I

# 1

## CUBAN SUNSET

*Manicaragua, Cuba*
*1958*

I was about seven years old when I experienced my first firefight.

It started like any average weekend evening in our little Cuban mountainside town. My parents had dressed to go out to the nearby city of Santa Clara, leaving me in the care of Crucita, my sixteen-year-old nanny. My mom hugged me, then my dad ushered her into our family's pride and joy, a factory-fresh 1957 Pontiac two-door hardtop. The year before, my dad paid $2,500 to bring it home. Kenya ivory with a beautiful two-tone interior, it was a symbol of our rising station in Manicaragua.

My dad loved cars almost as much as he loved horses, and he never missed an opportunity to take us someplace in our new ride. I'd climb up on the package tray under the rear window and stare at the passing trees whose branches formed a tangled green arch over the main road in our province as my father told stories from his rough-and-tumble youth.

I watched its taillights disappear into the night as they drove away, wishing I could go with them.

It was a warm weekend evening. A fan pushed air around in our living room while Crucita and I sat watching television on our thirteen-inch, black-and-white screen. Our semi-paved street was quiet and filled with family, a small enclave of the extended Prado clan and our businesses.

Our little green-and-blue brick house was actually a duplex. My dad's sister lived next door. Across the street stood my paternal grandfather's gas station and garage with his cigar-rolling business in an outbuilding. My dad's coffee company was located next door to us. Each morning, my parents would jump next door and open for business. Dad ran the enterprise, while my mom served as the bookkeeper and head of sales.

We were a tight-knit family in a community of tight-knit families. Nestled in this middle-class capitalist home that my mother so lovingly decorated, I always felt a sense of peace and security.

To be honest, this often wore on me. My dad had been a wild one in his youth, and I shared his DNA. My mother tried to temper that streak with rules and order, structure and polish. I was her only child, delivered after a difficult birth that ensured she could have no more babies after me. This made her overprotective at times, something my dad saw and balanced out with man-to-man talks and trips into the local Escambray Mountains to visit coffee plantations in his business's World War II–surplus U.S. Army jeep.

Being seven, I had no idea that Cuba was in the throes of a revolution. Sure, we'd heard stories of occasional raids outside of town, and the mountains were supposedly rife with guerillas living in the jungle. Here in Manicaragua, such things seemed remote—the stuff of school-yard legends that filled us with excitement.

As Crucita and I watched the evening television shows, a sudden commotion broke out in our street. I craned my neck to look out our front windows. I saw the three-foot-high brick wall that abutted our front porch, but nothing else in the darkness beyond.

Suddenly, gunshots echoed through the neighborhood. A few stray ones at first, then a swelling rash as automatic weapons joined the fight.

We sat, rooted in place by our TV, listening to the cacophony as muzzle flashes strobed in the street beyond and cast crazy shadows through the living room.

I jumped up, eager to see what was going on, oblivious to the danger, and rushed to the front windows. They moved with the use of a hand crank. I grabbed the handle and started spinning it in circles. Window open, I peered out into the night.

Right below my nose, a guerrilla, dressed in ragged green camo, lay prone on our porch. Just as I noticed him, he rose to a knee and triggered a full burst from his assault rifle at a nearby bar frequented by police and soldiers. The din was deafening, terrifying. Enthralling. I was engulfed by the moment, staring raptly at the fighter below me. His weapon to his shoulder, he pulled the trigger and sent another stream of automatic weapons fire downrange. Spent shell casings flew from his receiver to ricochet off our front windows with a sharp *tink-tink-tink*—a sound that is tattooed in the back of my brain even today some sixty years later.

I probably would have just remained transfixed in the window frame, but my panic-stricken nanny suddenly grabbed me from behind and yanked me away to the back of the living room.

*Tink-tink-tink.* More shells hit the glass as the revolutionary drained his magazine.

We listened, huddled together in nervous excitement as the bullets flew. Then, like an ebb tide, the sounds of battle grew distant until a few last angry shots echoed through the neighborhood. As quickly as it started, it was over. Silence filled the night.

Like wraiths, the guerrillas melted back into the countryside and escaped to their jungle refuge in the Escambray Mountains. For all the excitement and shooting, nobody was hurt. I was too young to know the difference between an assault and a hit-and-run raid, but this was certainly the latter.

I would learn what a full assault looked like later.

This may have been my first firefight, but I'd been around guns most of my young life. My dad, being a successful small businessman, often received threats. At the behest of his Masonic lodge brothers, he purchased a World War II–era German Luger pistol. To introduce me to firearms, he purchased a Daisy BB rifle and taught me how to shoot with it. He would sometimes practice with the BB gun by setting up a sawhorse behind the house, laying Coke bottles on their sides, then shooting right through their mouths to blow out their bottoms. It was a feat of marksmanship I could never match, but that was my dad. He was our protector.

Resourceful, rugged, and highly intelligent, his many wild barroom brawls in his youth before he met my mom transformed him into a man who was calm and fearless in a fight. After he fell in love, he channeled that energy into building a life for his family. He was a great businessman, an artisan who could work equally well with his hands, and even in middle age, standing all of five foot six, he was hard as oak. I wanted to be just like him.

When my parents came home that night of the firefight, I'd sworn to Crucita that I would say nothing of what had happened. She feared losing her job for letting me go to the window, though my folks would never have fired her for that. They knew I was always drawn to adventure. But a promise was a promise, and I didn't mention the firefight until a half century later. By then, I'd been in so many tighter spots that this one only stood out for being the first.

That night represented a turning point for us average Cubans. It was the moment that things began to change for us. An ideological war raged, pitting Castro's Marxist revolutionaries against Batista's government forces. Castro's men now gained the upper hand as the Batista regime began to collapse under the weight of its own corruption.

Our quiet days of horseback riding, church on Sundays, and school during the week look idyllic in retrospect, and the photos I have from that time show a happy, middle-class Cuban family built around the love my parents shared. We didn't realize that these were the last days of a dying era. Those determined guerrillas loyal to Castro would soon usher in a new one at bayonet point.

It was in this turbulent time that I learned my first lesson in counterintelligence tradecraft, though at the time I had no idea what it was called.

One night a few months after that first firefight, a cousin of my father's slipped into town unnoticed. Manuel was one of Castro's fighters, but he was also loyal to his family and knew my dad was apolitical. Sometime after midnight, Manuel's knock at our door roused the entire family. We let him in, and we gathered around our table to hear what he had to say. I sat next to him. Suddenly, he unslung his Thompson submachine gun and lowered it onto my lap. It was heavy—ten pounds—with a wood stock and a U.S.-military issue magazine. As he spoke, I clutched the weapon with both hands, feeling its weight, intuiting its power. It sent a surge of excitement through me like an electrical current. That moment, I knew that whatever my path would be, weapons like this one would be part of it.

As I stared at the tommy gun in my lap, I heard Manuel's warning to my parents. He revealed that Castro's revolutionaries planned to assault and capture our town in the next few days.

The adults debated what to do. My dad was well known in town. The police and soldiers were everywhere. If he fled the area with his whole family, the authorities would take notice and there probably would be retaliation. Worse, the revolutionaries knew their family connection. If my parents fled, he would be suspected of tipping them off, and *everyone* would get hurt.

"At least get your son out," Manuel said.

My parents discussed this. I'd been going to school about thirty kilometers away in Santa Clara, staying with my godmother during the weeks, coming home on the weekends. My departure would arouse no suspicions, and I would be safe.

It was decided I would leave immediately with Abuelo Emilin, my grandfather. Manuel retrieved his Thompson and disappeared into the darkness to return to his camp. At first light, my parents called a cab. The driver arrived, and my grandfather and I climbed in back wondering if we would ever see my parents again. A quick goodbye, and the cabbie whisked us away, across a bridge over a deep ravine with a rock-chocked river snaking through it. A moment later, we were in the countryside, bound for the illusion of safety in Santa Clara.

Manuel's intel tip served my family well. In my absence, my father prepared the house for war. He lugged sacks of coffee from his company and used them like sandbags to transform our bathroom into a bomb shelter. All the while, he had to pretend he did not know our town's impending fate.

The revolutionaries attacked soon after, sweeping through Manicaragua and driving the government forces back in disarray. They fled across the bridge over the ravine to reassemble outside of town and prepare a counterattack.

My family emerged unscathed from that short, sharp fight, but soon the uprising threatened to engulf Santa Clara as well. My father called my grandfather and told him to come home as soon as possible.

Once again, we tried to escape the war. We drove back toward Manicaragua until our cab reached the bridge over the ravine, where we discovered the guerrillas had pulled up its planks as a defense against the coming government offensive.

The cabbie told us to get out. We dismounted and watched him head back down the road for Santa Clara. That day, there seemed to be no safe places.

Except with my grandfather. Born in 1900, he was a baby at the start of the Cuban rebellion against Spain. One night, rebels broke into his family's home and stole a mattress—with him still swaddled in it. Fortunately, the rebels returned him to his parents unharmed. He grew up hard and proud. Like my dad, he was stoic, unflappable, and wise.

He looked down at me with lapis-colored eyes that seemed almost fluorescent and asked me, man to man, "We will have to cross the bridge. You afraid?"

I looked down the steep ravine, saw the water swirling through rocky rapids. A fall from the bridge would surely be fatal.

"No, Abuelo."

"Good. Come, then."

He grabbed my right wrist and held it firmly as we eased out onto the skeletonized bridge. We inched along a narrow beam; I had a death grip on the railing with my free hand looking down at the jagged rocks and foaming current. We made it across, and instead of fear, I felt a sense of exultation. For as dangerous as this situation was for us both, it was the type of adventure I craved despite my mother's best efforts to temper that impulse.

We walked home to find rebels sitting on our front porch wall, drinking coffee our young maid was serving them. They were a motley bunch with sweat-stained shirts, red bandannas, and shaggy beards. They smoked home-rolled cigars. A few of these Marxists toyed with rosary beads. So holy.

We had not been home long when the army's counterattack began with several air strikes. My dad hustled all of us into our makeshift coffee bag shelter in the bathroom, where we listened to the buzzing planes passing by overhead. Distant thumps and machine-gun fire punctuated the moment. We clutched each other and prayed for better days.

The army's counterattack failed. Castro's ragtag force held the government soldiers at bay, then continued their own advance. In a swift, sharp fight, they captured Santa Clara. The tide was turning against Batista.

My parents and grandfather agonized over what to do to keep us safe. I remember lying on my parents' bed, staring at a painting of Jesus on their wall as I listened to them puzzle through this impossible situation.

"That man, Castro. He will be the ruin of our country!" my grandfather said.

"Aw, Dad, how can you say that?" my mom asked. We had family who supported Castro, fought with him. My godmother's husband was a committed Marxist. Castro was supposed to be our nation's salvation from the corruption of the Batista regime. We were all in for a terrible surprise.

My grandfather was right. Instead of our salvation, Castro was our destruction.

Within days, the purges began. Anyone associated with the Batista regime was persecuted, jailed, and some even hanged from nearby trees.

# 2

## THE SILVER SPURS

*Cuba*

*1959–1962*

A few days after I returned home, revolutionary forces led by Che Guevara launched a three-pronged assault on Santa Clara. The fighting engulfed my godmother's city, and on New Year's Eve 1958, Batista's troops broke and ran. That was the final nail for the Batista regime, and the dictator fled the country for the Dominican Republic a few hours later on January 1, 1959.

The revolution, dubbed the 26th of July Movement, swept Castro into power, and overnight, life changed for my family. In Santa Clara, the effects of the recent battle were evident everywhere, including in my godmother's small duplex. During the fighting, one of Batista's World War II–era American-made M3 Stuart light tanks put a 37mm armor-piercing round right through their living room and demolished their couch.

Fortunately, nobody was hurt. I remember my cousin showing me the solid, unexploded round, which he'd found in the living room and kept as a souvenir. It was bigger than my hand.

If the aftermath of the revolution was evident in the streets, the new way of life for us kids began at school. We were ordered to join the Cuban Revolutionary Youth, dubbed the "Castro Youth." It was loosely based on the organization of the Boy Scouts, but instead of learning to camp, the Castro Youth tried to mold us into compliant Marxist ideologues. We wore our uniforms every day—shorts and white shirts with a neckerchief whose color denoted what level you were in the organization. We were sent out into the countryside to be foot soldiers in Castro's new literacy program. At age eight, I was expected to teach hardscrabble peasant farmers how to read. That was my first direct contact with the absurdity of the new Marxist regime.

In school, our teachers told us to watch each other and our families. If we heard anyone saying anything against Castro, we were to report it at once. The new regime weaponized us against our own families in perfect *1984*-esque fashion. Around town, every block had a designated official who recorded his neighbors' movements. Ears were always open, listening to the slightest critique of Castro, his revolution, or of Marxism in general. Once reported, those people vanished, taken in the night by the storm troopers of the 26th of July Movement.

As Marxist indoctrination soon dominated every aspect of our lives in school, life back home in Manicaragua became a growing nightmare for the middle class. A lot of people in town had always been jealous of my family's success. We'd endured threats before, but this seemed different. Various revolutionary committees were formed, led by some of the true dregs in our city. Now that they had achieved a level of power they hadn't had under a capitalist system, they took revenge on those more successful.

It didn't take long for some of the local guerrillas who had fought loyally with Castro to see this would soon spin out of control. They broke with the revolution and headed back up into the Escambray Mountains to carry on a new struggle against their former leader. Castro's loyalists showed no mercy to these "traitors," who were hunted down and killed over the next four years.

While new skirmishes raged outside of town, my father found it increasingly difficult to run his business under the new regime. In June of 1959, one of the newly appointed committees showed up at our family's business and declared it "confiscated in the name of the people." My mother tried to go back in and get her sweater, which was draped over her office chair, but the committee stopped her, declaring that even the sweater was now property of the state.

Across the street, they came for my grandfather's cigar-rolling business and his gas station. Overnight, we went from prosperous and hardworking to a family officially robbed by the new regime. The committee "generously" asked my father to manage the people's coffee roasting concern, but he refused. Though he was apolitical and had never expressed his views on Castro, after his livelihood had been stolen, he was far too proud a man to run it for these thieves.

About the same time, my godmother's husband sat my father down to give him a warning. Though he was a professor and lifelong Marxist himself, he could see the devastation the revolution was having on us and wanted to help. The news he conveyed was not good. My school in Santa Clara had been tasked with selecting several of its most promising students to be sent to the Soviet Union for further education. My name was on that list. This would not be optional; the government would simply put me on a plane to the Soviet Union, whether my parents agreed or not.

I was about to be torn from my parents to be brainwashed in a foreign land so I could someday become part of the revolutionary vanguard itself.

In the years since, I've often wondered what would have happened to me if we had not received that tip. Would I have ended up a Marxist, too? Would I have joined an intelligence service like Cuba's version of the KGB, the 02? I'd like to think not, but the indoctrination those children were subjected to in the Soviet Union transformed most of them into apostles of the revolutionary Marxism who later held positions of importance in the regime.

Losing his business was bad enough. My father was not about to lose his only son to the state as well. He pulled me out of school at once and returned me home to Manicaragua, where the tension ran high. At night, my parents would whisper to each other, planning and working through what to do. Already, the coffee business was being run into the ground by the revolutionary committee. They asked my father to come back and manage it again. He refused. It went out of business not long after.

The family limped through the next year in our home, watching conditions deteriorate. In April 1961, CIA-backed counterrevolutionaries landed on the Bay of Pigs, adjacent to La Planchita, one of the beaches my family used to vacation at in better times. I remember it being a place of great memories for my family, where the seafloor was carpeted with blue crabs and my dad would take me shrimping. Now, as the anti-Castro forces landed and tried to push ashore, revolutionary troops throughout the island mobilized to fight them. "The gringos are coming!" were the words on everyone's lips in those days.

The CIA-organized Bay of Pigs Invasion lasted three days and ended in a complete fiasco due to the betrayal and broken promises of the Kennedy administration. That costly failure both solidified Castro's status as a national hero and humiliated the United States. There would be no breaking Castro's stranglehold on power now.

My father and mother saw the writing on the wall. Our position had grown more acutely vulnerable every day and our family's options grew limited. It was time to leave town and try to get out of Cuba.

The new regime did not ban emigration, but anyone wanting to leave Cuba was required to leave all their possessions and resources behind. In the days before we departed for Havana, the local committee reappeared at our house, inventorying every possession inside. In front of us, they argued over who would get what item. It was revolting— legalized theft.

We packed a few clothes and decamped to Havana's Bristol Hotel, where we joined many families in similar straits. My father soon discovered that while it was possible to get out of Cuba, getting the exit permits needed to do so was an exceptionally difficult and corrupt process. He spent months cultivating contacts, trying to cut loose the necessary documentation. Meanwhile, we lived a life of waiting in the hotel.

It became clear we could not get the entire family out at once. My parents looked for options, growing ever-more concerned about the excesses of the Castro regime, fearing more violence and crackdowns aimed at people like us.

They had cause for such worry. When we first arrived in Havana, we turned onto one street to discover bodies hanging from the light poles. My mother gasped and screamed, "Don't look!" as she twisted around and dived over the front seat to try to hide the scene from me. Too late, I saw it. Buffered by a child's innocence, I was surprisingly not disgusted. It would be years before I understood that horror.

Those bodies hung there as reminders of what happened to enemies of the revolution. If we had not already started to hate Castro, this was the turning point for us.

In the hotel, my parents impressed on me the need for caution. I learned not to talk to other kids about any of our family's plans. They frequently repeated things to their parents or the regime's watchers. This new Cuba was fraught with new dangers.

We would have no freedom here. All the talk about agrarian reform, health care for all, literacy—it meant nothing in a country that no longer let you keep the fruits of your own labor, confiscated your possessions, and made everyone paranoid to even say one critical word about the regime.

There was only one place to go: America. We didn't know much about it. My parents had never been outside of Cuba, nor had anyone else in the family. But in the context of the Cold War, there was only one place of hope for people in our situation: the United States. Despite the Bay of Pigs and the fear of an American invasion it triggered, the truth is most Cubans had a generally favorable view of the U.S. and its people.

When it became impossible to get all three of us out at once, my father discovered the Peter Pan Program. Founded by a Catholic priest named Father Bryan Walsh in 1960, Operation Peter Pan was originally an effort to get the children of Batista loyalists out of the country so their parents could continue the fight against Castro while knowing their kids were safe. However, after the failed invasion, it quickly evolved into a U.S.-funded evacuation of whoever could or wanted to get their children out.

The exit visa process was managed by corrupt Castro bureaucrats in Havana. The necessary paperwork could be handled—for a price. My father developed the right contacts and got me an exit permit and a twenty-five-dollar plane ticket to America.

The family talked it through over many nights. My parents were sending me to a different country, unsure if they would be able to follow. Given the situation in Cuba, my father deemed it the only chance for me to live a life free from oppression and violence. He wanted so much for me to live in freedom that he was willing to risk never seeing me again to ensure I got that chance.

My mother was heartbroken and terrified by the prospect of losing her little boy. My father comforted her as best he could. On our last night together in Havana, we went to dinner with our extended family to the Tropicana, dressed in our most formal remaining clothes. Somebody snapped a photo of us at the table. Our last family supper. I was the only one holding a smile. My parents and other family members all looked grim and tense.

No wonder. My parents had lost everything. The television, the Pontiac—those were just material items easily replaced. But the family heirlooms that were signposts of who we were and what we became, those were unique. They were precious to us, meaningless to the committee that simply assigned a monetary value to everything back in our once-tranquil town.

On the wall in our home hung a beautiful set of silver spurs. They belonged to my father in his youth, and they were among his most prized possessions. He rode with them, he worked with them, and he brawled with them. They symbolized his unbridled spirit, wild and ready for any adventure or challenge. Even after my mom tempered him in marriage, he burned with the need to achieve, learn new skills, try different things, and see distant places. That sense of adventure further connected the two of us. It was part of my DNA, too.

Someday, when I was old enough to recognize what they meant, my father intended to pass those silver spurs to me. I was to do the same someday when I had my own family, my own son. A shared legacy across three generations of Prados.

Now such things would never be shared.

The tangible items of our life here in Cuba had been erased. The committee robbed us of our heritage. That was a generational wound that never healed, and among most Cubans who escaped Castro, that deep sense of loss is shared to this day.

The morning after our night at the Tropicana, they helped me pack one small duffel bag—all that we were allowed. My father dressed me in a fine charcoal-gray suit, and we departed the hotel as a family for the last time.

In the street in front of the airport terminal, soldiers of the revolution patrolled with rifles. They were everywhere—a reminder of the new realities of the Marxist police state our country had become in less than three short years of Castro's rule. I doubt my parents even noticed them, though. They were too busy struggling to control their emotions.

At the front entrance to the terminal, we said our goodbyes. My father said to me, "We will follow as soon as we can. You're a man."

I was ten years old.

My mother crushed me in one final hug, her face revealing her heartbreak. "If you cry," I said to her, "I'm not going."

She hugged me tighter. Then I felt her arms release me. Numb, walking like a robot, I carried my duffel bag into the terminal.

After three long years that saw them lose their livelihood, their house, and their possessions, they were now losing their only child.

When I turned around for one last look of my parents, through the glass "fishbowl," I saw my mother sobbing uncontrollably. Beside her, my father was biting his lips, tears in his own eyes.

I'd never seen him cry before. Somehow, I did not cry myself. I headed for the gate and the plane for America waiting there.

# 3

## AMERICAN ORIGINS

*Florida, USA*
*1962*

Darkness. I lay on my cot in almost a state of shock. Around me, a dozen Cuban boys snored and sneezed through this first night in America. From time to time, I could hear the sniffles of someone overcome by homesickness. Dazed or not, I was not going to cry. My father told me I was a man. I would behave as one.

Before I left, my mother gave me a ring. I wore it on my right pinkie as a reminder of her love and guidance. Through the night, I nervously played with it. I'd never worn jewelry before. It felt both awkward and comforting on my finger.

My first plane flight was a blur. I have no memory of what followed, just a jumbled bunch of fragments like a puzzle with half the pieces missing. We reached Miami to find a priest waiting for the five of us Peter Pan refugees on board the plane. I remember a white van, going to a fast-food joint, and sitting inside for my first American meal: a burger with fries.

I paid for it that first night in Florida City. My stomach convulsed, unused to anything but my mom's and godmother's cooking. The sounds around me were all different, all new. I missed my parents. Missed my home. Even the hotel in Havana. The future looked uncertain, and it began to dawn on me how on my own I really was now.

This was my introduction to America. The stories of immigrant families going to New York, entranced by the sight of the Statue of Liberty—that was not our tale. Mine was of a terrified boy, numb with shock, moving like an automaton to the directions of a kindly priest.

Because of the large number of children being rescued from the clutches of communism, there were three sizable and permanent camps where the new orphans could be housed: Florida City, Matecumbe, and Opa-locka. These were made up mostly of quickly erected townhomes, supplemented with a few tents for dining areas and makeshift class-rooms. Florida City is where I was taken. Although initially created to be a more temporary camp, eventually it also became a long-term fix-ture. Some of the kids would find foster homes; others would be blessed with their parents' quick arrival.

Others would be there for the duration. A select few, like myself, would be sent to an orphanage. But what was for me supposed to be a few days in Florida City turned into nightmarish weeks as a measles outbreak swept through us boys.

I caught the virus early, so my first week in America was spent in quarantine. My body ached with fever; my back grew covered with sores. I was taken to the base infirmary and lay on another cot, where once a day a nurse scraped the scabs off my back and cleaned the open wounds with alcohol. We were a miserable, scared, and homesick lot of kids.

I stayed strong by remembering the strength of my father and grand-father. They had led by example all their lives. I watched and learned. They embodied the toughness I knew I needed to survive this, and my memories of them sustained me through the worst moments in the camp.

In my dad's wild days, he and his older brother, my godfather, settled into a village bar one night. They were the rough-and-tumble cowboys whose aura of adventure attracted the small-town ladies. The "campesino" men didn't take kindly to that, and a fight soon broke out. My dad never shied from using his fists, but one of the small-town boys took the brawl to a new level when he pulled a knife and drove it into my dad's arm. Undeterred, my dad grabbed a chair and slammed it over his head. That ended the fight.

Those old Prados did not lose. They did not break. They took no shit from anyone.

I guess a little of that must have rubbed off on me.

As a young kid of perhaps six, I remember getting into a scrap with a neighbor boy who had called me names. It was as much of a fight as two six-year-olds could muster, until his father came out and chased me around the block, trying to hit me with a switch. When I dashed up to the house, I found my maternal grandfather, Emilin, watching me from the porch. The other kid's dad saw him and abandoned his pursuit.

"What happened?" my grandfather asked.

I told him the neighbor boy called me a son of a bitch. So I belted him.

My grandfather smiled, tousled my hair, and gave me a peso.

Lesson learned. Don't take crap. True pride requires the courage and honor to defend yourself.

That Christmas, my father got me a Daisy Red Ryder spring-powered BB gun. After a distant cousin kept calling me names, I decided on an ambush. I lay in wait for him around the neighborhood and sniped him with the Red Ryder. He'd take the hit and look around for me, but I had already melted away like a six-year-old paramilitary warrior in the making.

It did not take me long to realize those lessons from home applied in my new life on my own in America.

When the measles outbreak ended and we returned to full health, the church began sending us to more permanent placements. Some of the kids went to foster homes. Some stayed there in the camp. Just a few were farmed out to orphanages around the country.

I was one of those kids. With the measle scars still fresh on my back,

I packed my meager duffel bag and took another ride in the white van to the Miami airport. I spoke no English, the people at the airport spoke no Spanish. I just knew they were sending me to some place called Denver.

I'd never heard of Denver.

Aboard the plane—a bigger, fancier jet than the one I remembered boarding in Cuba—I fiddled nervously with my ring. After we took off, it slipped off my finger and fell into an air conditioner vent. I tried to retrieve it, but my fingers were too big to fit through the grate. I tried to explain to the flight attendant what had happened, but she didn't speak Spanish.

I had to leave the ring on board that airplane stuck somewhere in its ventilation system.

Denver's tall, snowcapped mountains proved the first of many culture shocks for me in Colorado. Another priest waited for me as I deplaned, and another van ride took me through the Rockies. I stared out at the passing countryside in a mix of fear and awe.

Rugged, towering mountains simply did not exist in Cuba. Neither did snow. The very scale and vastness of Colorado after life on an island was like watching a Disney movie. I was enthralled, and to this day, I love visiting those sites.

This new priest drove me into Pueblo and parked the van in front of a redbrick, four-story building. The sign out front read *Sacred Heart Orphanage*. With its bell tower and sweeping arch over the front steps, it was a dramatic-looking place, designed and built in the Romanesque Revival style that became popular throughout the West at the turn of the century.

I was led up those front stairs into the first floor, where the chapel and offices were located. Given bedding and some basic supplies in this shelter of God, I was shown to my new home on the second floor by a nun. I followed her up a narrow, winding staircase past stained glass windows until we came to the second-floor landing. Through a doorway, I found a broad, open bay furnished with World War II–era metal beds spaced a few feet apart—a room crammed with boys of varying ages.

The nuns who ran the orphanage lived on the floor above. Top floor was the girls' dormitory. There was also a pool, and beside the orphanage's outer wall on one side stretched a cemetery. Out back, the church had placed a series of temporary structures that served as classrooms.

What followed was a rigid routine carefully orchestrated by the nuns. We started mornings with Mass after breakfast, school during the day. At night, we had a television in each dormitory we could watch. Of course, the shows were in English, and I understood little, at first. Most were westerns that excited me with their action—*Bonanza, Gunsmoke, Rawhide*. And of course, the Three Stooges made us all laugh. If we got out of line, the nuns had no issues smacking us. We found them to be tough on us, but in a caring, not capricious way.

There were only a few Cubans at the orphanage. A couple of Mexican kids who also spoke Spanish were the only people we could communicate with at first. But the nuns set about teaching us English right from the first day we arrived. *See Spot Run* books were the source of my first words of English.

Early on, I befriended an older kid named Christopher. He was proud of his Mexican heritage. He was tougher and bigger than most of the other kids, and he spoke Spanish. Sometimes at night, we would grab some of the other kids and sneak out via the fire escape to go play hide-and-seek in the cemetery. If the nuns or our priest knew about it, they never said anything. It was one of the few ways to feel adventurous while institutionalized. I guess it fed that part of me I inherited from my father; a little mischief can be exhilarating.

One night, I was alone in the shower when three white kids came in, fanned out around me, and asked, "Do you like Mexicans?"

I was not quite sure why they asked, but the Mexican kids were my friends, so I shrugged and said, "Yeah."

Wrong answer for them. The three started shoving me around. I tried to stand my ground and got a few licks in, but it wasn't a fair fight.

It was an ugly moment, even if eleven-year-old kids can't really do much damage to each other in such a brawl. Still, it taught me a valuable lesson: if you don't fight back against bullies, they will only continue to target you.

The next morning, I told Christopher what happened. He gathered the Spanish-speaking kids together, and we discussed the situation. That night, a select three, including me, entered the showers. All three of the white kids were there. I picked them out, and we paid them back and then some. Of course, Christopher did most of the damage. By the time the fight was over, it was clear nobody would mess with us again.

Nobody did. Therein lay the lesson. My father and grandfather showed me the importance of pride. Of honor and courage. Those were integral parts of being a man and a Cuban. But there was a practical side to this I don't think I recognized until those two fights at the orphanage. Bullies will take your self-respect, your pride, and your dignity while they work you over day after day. What is the answer? Maintain your pride and honor by fighting back. If they have numbers, find allies. If they are stronger, you fight smarter. You make them pay for messing with you, and they will never mess with you again.

That was the true reason my grandfather gave me that peso. I never teased or bullied anyone, but I was damned sure never going to take a pounding without doing something about it. I think the principle applies to nations just as it does with schoolyard politics. In the years ahead, as I began my journey into the shadow world of paramilitary and counterterrorism operations, I saw the same lesson many times. They will leave you alone if you prove too dangerous to mess with.

Months passed. At times, I felt like I was sleepwalking through my new routine. We were encouraged to go to confession every other day, but what ten-year-old has so many sins to atone for? The steady diet of religious indoctrination kept me from feeling truly spiritual. I always liked going to church back in Cuba, taking Sundays to go with my family to the little church in Manicaragua that formed the center of our town square.

There was comfort there, a sense of belonging and family. To this day, I enjoy going to church, only these days I prefer to go alone. Spirituality is a personal aspect of my life, shared only between God and me. Over the years, I found that priests and parishioners only interfere with that connection.

Often at night across the dormitory, sadness was palpable. Every boy there had a tragic tale. Some had been abandoned. Some had lost their parents. Others were given to the orphanage at birth and never knew anything but life according to the church.

Whatever path they had followed to this place, they all felt a void. There was nobody waiting for them, eager to get them out of this place. No family. They were castaways and they knew it. With this realization in their minds, you could feel their mood turn like the autumn chill that crept through the old, wooden windows. Boys who posed as solid, tough, and resourceful in daylight would often be reduced to tears in the darkness.

Those were the hardest moments for me, lying on my army surplus hospital bed. But again, I was different. I knew my mom and pops would come for me. That faith was never threatened, even as the days dragged into weeks, and the weeks into months. My father would find a way to get to America and reunite with his only son. The others around me? I knew I was the fortunate one, a point driven home through the toughest nights when I heard even Christopher trying to stifle his own tears a few beds over from mine.

Thoughts of home would always dominate my mind in those moments. The horse my parents gave me. We named him Candela, "the Flame," and my father taught me to ride with him. I missed the little community we had set within our town. My grandfather's place across the street, my great-grandmother's not much farther away.

Family ties meant everything to us. Feeling severed from those roots left me pining for home.

I missed the smells of home. In the mornings, as my father opened for business, the rich aroma of coffee always filled the house. To this day, the smell of freshly roasted coffee and leather can take me right back to my childhood home. If I walked down the street, a saddle shop and tannery stood at the corner. The smell of leather always made me stop. To me, it was the scent of adventure and the many explorations I made while riding the Flame.

In the mornings, the sadness was packed away and the daily grind of learning English began anew. The *See Spot Run* books were a valuable gift the nuns gave to me. Learning the language of our adopted country would be our ticket to a better life. To this day, many friends wonder at the fact that I have little to no accent in my English.

Far beyond my horizon, the relationship between Castro's Cuba and Kennedy's America steadily declined. Tension grew, and Castro began importing Soviet military equipment and advisors. The threat this posed to the United States would become clear later that year with the Cuban Missile Crisis and the world's whisker-close brush with World War III and Armageddon that nearly followed President Kennedy's decision to impose a blockade. But through the summer, the deteriorating relationship between the two countries prevented many families from getting out of Cuba. Some of the Peter Pan kids were never reunited with their families. For others, it took years and the establishment of the Freedom Flights, which pulled some three hundred thousand Cubans out of the country and brought them to the United States.

Even then, about 10 percent of the Peter Pans languished in orphanages or camps like Matecumbe and Florida City. Others went to foster homes. Some, I am sure, endured abuse or emotional neglect. Ultimately, about fourteen hundred Peter Pans never saw their families again.

One early evening during the late fall of 1962, we'd had our supper and were given a little free time in the yard to play team sports. I was on one of the basketball courts when a nun came to escort me to the rectory.

I walked over there with her, and upon entering found our priest waiting, the coal-black office phone off its cradle, handset lying on his desk. The nun handed it to me.

"Hello?" I said tentatively in Spanish.

"Son," my father's reassuring voice said, "we're in Miami. We'll be getting you home soon."

I never doubted he would.

# 4

## STARTING FROM THE BOTTOM

*Miami, Florida*
*Late 1962*

My parents made it to Florida just before the whole world nearly exploded in October 1962. It was a near-run escape, at the height of the Cuban Missile Crisis, their movement greased with the last of the family's resources to ensure they'd have a ticket to freedom.

They reached Miami with nothing but a few changes of clothes. With lots of help and guidance from Humberto, my mom's cousin, they obtained our first living quarters in a ramshackle apartment complex just off of Biscayne Boulevard and Twenty-second Street. My dad's days of respected middle-class entrepreneurship were left back on Cuban shores. He had nothing to start with but his street smarts and his hands. A new nation, new language to learn, new customs in an unfamiliar city—that was their reality in those early weeks in America. To some, it may have felt overwhelming. But my folks rose to the challenge with courage and energy.

I saw our new reality that fall after my folks retrieved me from the orphanage. A church van dropped me off in front of the place, which virtually was a ghetto back then (it has been gentrified in recent years).

Inside, the three Prados plus Tia Tere and my two cousins, Manny and Margarita, existed in a tiny one-bedroom space designed for two people. Closet-size kitchen, bare-bones furniture. I remember a Formica-topped aluminum table wedged into the kitchen, a couple of ancient chairs tucked underneath. Stained sink beside a Depression-era stove. A shower/toilet area smaller than most present-day closets lay beyond the kitchen. We *gusanos* ("worms," as Castro named those who deserted the revolution) knew what starting over felt like. And we knew we were blessed to be in America.

My folks slept in the nook that passed for a living room. Every night, they took the couch cushions and laid them out on the floor, then fell asleep together under threadbare sheets. Being the tropics and Florida, cockroaches were a constant problem. We could hear them scuttling around us at night.

My dad never took a welfare check. Instead, he found any work he could get. He mowed lawns, unloaded trucks while I sold newspapers for a few extra pennies. It was not enough. My mother soon went to work at a sweatshop making shirts. Day in, day out, she labored in a sweltering warehouse sewing buttons on clothing my family could not afford.

Nobody complained. My uncle was an electrical engineer at the power plant in Santa Clara. Though his children and wife had left for the States, the regime deemed his skills too critical to lose. They would not let him emigrate. Desperate to be reunited with his family, he tried to escape by boat. He spent six days at sea before grounding on a reef and being rescued by the U.S. Coast Guard.

In retrospect, the best thing that happened to me personally was the Cuban Revolution. I became an American and had the opportunity to make the most out of my life. But in those first years in our adopted country, my parents paid the price.

Yet I never saw them quarrel. Their loyalty and love for each other held the family together. They sustained us in a way that sometimes made others envious. In later years, I used to say that anyone who tried to judge their own marriage by my folks would fall way short—even my own wonderful marriage of thirty-nine years as of this writing. I never saw anyone match the connection they shared.

There were many despairing moments along the way. Large and small, each was a test of my parents' resolve. Most of the time, we adapted. We made do without. We survived. But occasionally, there would be a moment that served as a reminder of all that we had lost thanks to the communists back home.

I remember playing with my cousin Manny (who became the closest thing I have to a blood brother) in the street outside our apartment one evening, waiting for my dad to come home from work. Just as he wearily arrived, an ice cream truck puttered down NE Twenty-second Street. My cousin Manny and I asked my dad if we could get an ice cream.

He said nothing for a long moment as he looked at the two of us. Then he quietly began to cry.

The prosperous business owner from Manicaragua had been reduced to such poverty that he did not even have a dime to give to his son and nephew for a treat.

When my uncle came a few months later, we scraped together enough money to move the family across town to a rough-and-tumble lower-middle-class neighborhood in northwest Miami near what is now Liberty City. Another ghetto, but an improvement for us. Our new, slightly larger apartment was still a shoebox, but after Biscayne Boulevard, it felt like the Hamptons to us.

Life settled down a bit for us there. We found a church, Corpus Christi, where I sang in the choir on Sundays. A priest who noticed my attendance pulled my parents aside and offered me a free education and uniforms at the adjacent Catholic school. I was attending there when John F. Kennedy was assassinated.

After a couple of more local moves in the racially mixed Miami area, my father scraped up just enough money to buy a small house in

Hialeah, a new suburb of Miami, Dade County, which most considered the hinterlands. It was a whopping $12,000 home.

I started school at Palm Springs Junior High, where the distinction of being Cuban and a new kid sometimes led to conflict with the native white kids. As my parents battled their way up the economic ladder, they encountered that racism, too. In the early days, some places would not rent to us because we were Cuban.

My family took that in stride. It was almost like paying dues. You take the heat; you keep pushing on. My dad never lost sight of his objective: a better life for his family. And as he secured better employment, his sheer industriousness opened doors that guaranteed we would get where he wanted us to be.

He got a job on a small boatyard on the Miami River. With his first paycheck, he bought a hammer, saw, hand drill, and some screwdrivers. Those tools became his prized possessions. He used them constantly, working jobs at night building things for other people. If he didn't have a job after his shift at the yard, he'd store his tools there. One night, a fire broke out and burned the storage area to the ground. The next morning, my dad discovered that he'd miraculously forgotten to put his tools away. He'd left them in the boat he'd been building. That boat burned to the waterline, but his prized tools were intact.

Those little lucky moments became our family's saving grace.

Subsequently, his work ethic landed him a job at the prestigious Chris-Craft Corporation, making luxurious boats. He was an exceptional carpenter, and back then, most of the boats were still made of wood. We were starting to live the American dream: you work hard, you get to enjoy the fruit of your labor.

In time, he bought a van to carry his tools from site to site. Inside, he meticulously organized his equipment. Everything had an exact place, and when I began going with him to help on projects, I had to learn where every tool belonged in that van. That level of organization stuck with me and would play an important role later in my life when I was helping my beloved Contras fight in the jungles of Central America, or with my CTC colleagues planning the demise of an international terrorist. Through those tools and that van, I learned to be organized and meticulous.

In two and a half years, my father went from a penniless immigrant living in a dump to a modest homeowner in his new country. The down payment for that $12,000 house stretched us to the limit, but every spare moment he devoted to improving it. He built a two-car garage, added an extra bedroom, bath, and even a sunroom off the back of the house.

For several years, my father and I worked on weekends together, doing odd carpentry jobs for people, painting, and cabinetry. Once, while I was painting a pair of louvered closet doors in an empty apartment, I came across a beautiful Gurkha knife sitting on one of the closet shelves. I showed my father, asking if we could keep it. It had clearly been abandoned by the previous tenant. But my dad said no. He was a man of honor, and his code forbade him from taking another's possession, even if it had been left behind and forgotten.

My mother and father loved America and all its promise. They earned legal resident status, then received their citizenship in record time. They became ardent patriots who never missed voting in an election. Here, we could work as we wished, worship as we wished, and be left alone to do it. Nobody threatened us. Nobody tried to seize our property or steal my father's livelihood. He didn't fear his only son might be kidnapped and held for ransom. Air strikes and raging battles that put tank rounds through our family's furniture were a thing of the past.

He made the most of this second chance.

My mother did, too, though she probably suffered more than any of us. Long hours in the sweatshop never dimmed her spirit. She learned to do without. She learned to stretch the family's food budget.

In the sweatshop, she was surrounded by heavy machinery and huge fans that did little more than push the hot air around. It was a piecework job, meaning the more she produced, the more she made. A finished shirt netted her five cents. She could work all day as fast as humanly possible and make only a few dollars. Yet every nickel counted, so day after day, she returned to that factory even as it robbed her of her health. She developed hip and leg problems as a result of the repetitive motions required to do her job. Much later, they allowed her to work at home, dropping off work in the morning and picking it up at close of business. She did detail work then—embroidery, making buttonholes, and so on.

Despite the physical demands her new job placed on her, she always brought a softness to the harder edges of the family—the yin to my father's yang. She never left the house without being meticulously coiffed and dressed. From her, I learned the value of clothing and style, and that part of her remains with me to this day. Her spirit was irrepressible. In the worst moments of our leanest times, I never once saw her despair.

Even at our poorest, my mom made sure we had books in our house. She was a voracious reader, consuming every Spanish newspaper we could get in Miami. I picked up her reading habit, too. In those darkest moments of my family's struggle to get established in America, I escaped into dime novels. They fed my suppressed thirst for adventure, and I found kindred spirits in the likes of Ian Fleming's 007 spy series, Edgar Rice Burrough's Tarzan, but especially World War II spy novels about the Office of Strategic Services (OSS) and the exploits of its agents. It was through those latter books I learned about the legendary real-life spy, William "Wild Bill" Donovan—the head of the wartime OSS. He was a larger-than-life figure, a man of action imbued with courage and the conviction of a dedicated patriot whose lifetime of service to the United States ran the gamut from infantry officer in World War I to antitrust lawyer, diplomat, and spy. His career peaked when he was made the first director of the Central Intelligence Agency upon its establishment after World War II.

I spent many late nights in our humble homes, poring over those books. They were a window to a different world. Without them, I may have never seen beyond the one I knew in Miami—the rugged streets, school, and the weekends spent working with my father.

Three years after arriving with nothing, my folks had carved out a successful life for themselves. We were established, chasing our own American dream. But just as things were going well for my parents, I started to cause them heartache.

As we clawed our way out of poverty, I learned some hard lessons on the streets of Hialeah. If you didn't have a close group of friends around you who had your back, you became a target. White kids and Black kids coalesced into their own tribes. We Cubans did the same. We looked out for each other. If one of our own was caught and pummeled by the other street kids, we'd make sure to exact a price from those responsible. It was a bare-knuckle path to high school that made us hard and taught us the value of loyalty.

The summer before my freshman year in high school, my dad landed a second job working for an eccentric millionaire named Edgar Gabor. He owned a company called Cadillac Steel Works, but it was his side project for which he hired my father. Edgar had gone into the navy during World War II, serving on PT boats. Somehow, he'd found a war-surplus PT boat and wanted to turn it into a private yacht. Those little torpedo boats were made almost entirely from wood, so the reconstruction was tailor-made for my dad's skills.

He took me to work on the evenings and weekends that summer, and it was on that job I met Edgar's personal pilot, Jay, an air force veteran who was into martial arts. He showed me some basic judo moves, then gave me a little red illustrated book on the subject. I studied it constantly, practicing kicks and sweeps with my neighborhood friends. I filled a duffel bag full of sawdust, hung it in the garage my dad built, and spent hours working out, beating the bag with the moves Jay taught me. It was the first time I'd been introduced to a disciplined method of self-defense. I was hooked.

My freshman year in high school, I discovered girls and SCUBA diving. My grades tanked. My parents watched with alarm as I started sliding off the path, spending more and more time chasing girls and cutting school to go dive, all while getting in a scrap or two.

Karate became my saving grace. With the pennies I saved, I joined a karate school owned by a World War II Marine named Leo Thalassites and his junior partner, a Vietnam War Marine Raider named Jim Alfano. Jim saw potential in me and developed into a mentor through my first year of high school. He kept me from going totally to the street, where many of my junior high friends were already headed.

I thrived in Jim's world of hard work, mindfulness, and pride. He developed us as full individuals, teaching us a philosophy of constant self-improvement. At the heart of our dojo was a style of karate called Kyokushin that focused on supreme aggression—one kick, one punch to defeat a foe.

Our class would sometimes do demonstrations of this discipline of karate. Once, we were invited to do one for a local army reserve Special Forces unit. At the end of it, I broke a brick with my bare knuckles, a feat that impressed the Green Berets.

Not long after, Jim told me he'd lined up a demonstration at my high school. The news excited me. My parents never approved of organized sports, so this would be my chance to show my peers some of the skills I'd learned. But the night before the demonstration, my father came home from work and asked me to stay home from school the following day. He had acquired a free load of cement from a work colleague, and he needed me home to help his friend pour our new patio floor. I had no choice. I obeyed my father.

When I failed to show up for the karate demonstration the next day, Jim was furious. To him, my no-show was a breach of discipline, of loyalty. In reality, it was anything but. I'd sacrificed my chance to earn some social standing at the high school to obey my father's request. It didn't matter. Without asking me for an explanation, Jim ostracized me from his inner circle and barely acknowledged me again. I was as broken-hearted as a fifteen-year-old could be by that treatment.

I'd thrived in the program, and Jim's mentorship had meant a great deal to me. With his guidance, my trajectory was heading in the right direction. I probably would have ended up in the marines, or maybe the Miami PD.

All that changed with that one no-show. The rejection devastated me and left me embittered. In retrospect, I suppose I could have gone to Jim and explained what had happened, but I had too much pride to do that. I suffered in silence, then finally left the program.

Thus began my tailspin into Miami's mean streets.

# 5

## EMBRACING AND ESCAPING THE STREET

*Hialeah, Florida*
*1965–1971*

We entered the McDonald's and saw them immediately, and I knew we were in for a rough time. Sitting in one corner of the fast-food joint was BD, our school's star running back. About half the team's offense clustered around him. These were the tallest, beefiest kids in our school, and they didn't have the slightest issue with throwing their weight around.

They saw me, the scrawny sixteen-year-old outcast from our high school. I was fast, agile, and becoming a decent martial artist, but I was also small, outnumbered, and with my then girlfriend, a beautiful, intelligent redhead named Carmen. A brawl was the last thing I wanted to expose her to, especially one that I couldn't win. Looking at the numbers, I knew if anything developed, I would surely take a beating.

I made eye contact with BD the running back. In that split second, I knew a hassle was coming. I could see the anticipation, the eagerness to stir something up. He'd always been a bully; much of the school feared him. I was smaller, with a prettier girl—an easy target in his mind.

The football players stood up in unison. Taking a cue from BD, they flung a few insults my way, then made crude remarks about my "smokin' hot" girlfriend.

I fired back with an earnestly delivered, "Fuck you." De-escalation was not my strong suit. BD's eyes lit up in indignant fury. The squad headed our way. I grabbed Carmen's hand, and we bolted from the burger joint at full speed. Sometimes, there's no point to getting beat down and getting the people around you hurt.

They chased after us, shouting and taunting, but we evaded their pursuit and made it a hundred or so yards to the Arby's restaurant where I'd been working. There, our manager Ron—a Vietnam veteran of the navy's legendary Underwater Demolition Teams—asked us what was going on.

We told him, and he grew angry. Ron was a huge man, tough as nails and always up for a good fight. He belonged to a local biker gang and brawled regularly on the weekends with his crew. Rumor had it that his dad was allegedly connected to the Mob.

Needless to say, when half a football team was looking to give you a beatdown, Ron was a solid guy to have in your corner. He waited for the football players to reach the Arby's parking lot, then went outside with one of his friends to confront them, where he demanded to know what they were doing. BD made the mistake of telling him they were looking for me. That was Ron's cue to get things going.

"Ric is my little brother," he announced as he calmly walked up to BD's posse of jocks. "You want a piece of Ric, you come through me!"

They wanted a piece, all right. Fists started flying, and football players started going down. Hard. Ron and his friend were like terminators. The jocks never stood a chance. Despite being heavily outnumbered, the two bikers beat them all to the pavement in a matter of seconds. I had never witnessed that kind of surgical violence or how quickly its application demoralized opponents.

Lesson learned. Avoid the fight if you can. But if you have no choice, go in for total destruction and take the fight out of your opponent. Half measures will only get you hurt.

The truth was, Ron wasn't overstating our relationship to those guys. He and I had worked together for almost a year, and he'd become the big brother I never had. He lived by a code of honor I respected while avoiding the criminal stuff other bikers got into. But he was always up for a good brawl, and if his knuckles weren't sore, it wasn't a good weekend.

The next day at school, the football players saw me in the hallway. I mentally prepared myself for a last stand. They turned around and went the other way. Knowing Ron was in my corner was money in the bank. They left me alone, knowing the inevitable retaliation would be way more heat than they could handle. Sadly, if I had not missed that karate demonstration at the high school, they never would have tried to confront me in the first place. Plus, I would not have left the dojo. Yet another peripheral lesson: shit happens for a reason!

Of course, in the moment, none of that eased my pain and resentment over being ostracized by Jim. There were no other dojos in town and no other organized martial arts classes to take. I had no outlet. Thanks to BD, I realized that survival in Hialeah would require that I get strong.

We had one gym in town. It happened to be in the same strip mall as the dojo. The gym rats were a tough crowd, pure street. They weren't there to get ripped for the beach. They were there to get buffed out to dominate in a fight.

I joined the gym and threw myself into daily workouts with the same zeal I did with karate. At the same time, I mowed through Arby's roast beef sandwiches and milkshakes in an effort to bulk up. Ron marveled at my appetite and encouraged it. He even started calling me "Chest," as my pecs were the first body part to show progress. Unlike at the dojo, I was building strength without an honorable purpose.

It was there at the gym I met Albert San Pedro, a.k.a. "Big Al," and his circle of friends. I suppose today they'd be called a gang. Really, they were a group of kids who banded together for sheer survival and venting of teenage testosterone. They'd gravitated together for mutual protection after getting trapped between the other two forces on the streets: the football players who bullied them and a nascent African American gang that had just taken root in our area. In our world, if you didn't have somebody to watch your back, you'd become a target by a lot of very dangerous people.

It wasn't the dojo, but with Albert and the rest of his friends, I felt like I had a place again. Loyalty was valued. We looked out for each other and our families. But as those friendships deepened, I was drawn deeper into the street. We ran hustles. We stole hubcaps and more. We protected each other. We later developed a strong association with the Miami Crowns, a much more developed street gang, of which I eventually became a full member.

My tanking grades and questionable friendships alarmed my parents. By the end of my freshman year, they decided to pull me out of Hialeah and send me to nearby Miami Springs High School.

Unbeknownst to them, Albert and the rest of his gym crew—el Chinito, Rubio, la Mona, Milton, Popeye, El Richard, and many more—all went to Miami Springs. The move to get me away from trouble actually solidified my connections to it. Of all the guys I ran with back then, Rubio became my only enduring friendship out of the bunch. He got smart early, moved away from the area, and built a good life and family for himself.

We've stayed in touch through the many decades since we rolled together with the Miami Springs crew.

The gym served as the nexus of our high school relationships. We hit it together almost every day after the final bell rang. By my senior year, I could bench-press 280 pounds, Albert over 320. I went from small and scrawny to solid, strong, and tough.

One day at school, the Miami Springs football players approached Albert and said, "We've got a fight coming with the Cubans. Are we going to have to worry about you?"

The football team wanted no beef with Albert's group. Albert said, "I don't give a fuck about those guys."

Thus sanctioned, the two sides squared off later in the week. We were left alone; everyone knew our rep. We were not afraid to fight and would always inflict damage.

Another afternoon, one of the "tough" guys at the school decided to target me. In the school's parking lot, he tried to bully me. I would have none of it and fired back. Fists flew, and the fight got furious. I kicked, punched, and grabbed the guy, flipped him onto a car. Easy day, right? I was going to pummel him against it. Out of desperation, he sank his teeth into my left middle finger and wouldn't let go. I kept hitting him, and he kept biting me, so I grabbed the car's radio antennae that we'd broken off in the fight and started whipping him with it. That did the trick. He stopped biting me, but by then, I had another issue: the car's owner.

I happened to choose the worst possible car in the parking lot to damage. It was owned by the biggest and toughest African American kid in the school. He asked around and found out I damaged his car. That afternoon, the school was abuzz with word that he and his pals were looking to exact revenge.

Albert came to me with a couple of his usual suspects. "Don't worry," he reassured me. "This is an opportunity to show them all who we are, nothing to fear." If we stood against the biggest kid in the school, Albert knew we'd be at the top of the heap. He'd be the leader of the toughest of the tough.

The end-of-the-day bell rang. We quickly assembled our five Hialeah boys. The African American kid met us on the front lawn of the school, flanked by four of his own pals. Fair fight. One on one. We went at it, swinging and dodging. The fight was one for the record books. We held our own, and by the end of it, we were still standing. We may not have won the crushing victory we wanted, but we did enough damage that afterward, the African American kids said we were square. It was a pivotal moment for us. The African American kids were a powerful bloc in the school, and now we'd secured our flank with them. As for everyone else, we showed them we had no fear and plenty of teeth. From then on, pretty much everyone left us alone. Albert was considered one of the top dogs, and we were his posse.

Unfortunately, Julito, a close friend of the finger-biter, ratted us out to the principal a few days later. I was suspended for fighting. My father was furious. After I told him what happened, he went down to the school to explain to the principal that I had not started the fight, I'd ended it. The principal was about to rescind the suspension, but right then, Julito was brought into the front office dazed and bleeding. Chinito had caught him in the halls and pummeled him for violating the first rule of the street: you never rat anyone out—even your worst enemies.

The principal looked at my father and said, "The suspension stands."

Funny note: this incident actually came up during the background investigation for my clearances into the CIA. Yes, that is how thorough and intrusive these BIs (background investigations) are.

▬▬▬▬▬▬▬

With our place now well established in the Miami Springs pecking order, Albert turned his attention to making money. At the time, I held multiple jobs, working at Doral Country Club as a maid's assistant, the lowest position on staff. I also spent some nights as an apprentice in a small shop learning how to cut and polish prescription glasses; my father wanted to make sure I developed some useful skills before I graduated. My junior year, I found work at Bart's Men's Wear, an upscale gentlemen's clothing store that sold high-end clothing and formal wear. The part of me cultivated by my mom really enjoyed that job. While I could hold my own in the street, I learned to clean up well, tie a tie, and wear GANT shirts and Weejuns penny loafers. In fact, it was my growing toughness and my "Ivy League" dress that got me accepted into the Crowns, where I met my lifelong friend, Max.

While I worked multiple jobs for barely minimum wage, Albert had an entrepreneur's mind. He figured out that if he could rent a meeting hall, he could host parties that we euphemistically called "open houses." He provided the entertainment, took the entry fee, and pretty soon he was running a veritable underground moveable party scene for the under-twenty-one Cuban set.

It grew and made more money. They were fun mixers, and Albert showed he had a shrewd, innate business instinct that he developed and refined in the years to come.

Meanwhile, on the side, we still got into a fair amount of low-level trouble. I could see far enough down the road to know this way of life would be a dead end. Drugs were just starting to hit the Miami scene. Other rival groups were starting to get into it. Things were getting rougher, and our rivals were getting more dangerous and well armed.

Things went bad pretty quickly once the guys graduated from high school. I avoided the worst of it, mainly because of my love of marine science, which drove me into the college path. Ron had taught me how to SCUBA dive, and that became the passion that saved me. While others were buying dope and experimenting with all the stuff starting to flood the streets, I was saving every dime I had either for protein shakes to help me bulk up or for SCUBA gear. Others cut school to party; I'd sneak away to go diving—with a girlfriend, of course!

After that terrible first year at Hialeah High, I became a solid B student, despite the brawling and the trouble we got into around town. School was interesting to me. I liked to learn, and when I applied myself, I did well.

After graduation, I started at Miami Dade Junior College in the Marine Science Technician program. It was a demanding curriculum, taught by a former U.S. Navy dive instructor who expected us to grasp complex biological concepts very quickly. I scrambled to keep up and worked hard. Yet there were times I still rolled with the Crowns and Big Al after classes.

Once, a group of antiwar student protesters decided to stage a rally and burn the American flag on campus. I was outraged. We may have had things rough since coming to Florida, but this country gave us every opportunity to succeed. My family had long since became ardent patriots. Burning the flag was not okay.

So I called Flaco. He and some of our Crowns agreed this was a worthwhile fight. The next day, we crashed their flag-burning party like hell on wheels. After it was over, there were plenty of broken protest signs and bead necklaces on the ground, no hippies in sight, and the flag flew proudly over the campus. The school bulletin ran a piece mentioning how some Cuban refugees had defended the flag.

That was a watershed moment for me. A lot of the time I spent in the streets I felt a sense of guilt for the stupid crap we were doing. I knew the petty theft and the open-house parties weren't my path. The fighting that came along with defending honor, pride, and a chunk of the 'hood had no higher purpose beyond loyalty to my friends and the thrill of a good scrap. The campus scrum was different. It gave me a true sense of satisfaction. Defending our country from people who wanted to tear it down? That stirred something in me.

Not long afterward, I was sitting in one of the oceanography classes with a fellow student named Glenn Richardson. Glenn looked like a young version of the Marlboro Man, rugged and outdoorsy. We'd known each other casually since I'd started at Miami Dade, and we usually made small talk before class. This time, I noticed he was wearing a green flight jacket that looked supercool. I wanted one immediately.

"Hey, Glenn, where did you buy that?" I asked.

Glenn looked indignant. "You don't buy these, you earn them!" he replied.

"Whoa, cowboy! No offense, bro! What the hell do you mean?"

He started telling me about the U.S. Air Force Pararescue Jumper (PJ) program that he had joined. He explained he'd learned combat rescue and medical skills. He got to jump out of airplanes. He got to practice rescues at sea. He told me they even got to do SCUBA and underwater operations. Those who joined and became PJs also received the honor of wearing the coveted maroon beret.

As Glenn described the life of a PJ, it fed all my James Bond / Ian

Fleming fantasies of a life of adventure and daring. He saw how it energized me, so he invited me over to his house to show me photos of the training and his life in the PJs. By then, he belonged to a reserve unit.

During their next drill weekend, he brought me out and introduced me to his brotherhood. A well-muscled PJ, Alan "Al" Stanek, gave me a short history of the PJs. After World War II, the U.S. Army Air Forces recognized the need for a unified organization to perform search and rescue. The Air Rescue Service was born from that need in 1946. The following year, the air force established the Pararescue program. This authorized pararescue teams, along with the creation of the Pararescue and Survival School at MacDill Air Force Base in Florida. The commandant of that first school was a pilot, First Lieutenant Perry C. Emmons, who had been assigned to the Office of Strategic Services (OSS) during World War II.

The Vietnam War gave the air rescue program the primary mission for saving our pilots shot down behind enemy lines, often doing so while under fire. But the PJs soon expanded that role to assist any American soldier in harm's way, and it eventually became known as *Combat Search and Rescue.*

The PJ teams would go out on their missions in two helicopters, one a "high bird," which provided backup firepower and often rescue for the "low bird," which actually facilitated for the PJ to do his rescue mission on the ground. Initially, they flew in Bell UH-1 Hueys—the iconic chopper of the Vietnam era. Later, the teams received Jolly Greens, larger birds with more capabilities, including a refueling probe that extended their range with air-to-air tanking. The Jolly Greens carried two wicked "mini-guns" (the M134 Minigun is a 7.62×51mm NATO six-barrel rotary machine gun with a high, sustained rate of fire of two thousand to six thousand rounds per minute; it features a Gatling-style rotating barrel assembly with an external power source). The PJs would get on the ground, assist the downed aviators—oftentimes the pilots were wounded—and get them into the hovering bird overhead.

Rescuing crews who went down at sea became another major role of the PJs. The brotherhood was a tight one. They were elite, honed with excellent training, and tempered in the furious air-ground fire-fights over North Vietnam.

When Alan finished with the history lesson, he read to me the pararescue motto: "This we do, that others may live!" From that point on, I knew this was the life I wanted. I had found my purpose.

Without telling my folks, I went and enlisted, with a guaranteed shot at trying out for pararescue, but no guarantees of making it. I passed the written exams and the PT test, and I was accepted into the PJ entry program. I would report for basic training the day after Christmas of 1971.

I knew this was going to be a battle. Between my high draft number and my student status, my parents were not concerned with me being conscripted into the army. My mom was still overprotective, and the idea of losing her son to the military during the Vietnam War was going to be tough on her. I wasn't sure how to tell them, so I kept quiet about it until early December. I broke the news probably a bit harshly, telling them, "By the way, I joined the air force. I leave December 26 for basic training."

The shit hit the fan. My father was furious, my mom broke down in tears. It turned ugly. Fortunately, my "big brother," Ron, stepped in and helped smooth some of this over, talking to my folks about the advantages the military offered. He and my dad had several long conversations. Ultimately, they had to accept it. Their son was leaving the nest for a life that seemed only a distant dime-novel dream a few months before. I couldn't wait to get started. My folks could only watch me depart and start my own path into the world. Looking back, I realized that break from home was terribly hard on my mother.

She'd lost me once to an orphanage in a foreign country. Now, as an adult, I was leaving them behind for a life I wanted more than anything else.

It was a tough way to say goodbye. But it pulled me away from the

Crowns and their increasing descent into a life of hardened crime. For that, I know my father was grateful. The allure of the barroom brawl, of those wild nights infused with the passion of youth—those were his glory days. He knew their power. He'd overcome it himself only by falling in love with my mom. That connection put him on a better path.

The air force, not love, served that purpose for me.

After I left, the Crowns generally went one of two ways. A few became cops. Others stayed street and embraced a full-time life of crime. Many died in the process. Albert made a lot of money in various enterprises. He ended up connected to mayors, police chiefs, and had his fingers in many pies. He became a millionaire with his business dealings, and he used the money to consolidate and grow his power throughout South Florida. It came at a heavy cost.

Several years later, Albert did time in prison for unrelated charges, I heard later that he emerged from that experience and went straight. He became a legitimate businessman using his streetwise entrepreneurial instinct to build a successful life for himself and his family.

All of this went down long after I joined the air force and left the scene. We all remained friendly—people from home always have a role in your life—but in the years ahead, we saw each other only sparingly at funerals or other formal events. They were still my brothers, but our paths diverged so completely that, ultimately, we had little left in common.

I was to travel the planet; they stayed in Hialeah. It created a divide even our shared experiences and memories could not bridge.

Yet almost two decades after I left home, those teenage friendships almost derailed my career at the CIA.

# PART II

# 6

## RUNNING THROUGH THE SHADE

*Miami Springs, Florida*
*Fall 1980*

I stepped out of my little house in Miami Springs and checked the late-afternoon sun. It already hung low on the horizon to the west, casting long shadows across my quiet neighborhood's tree-lined streets. Clear skies. A beautiful day was brewing, but I was in a foul, dark mood. I checked my watch and did some math. I had fifty-five minutes to do seven miles.

I jogged off the porch and hit the street. Thanks to the trees, there is always shade in Miami Springs. I never ran a set route, just always chased that shade.

Nine years and half a lifetime had passed since I first left home for the military. The air force sent me to Lackland for my initial training that weeded out some of the prospective PJs. I learned that while I was a capable swimmer underwater, swimming on the surface with my head up was slowing me down. It took a lot of effort to retrain myself to do that, but I was helped by my PJ classmate Steve Hutchinson, a state champion swimmer. I was far from the fastest surface swimmer in my class, but I was strong and could stroke forever. I was sent to Key West for U.S. Naval Underwater Swimmers School, where I most certainly did not tell the instructors that I was civilian SCUBA qualified. My first PJ sergeant at Lackland, the legendary Jon Hoberg, had told me to keep that to myself or I'd get hazed mercilessly. After finishing there, I went on to Benning for airborne school, where I learned to love to parachute out of C-130 transport aircraft. The visceral thrill of every jump gave me a wicked rush. Parachuting and subsequently skydiving became a lifelong passion as a result, though I was never that great at it.

I turned down a shady street and picked up my pace. The sun was fading faster now. I checked my watch. Forty minutes, then I'd have to be home and hit the sack early for my shift at the firehouse at 0630 the next morning.

Dark mood, dark times. I loved being a PJ, I loved being in the military. It was adrenaline rushes for an altruistic purpose—to save lives. Everything had fallen into place, and I was happy.

How did it go so wrong? I didn't want to think about that.

From U.S. Army Airborne School, I got orders to Spokane, Washington, to attend the Survival, Evasion, Resistance, and Escape (SERE) program. There, we learned what to do if a rescue went bad and we were trapped behind enemy lines. We practiced escape and evasion techniques, then spent the second half of the course in a simulated prisoner of war camp. We learned to resist interrogation and how to work together to escape. During one effort, my fellow prisoners simulated a race riot and began a fight. Our guards rushed to break it up, and during the melee, I slipped away. The first time we tried this, the guards hunted me down with dogs and caught me. This time, I made it out, scored a bologna sandwich from the instructors, then was put back in the camp to undergo the rest of the exercise.[1]

1. The much-maligned enhanced interrogations that my Agency sparingly performed on known terrorists were wholly based on this SERE training. The politics that followed negatively impacted on the lives of many dedicated Agency officers—especially that of my dear friend and former boss Jose Ro-

I ran through the pockets of the golden rays of dusk as I heard airliners landing at the nearby airport. They passed overhead with a whining roar as they made their final approaches to the runway. Miami Springs was an otherwise quiet little community tucked between the airport and Hialeah. It was a great, middle-class kind of town with its own police force and good schools. It would have been a perfect place to raise a family.

I lived alone in the house I'd purchased.

A few years before, I'd met and soon married a younger girl. We had no idea what marriage entailed, being young and totally unready for the commitment. The house was to be where I'd raise my family. We had a daughter together, but not long after she was born, our marriage collapsed. I fought to gain custody of my daughter, but that was a no-win fight with the court system of the day, which favored the mother at every turn.

The end of the marriage was difficult enough, but I loved my little girl in a way I never knew I could connect before she arrived in my life. Having that bond eviscerated me. The pain morphed to anger. I dealt with it by working out fanatically. I lifted weights every other day, ran four times a week. Yet even that exhausting regimen wasn't helping. Each day, I sank deeper and deeper into anger and depression. I just wanted my daughter back.

When we finished SERE school, those of us left went through our final phase of our program, then called *transition training*. We became fully certified combat medics—EMT-2s.

The most challenging training was the Mountain Phase. Here we mastered sophisticated climbing disciplines and finished that phase with a weeklong exercise knee-deep in Utah snow. Yes, my first time ever in snow was wearing snowshoes and lugging seventy pounds of gear. Easy day.

---

driguez, arguably *the* most beloved leader in my generation of officers at the CIA.

The training culminated with a night SCUBA jump from a C-130. Once we did that, we would be welcomed into the brotherhood of PJs.

That night for us came in late November 1972. It was cold as balls, and the wind was blowing at over twenty miles an hour. We'd already scrubbed the jump three times due to weather. One more, and our instructors told us they'd send us home for the holidays and we'd have to return to finish the program in January. Going home without our coveted maroon berets? Hell no!

We all begged our sergeant to let us take the risk of the beyond-regulation winds. I leaped out of that C-130 into a pitch-black winter night, falling toward an unseen Utah lake two thousand feet below, wearing a full SCUBA kit that weighed about 130 pounds. My chute opened; I swung down and hit the lake to be instantly bathed in near-freezing water. My partner, Steve Birkland (a.k.a. Jolly Green), splashed down nearby, and we swam quickly to each other. In seconds, the intense cold rendered our hands useless. We fumbled around, helping each other out of our chutes, shivering from the cold. Just as things started getting really dicey, our rescue boat showed up and the crew pulled us aboard. We unzipped our wetsuits just enough to cram our throbbing hands under our armpits. They felt like ice cubes.

A moment later, PJ Sergeant "Rusty" Atkins handed us a flask. "Congratulations and welcome aboard, PJs!" I still get goose bumps when I relive that moment, and not because of the cold.

Sadly, a few years later, Rusty took his own life. In the long run, the scars from what warriors witness are not always survivable.

In my head, I was there in the Utah night, freezing my ass off. But as I ran in Miami Springs that early evening, it was still hot. That sticky, humid Miami heat that I'd lived in most of my life. I was used to the tropical climate, but I still didn't like to run in direct sun, so I hopscotched from shade patch to shade patch, zigzagging through the neighborhood as more planes began taking off and landing from our airport.

By the time I was assigned to my first PJ unit, the Vietnam War was over. I had been ready to go, wanting to do my part. Fortunately, for my mom's sake, that didn't happen. Instead, the air force sent me to the 301st Air Rescue Squadron at Homestead Air Reserve Base, just south of Miami. I was going home, now part of one of the most elite outfits in the military.

I served a total of two years on active duty, then transferred to the 301st on reserve-only status. Jim Wilson was a fellow PJ and one of my mentors in the unit back then. In his civilian life, he was the fire captain for the then Metro Dade Fire Rescue. He talked me into joining. That was not a path I ever would have explored on my own, but Jim knew I was always looking for action, and he assured me the life of a firefighter/paramedic would never disappoint.

He was not joking.

I checked my watch. Ten minutes left. I was almost home now anyway, so I pushed the pace even harder for this final stretch. I made it back to the house and went inside for a quick shower and a light meal, then hit the sack.

At the firehouse, we worked twenty-four-hour shifts followed by two days off. One on, two off. That sounds like a great life, but there was a reason. Nothing I'd ever experienced in the military or in the streets of Miami prepared me for the things we saw and did during those days riding rescue in the violent streets of greater Miami. As an EMT, I rode to scenes of horrific violence and tragic accidents. We saved some, lost others. I tried to wall off the losses, but sometimes I revisited them in my sleep.

The worst of the worst came on a day we responded to a scene where a boy of about ten had slipped and fallen into a backyard swimming pool while drinking a glass of orange juice. He hit his head and was knocked unconscious. His mom found him floating facedown in the pool. We rushed to the house, and I started mouth-to-mouth resuscitation while my partner did chest compressions. We got him to the ambulance. His mom rode shotgun.

My partner kept up with the CPR. I got on my knees in the back of the ambulance, whose floor was an easily cleaned diamond-pattern metal grate.

As the mom watched, panic-stricken from the front of the ambulance, her son vomited three times into my mouth. Each time, I turned and spit out bile and orange juice, then continued working on him. Our driver sped through the streets breaking every law of the road to get us to the hospital. When we skidded to a stop and flung the doors open, some nurses with a gurney were there waiting for us. We laid him on it and rushed him into the emergency room, where the docs were ready and prepped for him. One of the docs looked him over and said, "Good job, guys; he's nice and pink. We'll take it from here."

As I stumbled out of the emergency room, pants torn and knees bleeding from the cheese-grater floor in the back of the ambulance, my nose picked up the rancid scent the adrenaline had blocked. A nurse saw me and asked me if I was okay.

"Yeah . . . ," I mumbled. She could see I wasn't. She rushed over and stuck some smelling salts under my nose. Just for a second, but it was enough to bring me back from the shock I was falling into. A moment later, the boy's father pulled up and sprinted through the ER doors.

When we got back to the firehouse, we learned the kid didn't make it.

I've had nightmares about that call ever since. Sometimes months go by, sometimes years. But I've never been able to shake that one. The boy always returns. I still hope and pray that he somehow knows how hard we tried to save him.

For all the bad days, I still loved the work; it was rewarding, and every call brought a new adventure. There were moments of levity and moments where we saved a life. Once, we responded to a 911 call to find a man high on PCP flinging a couple of cops around like rag dolls. His girlfriend lay bleeding from a gunshot wound on the bed behind him. To get to her, we knew we had to help subdue the boyfriend first. My partner, Frank, went high, and I went low. We careened into the drug-crazed madman, knocked him off his feet, and held him down so one of the cops could cuff him. It took four of us to do it—two EMTs and two cops. But we got to the girlfriend in time, stabilized her, and sped her to the hospital in our rescue truck, where the docs saved her life.

Between shifts, I continued my military career with the air rescue unit at Homestead. But by 1978, I'd gone to nearly every course they could send me to except German Ski School and Arctic Survival School. I applied for both for four years and kept getting denied. "What does a PJ in South Florida need with cold-weather classes?" was the invariable response. I tried to reason with them. "How many wars are fought in Florida?" But it did no good.

Finally, I'd had enough. I left the air force and joined the National Guard, joining the Twentieth Special Forces Group, and aspiring to earn the coveted Green Beret. I was slated to go to the legendary Q Course but hadn't received a slot yet.

Still, I wanted something more. The action is the juice, and I always chased that rush. Still, this time was different. I didn't feel like I was on the right path. I was drifting into a life I never asked for that seemed to be somebody else's destiny, not my own.

I also needed to get out of Florida. Home had become a painful grind, and I thought a change of venue might help, along with a new challenge that could absorb my attention.

I sent in handwritten applications to the CIA and the Secret Service; I even tested for the latter. But this was right after the Senate's Church Committee hearings had badly damaged the CIA after it revealed some of the Agency's excesses during the 1950s and '60s. The practical upshot from the hearings led to restrictions in the way the CIA could operate. Gerald Ford issued Executive Order 11905, which banned political assassinations. Jimmy Carter expanded that with EO 12036 a few years later.

Additionally, the means through which the Agency was allowed to collect intelligence was restricted following the hearings.

The bad press and the new limitations left the CIA badly damaged politically and practically.

I ended up applying to the Secret Service after the CIA told me it had no full-time positions available that matched my skill sets. Yet in the spring of 1980, the Agency reached out looking for a medic who could work a short-term contract supporting the famed Special Activities Division (SAD). Responsible for all covert and paramilitary operations, SAD was the elite part of the CIA that carried out the more kinetic stuff. It was where the action was, and I loved being a part of it.

Initially, I worked out of the medical offices in Langley. We built med kits, and I did some lab work. Then in late June 1980, I flew to Arizona to support a two-week desert survival course where I worked with actual operators and officers. It was the chance of a lifetime.

I was young and fit and eager to impress, so beyond teaching some medical aspects of desert survival, I took on every extra duty I could. At night, I would test the students' situational awareness as they were out trying to escape and evade the instructors. It was a lot like SERE school in some respects, so I would find some high ground and watch them disperse in pairs. I'd sketch a map of their approximate locations, then go sneak up on them after dark.

Once, I crept within a few feet of two students and heard them chatting back and forth to each other. When one of them said, "Man, I'd give anything for a pizza right now," I jumped out of a thornbush and shouted, "*Pizza delivery!*"

They pretty much shat themselves. I slipped away just as their shock turned to laughter. But lesson learned: you gotta be vigilant. Not knowing I was cheating, the students thought I was some sort of CIA Native American tracker!

A few days later, we'd guided a class to a nearby well, where they were to hunker down for the night. The day had been well over 120 degrees, and the water source was obviously much appreciated—at first.

The students discovered a dead mouse in the well's bucket. The stench was considerable. They could not bring themselves to drink from it. They protested to me, demanding fresh water. I asked them if they'd boiled the well water and put iodine in it. They said yes. So I asked for one of their canteens, drank half of it, then poured the other half down my pants.

"If it's clean enough for my crotch and my throat, it should be good enough for you." I handed back the canteen and walked off.

At the end of the two weeks, I emerged from the desert and called home on the Fourth of July. My mom answered, sobbing. My beloved Abuelo Emilin had died that very morning in Cuba. My grandmother had woken up to find him holding her hand after passing in his sleep.

I returned to an empty house in Miami Springs filled with a deep sense of loss and a profound loneliness. The dark anger and pain I'd been feeling for months turned even more acidic. Instead of a refuge, the house served as a constant reminder of the heartbreak and pain I'd been dealing with for almost a year now. I didn't fear physical pain. But heartbreak? I had no answer for it.

The next morning after my shift at the firehouse, I went for my run through the shade. I got back bathed in sweat, still unable to get out of my own head. If I didn't figure out something, it was going to come out in some volcanic, very bad way. For weeks, I'd been snapping at people who were only being social. I was looking for a fight, some outlet to blow off the steam. Nothing was working. I didn't know what to do.

I poured a glass of water and went out to the porch to sit in the sun, frustrated that I couldn't break out of this darkness.

Inside, the phone rang. The interruption annoyed me, but I got up to answer it anyway.

"Prado."

"Hey, Ric, this is Russ," came a voice. I recognized him as one of the CIA officers from Special Activities Division whom I had just worked with in Arizona. "Not sure you remember me—"

"I remember you," I said.

"I have a really important job that you may be interested in. Would you be willing to come up and talk about some work?" he asked.

*Hell yes, I would. Get me the hell out of here.*

"Short or long term?" I asked.

A pause. "Long term."

I didn't hesitate. "I'm in."

"Great. When can you get to D.C.?"

It was a Thursday. Heart racing, excitement building, I replied, "Will Monday work?"

"Excellent. See you then."

I was bound for Langley at last, and soon enough I would leave this empty house behind forever.

# 7

## AGENCY MAN

*Langley, Virginia*
*Fall 1980*

Walking up the steps of the Agency's headquarters building, I felt six feet tall. Ever since my first encounter with espionage and World War II novels, I had dreamed of living the life of a spy. Those years of escapist reading as a kid fostered a vision of what spies do.

Would I be fitted for a tux? Taught the art of Sean Connery–esque seduction? My martinis shaken, not stirred? I didn't know what to expect, but the preconceptions I entered the building with would soon enough be torn down by the reality of the job.

Fortunately, this was one of those rare times in life where the reality was better than the preconceptions.

When my family had nothing in those first years in Florida, I learned to savor every good moment that came along. My stride slowed, I looked up at the entrance to the headquarters building and tried to breathe an eternity into this moment. Now, here I was, a once-orphaned Cuban refugee from the streets of Miami about to join the storied Central Intelligence Agency.

When I reached the glass doors I paused, stretching a final second or two out of this moment. As I did, I saw through the glass the CIA's famous seal embossed on the marble lobby floor in gray and white. In its center, above the star and shield, was the symbol of my adopted country, the eagle. He looked proud, resolute, and rugged as hell.

*Don't mess with us!*

Into the lobby I went, but I skirted the seal, thinking it would be sacrilegious to walk on it. That became a ritual of mine for the next thirty years.

The lobby possessed a blend of grandeur and history that left me mesmerized. It felt dreamlike just to be there, among the columns, the busy suits hurrying this way and that, and of course the Memorial Wall to my right where chiseled into the marble were the words, "IN HONOR OF THOSE MEMBERS OF THE CENTRAL INTELLIGENCE AGENCY WHO GAVE THEIR LIVES IN THE SERVICE OF THEIR COUNTRY."

Below the words were five rows of stars, each one representing an officer lost. Flanking the stars was an American flag on the left, an Agency flag on the right.

Looking at it gave me chills. Most of those stars had no names attached below them. Men and women so devoted that they gave their lives for a country whose people would likely never learn their names or know their deeds. Quiet heroes, anonymous but remembered, silent to the end.

But not forgotten.

I checked in and announced who I was and who I was there to see. While I waited for my point of contact to come escort me, I noticed a statue on the left side of the lobby. I walked over to it.

Wild Bill Donovan.

He was a major childhood hero of mine, along with Teddy Roosevelt and Wyatt Earp. When he founded the OSS—the CIA's World War II forerunner—he told President Roosevelt he'd fill the ranks with "calculatingly reckless men of disciplined daring . . . and that they would be trained for aggressive action."

I promised myself that in the months and years ahead, I would measure up to the example of those pioneers.

My point of contact arrived, escorted me behind the stars to the badge office. I filled out some paperwork and was led to the Special Activities Division. There, I learned that they needed a Spanish-speaking paramilitary officer but had no one in-house who fit that bill. Then somebody remembered me, the "Cuban PJ" from the field training exercises over the previous summer. I'd made a good impression, and while at the time they'd told me they had no openings, they'd kept me in mind for when something came up.

Came up it did. I was led into a small conference room to be briefed on my new role.

Anastasio Somoza had long been considered one of the worst despots in Central America, ruling Nicaragua from 1967 until 1979. His regime had grown so corrupt and oppressive that the Carter administration withdrew its support and forced most of Somoza's allies to follow suit. Since the early 1960s, a Soviet- and Cuban-backed communist insurgency had flourished in the Nicaraguan countryside. Following a massive earthquake that devastated much of Nicaragua, the Sandinistas, as the insurgents were known, gained the upper hand. After Carter turned against him, Somoza was doomed. He fled the country in 1979 after looting its treasury. Allegedly, when the Sandinistas took power, they were left with less than $2 million with which to run the country.

Shortly before I arrived in Langley, a Sandinista hit squad assassinated Somoza while he was living in exile in Paraguay in what was called Operation Reptile.

The Sandinistas quickly consolidated their power through a Nazi-like pogrom and oppression of their own. The regime followed the same path Castro had—purging less ideologically committed allies, throwing opposition members into prisons, or killing them outright. The country was bankrupt, and people in the countryside were starving. Meanwhile, Daniel Ortega, the new pro-Soviet dictator of Nicaragua, had opened the door to communist influence. Economic and military aid from the Eastern Bloc was flowing into Central America via Cuba, and the Sandinistas began to stoke Marxist insurgencies in other nations, including El Salvador. Central America was fast approaching a tipping point.

At stake was more than just one nation's swing to the Soviets. American foreign policy for a century and a half had been predicated on the Monroe Doctrine, which aggressively sought to keep foreign influence out of the Western Hemisphere. The Soviets had found a foothold in our part of the globe through Cuba. Now they were exploiting another domino in Nicaragua. El Salvador, Guatemala, and Honduras were in their crosshairs, too.

Here, in one of the darkest hours of the Cold War, the spread of communism through Central and South America became a dire threat to the security of the United States.

Castro's Marxists had destroyed everything my family had built. America had given us the opportunity to rebuild and start our lives anew. Now, my adopted nation was giving me a chance to strike back at those who had upended and stolen my family's lives. As I listened to the briefing, I saw in my mind's eye the countless families whose hard work would be appropriated by the new Nicaraguan state, whose land would be stolen, whose factories and livelihoods would be robbed with official sanction. They were in for a repeat of what we Cubans had already endured.

In fact, it was already happening. Like Orwell's *Animal Farm,* the revolution's leaders simply became the new communist elite, living high on the backs of the peasants and workers while appropriating what little wealth remained in Nicaragua. The plunderer Somoza had simply been replaced by a plunderer with a different ideology.

Meanwhile, a few desperate men and women had fled across the northern border to Honduras, where they were living in dilapidated refugee camps. They'd seen their farms pillaged, their families destroyed. Others who had been part of Somoza's military escaped to Honduras after they saw what happened to their defeated comrades: executions or imprisonment. They formed the core leadership of this ragtag force, which became known as *the Contras*.

They were willing to fight—not for the Somoza family but for their own families and communities. The problem: they had virtually no training, little support, few supplies, and virtually no weapons. In this condition, the Contras had no hope of beating the Soviet-backed regime.

The CIA was directed by incoming President Ronald Reagan to change that. But they had no native Spanish-speaking paramilitary officers down there. My job was to help provide training to this nascent insurgency. Medical. Military. Whatever I could teach them. "Get your ass to Honduras. Make them love you and trust you. Listen to your bosses. Do what they say. Get them into the fight."

The years of reading I'd done paid off in that moment. I immediately thought, *This is like being an OSS officer trying to train and supply the French resistance to the Germans during World War II*. I understood what I would have to do.

The briefing was short and didn't dwell on the details. When they finished giving me the thirty-thousand-foot overview of the situation, somebody added that I would be on my own. Expendable.

There was no time for me to go through any Agency training. I was to depart in a little over a week. In the interim, I was ordered to check into a local hotel and deal with some admin crap that is never written about in the spy novels: insurance, medical exams, setting up my credit union account, and a myriad of other paperwork.

As I prepared to deploy abroad, I was given my first alias: Alex. My true identity was tucked away. In return, I received identification, credit cards, passport, and other documents.

I failed my first test of fieldcraft just after getting my new identity. I checked into a new hotel in Virginia under my alias, but I signed the registration form "Ric Prado." Just before handing it back to the clerk, I realized what I'd done, tore it up, and had to ask for another one. Fortunately, the clerk didn't suspect anything. Nevertheless, it was a wake-up call for me. In this new life I suddenly had in front of me, such mistakes could get me killed. I would have to be more meticulous in the future.

A few days into the administrative process, it began to dawn on me how different my life would be from now on. My running days in Miami Springs were over. So was the comradery of the firehouse. Most important, I would be far from my little girl and my parents. I could not tell anybody what I was doing, or even where I was.

Before I left for Langley, I'd taken my dad aside and told him I'd been offered a civilian job in the military. I never mentioned the Agency, but he knew his son. He knew I wouldn't leave the military reserves and the firehouse for a job as a bookkeeper for the Department of Defense. He knew I was running toward trouble, legal, but trouble, nonetheless. He also knew not to mention that fact to my mother.

Ten days after being hired by the CIA, I was booked onto a flight to Tegucigalpa, Honduras. Since arriving in Florida from Cuba and one temporary duty assignment (TDY) to Panama for the Jungle Warfare Training Center, I had not been outside of the United States. It happened so quickly I had no time to go see my parents or to somehow find a way to say goodbye to my little girl. With one bag and one suitcase, I stepped onto my third international flight that would carry me to a new life.

I touched down in the Honduran capital expecting that somebody from the CIA crew would be waiting for me. I wandered through the terminal and recovered my suitcase. I didn't see anyone. Was I expecting somebody to be standing there with a sign that read "Alex"? Probably not, but I thought for sure they'd have somebody there to meet me.

After a thorough trip through the terminal, it was clear I was on my own. As the other passengers departed, I found myself virtually alone. Honduras in 1980 was not a big travel destination. The terminal had one pay phone, but I had no number to call, so all I could do was hang around and wait. Eventually, the airport closed, and I was left there alone.

For three hours, I stood outside the terminal, leaning against its wall. I could not have stuck out more if I'd written *I do not belong here* on my forehead.

Finally, two guys from the "base" showed up. They led me to a sedan, and we set off into town.

Honduras was and sadly remains an impoverished nation. The capital was over four hundred years old, nestled between a series of hills. Over the centuries, it grew to include about a million people, but the urban planners failed to keep up with the swelling population. I thought I'd seen poverty before, but that first drive through Tegucigalpa opened my eyes to the desperation so many people face.

There was little sign of American influence here. Later, I would see fast-food restaurants like Burger King and McDonald's in El Salvador and other places I visited throughout Central and South America. Honduras had nothing like that. There was a Holiday Inn downtown, but that was too obvious a place for the likes of me to stay. Instead, they drove me to a quiet place called the Hotel Alameda, located minutes away from our base. It was decent lodging and included a security wall and pool in an inner courtyard.

I checked in, got to my room, and my new friends told me, "We are also staying here; join us for dinner and drinks. You start work tomorrow."

The next morning, I was brought to the operation's safe house—basically a nondescript building with offices inside for us to work. There I was introduced to the team and my role in it. In these early days, there were only five CIA officers who interfaced directly with the Contras in Tegucigalpa; none were yet in the field. My job was to go into the ten camps that lay scattered along the Honduran-Nicaraguan border and help train and organize them while building trust. This would be a tall order. The camps were located in remote sections of the jungle or high mountains, only accessible via poorly developed roads, or by helicopters, which we did not initially have access to.

The Contras were divided internally between rival factions and leaders, as well as along ethnic grounds. On the east coast, the Miskito Indians were willing to fight against Ortega, but the other Contra groups mistrusted them because of their dreams of autonomy. The Miskito, in turn, mistrusted the "Spaniards," whose leaders all came from the former Somoza regime. Eventually, there would also emerge a southern front, which was largely populated by disaffected former Sandinistas. Layered into this Byzantine drama was a group of Argentinian army officers, sent north to assist in developing the Contras into a viable fighting force. Though the U.S. was paying for their presence, so far, they had done little to earn their pay. Most caroused in the capital and played favorites with the Contra factions, which made unifying them even more difficult for us.

There was competition among the camps for the available supplies—what little there was to be had. The Honduran army provided some support, but the Contras lacked weapons, food, clothing—even shoes. Still, from the initial briefings, I knew that they did not lack in grit. Anyone willing to live shoeless in the jungle on near-starvation rations had to be motivated.

Supplies and training—that's what they needed. Though I would be residing in the capital, most of my time would be spent in the camps, getting to know each faction, its leaders, and its needs. It would mean some of the most rugged and inhospitable terrain imaginable—and I would be doing it without any other American or Agency officer.

Over the course of the next few days, I was introduced to some of the Contra senior leadership and to our courageous Honduran counterparts in the capital as "Captain Alex." Once I finished the meet and briefs, I was asked, "When will you be ready to go see the camps?"

"How about yesterday?"

# 8

## THE MUCH-MALIGNED PATRIOTS

*Honduran Border*

*Late 1980*

The beat-up Toyota Hilux bounced along the jungle track, its suspension getting a workout as the vehicle pitched and rolled along. We'd been driving for hours, never getting above about thirty miles an hour as the track wound its way deeper into the Honduran outback. Palms and broad-leafed Spanish cedars, balsa, rosewood, and Castilla rubber trees towered over increasingly dense scrub to make a crowded canopy of foliage so thick that it virtually blocked out the sun. We forded fast-moving streams, inching the Hilux along in the current, watching as the front wheels nearly disappeared underwater.

This was some of the most unknown terrain on earth. Poorly mapped, not well explored because of the jungle's many dangers that ranged from pumas to dozens of insect-borne diseases not well understood by modem medical science. No wonder entire civilizations disappeared here, their cities overtaken and swallowed by the rain forest for centuries.

The border between Honduras and Nicaragua was unmarked, an

endless stretch of green, punctuated by an occasional village flanked by fields still tended by hand. Slash-and-burn farming was still predominant.

We drove south, winding along, gaining altitude. As we went higher, we left the jungle behind. The terrain became arid, rugged, and hot. Craggy hilltops and sawtooth mountain ridges replaced the rainforest landscape as we topped out at 5,500 feet. Pine trees stippled the slopes around us, making the place look a little like Mexico or Southern California.

Today, our destination was one of the westernmost camps, closest to the Pacific Ocean. It finally came into view, a collection of huts and makeshift structures stretched across a hillside cleared of trees. The few men and women there were rail-thin, wearing a collage of civilian checkered shirts, olive-drab uniform pants, and caps. A few wore fatigue jackets. As we inched up the slope of the hill to its entrance, I could see the guards carrying a variety of weapons—ancient bolt-action rifles and shotguns. Soon we would replace these with Belgian-made FN-FAL 7.62mm assault rifles.

Each of the ten camps situated along the border with Nicaragua housed perhaps a couple of hundred soldiers. Those in charge ran things because the men were loyal to them somehow. Each camp's leaders presided over a personal fiefdom and private force of loyalists. They were supposed to report to the Nicaraguan Democratic Force (FDN) senior leadership council in Tegucigalpa, on which they depended for the meager logistical support and the promise of better days to come.

We pulled into the camp and rolled to a stop. As I dismounted from the Hilux, I could see some of the men gathering to greet us did not even own shoes. They lived side by side in hellishly hot huts, lucky to have a cot to keep them off the ground, eating food that would make most humans gag. Homemade hammocks were stretched between the trees. All the camps I visited shared these commonalities. It was a crazy way to go to war. But that was what we were there to fix. And fix it we would.

While I made my rounds through the ten camps, the FDN logistics folks kept making overland resupply trips, and more and more of the USG-procured supplies were starting to trickle into the camps. Morale was improving, and so were the living conditions—albeit still Spartan by any third-world military standards.

When I again returned to the first camp I visited, I was greeted by the camp's leader, Commander Suicida, who was a former Nicaraguan National Guard sergeant named Pedro Pablo Ortiz Centeno. He had escaped to Honduras after the Sandinistas took over his country. He was rugged, charismatic, and led from the front, sometimes carrying an M60 machine gun as he fought alongside his men. In combat, he displayed a level of reckless courage that earned him the nickname "Commander Suicide." His personal example and personal magnetism engendered considerable loyalty among his men. They were a dedicated, tight-knit group wanting only to strike across the border at their Sandinista enemies.

Over the years, Suicida has been painted by the media and academics as a brutal killer who, among other things, deliberately assassinated Nicaraguan and Cuban members of a literacy program designed to teach peasants to read. How such Marxist propaganda infected the history of the Contra war is beyond credulity. Suicida was a warrior who fought to reclaim his country. Would he kill? Hell yes, he would, but only his sworn enemies, the Piricuaco—"Rabid Dogs"—as the Contras called the Sandinistas.

I slung my AR-15 rifle over one shoulder and told him we'd brought him a supply of Soviet-made 82mm ammunition along with a few mortar tubes with which to fire them. He sent one of his men to start unloading the supplies. I can still remember those wiry rebels hoisting the heavy boxes of mortar rounds up that steep, muddy hill. I was in damn good shape, and I was sucking the leaves off the trees while trying to make it up that hill.

Before we'd even finished our conversation, a sudden rash of gunfire erupted from the scrub pines on the southern slope of the hilltop.

Contras began running toward the gunfire, their leaders barking orders. Bullets whined and cracked. I unslung my AR-15 and rushed to join the fight.

An automatic weapon cut loose. More shouts and angry cries. The Contras began shooting back. The Sandinistas down the hill sprayed and prayed. The Contras did the same; not me—I aimed and shot. Then, as suddenly as it began, the enemy faded back into the trees and vanished. Time on target? One minute, but it felt like a lifetime.

I could see the Sandinistas didn't have much training, nor tactical acumen. Neither did the Contras, of course. The firefight was more a battle between armed mobs than two military formations.

None of my Contras were killed on the hilltop, but the raid made me angry. The Piricuacos had crossed into Honduras and attacked the people I was supposed to help. I quickly found out this was not an uncommon harassment tactic.

This needed to stop. It would also be an opportunity to earn street cred with the Contras, who'd seen other "leaders" like the Argentines come and go with little interest in living or fighting alongside them.

That was the first thing I tried to change. I lived with them, embracing the suck equally with them. When I began to show them how to use the mortars, they realized I might be useful to them.

Those 82mm mortars made for terrific jungle- and mountain-portable artillery weapons. They consisted of three main parts—the smooth bore tube, the baseplate, and the bipod. A small sight could be installed on the side of the tube. Altogether, the pieces weighed about 120 pounds. The mortar bombs contained about 420 grams of high explosives and themselves weighed about six pounds. The crew fired the weapon by feeding the round into the tube's muzzle. It would slide down the inside to a firing pin at the bottom that ignited the round's propelling charge, sending it flying out in a ballistic arc to the crew's target. They were deadly effective when employed properly.

During the day, I trained them to fight, showed them how to use the weaponry I could bring them. I taught them to push forward observers out to spot the fall of each mortar shell, and how to use radios to adjust fire.

Gradually, I got to know who these people were. They told me horrific stories of how their families had been slaughtered by the Sandinistas. They were farmers, artisans—peasants, really—who fled the oppression with nothing but the clothes on their backs. They weren't just poor; they were destitute.

Many were religious refugees—devout Catholics purged by the Marxists, who saw religious faith as an enemy of the state. These people of faith refused to submit to a government whose central premise was that the system itself should be worshipped, not a higher being.

Their lives were defined by this struggle. They wanted to fight for and avenge what had happened to their wives, their kids, churches, and villages. They told me harrowing stories of escape, how the Sandinistas marauded towns, raping and looting the terrified villagers. They played death games—men with guns tormenting people with nothing but a few farm animals that were soon to be stolen and eaten by these communist gangsters.

Listening to these stories, I understood why they were willing to endure so much privation in the camps. They'd lost everything to the communists. Now, they pinned their hopes on the rebellion. I didn't find anyone who was pro-Somoza, or any single unifying political ideology. To them, this was a personal war against those who stole their lives and families.

This well-earned fear and hatred for the Sandinista regime was the central rallying point that kept the Contras together. They were willing to suffer through things most Americans could never even fathom if only to get a chance to strike back at those who destroyed their world.

After some basic training on the mortars, Suicida led his men on a reprisal attack for the Sandinista raid. Our freshly minted forward observers infiltrated through the pine forest to the Sandinista camp, which was not far from the Contras'. Lax security on their part let our men creep close enough to get a good vantage point to reconnoiter their base.

I then led my Contras to launch a mortar barrage that caused total chaos and inflicted significant damage. We were lucky from the outset when our first few mortar rounds landed a bit long of target. This actually turned into an unintended benefit. With explosions going off behind their positions, the Sandinistas went to ground and we pinned them in place. After all, nobody wants to run away *through* a mortar barrage.

We adjusted fire and delivered a good dozen direct hits on the camp. Eventually, the Sandinista troops fled, taking only their dead and wounded. Though we suffered no losses that day, the Contras lacked the logistics to stay and occupy the territory. Reluctantly, Suicida led them back to the camp to live and raid another day. That was the best they could do with the minimal resources they had. To assault into Nicaraguan territory, hold it, and push deeper into the country in a sustained offensive required a logistical system that simply did not exist at that point. Any operation like that needed food, water, ammunition, medical support—and all with a means to deliver them through some of the most inhospitable terrain in the world. There were few roads, which made the logistical situation even more difficult.

An offensive would be beyond the ability of the Contras for several years. For now, the hit-and-run raids would be the only way to strike at the Sandinistas.

In the weeks that followed that indoctrination into combat, I again traveled to all ten camps, meeting and developing strong relationships with the leaders as well as the rebel soldiers, listening to whatever they wanted to tell me. Being a native Spanish speaker, I was told a lot.

I began to get a sense of the intrigue going on between the Contra field commanders and the FDN's leadership back in Tegucigalpa. My first briefing at our safe house mentioned this, but with a little time in country, I gained a greater appreciation of the sometimes savage internal infighting.

Layered into the intrigue was an Argentine Army contingent sent north to ostensibly train and equip the Contras. Their cadre was an eight-man team of sergeants and officers who rarely bothered to visit the camp. When they did, they never stayed overnight. They played favorites with supplies, provided little training, and stole money the Agency had allocated for the Contra field commanders and foot soldiers. For them, the assignment was a get-rich-quick scam with Uncle Sam as their mark.

Suicida in particular was furious with their behavior and made no effort to conceal it. Ultimately, that made him a target, and he knew the Argentines were machinating to get rid of him.

I heard similar things about the Argentines in the other camps I visited, including the Miskito Indian camp on the eastern end of the country. There, I got to know the Miskitos as fierce warriors who lived in the coastal lowland jungles and clung to their traditional way of life. The Miskitos were looked down on by the other Contra leaders. The Argentinians reflected that same racist sentiment and made sure the Miskitos received the barest of resupplies.

To compound matters, the Argentinians were unabashed anti-Semites. My first boss at the time was Jewish. This led to even more friction and trouble with the Argentinians. At one point, the Argentine general laughingly said to "Joel," my then boss, "Yeah, when we were having trouble in the army, we just shot every third soldier. Just like the Nazis with the Jews!"

Needless to say, the relationship between these thugs and the rest of the Agency's effort in Honduras was strained, to say the least. We were there to help the Contras reclaim their country and establish a new democracy. That was the last thing the Argentines were there to do.

Between my time in Tegucigalpa, I investigated the Argentines and met all of them. To a man, I found them to be useless parasites. They weren't teaching the Contras how to fight; I never once saw any of them conduct any training at the camps. They were taking American money and using it to whore and party in Tegucigalpa. Get a few drinks in some of them, and they would openly brag about being part of death squads back home in Argentina. They were men of the basest moral character—murderers and rank opportunists who used their military positions to service their own indulgences.

It was a reprehensible situation, but one I didn't have the authority to do anything about. All I could do was mitigate the damage their indulgences did to the Contra cause.

That damage was the severest at the Miskito camps. These men were fierce, committed anti-Sandinistas. More than any other group in the FDN, they suffered the worst *depredations* at the hands of the Sandinistas, who were just as racist and hate-filled as the Argentinians when it came to this small, indigenous population.

More than any other FDN faction, the Miskitos had one clear goal: retake their homeland along the coast and continue to lobby for their autonomy. Once that was done, they didn't care who ruled Nicaragua. They just wanted to be left alone by everyone.

They needed little from outsiders in ordinary times. They hunted and grew crops in sections of the jungle they cleared, and there were several key gold mines in their territory. Two of the largest ports in Nicaragua—Puerto Cabezas and Bluefields—were in the Mosquitia, and these provided trade and work for those who wanted it. They were a proud and pure people. I liked them immediately.

That was not reciprocated, at least not at first. After eating so many shit sandwiches from friend and foe alike, they didn't trust me much. Yet from the first moments I spent in their camp, I could tell they could be the most formidable and loyal fighters in the entire Contra movement. I would need to earn their trust and help get them better integrated into the overall FDN operation. No easy task.

The first step clearly would require getting supplies to these guys. The Argentines had a lock on that at FDN HQ. I would soon have to consult with my new boss on how to best confront that den of snakes. In the meantime, I brought them what weapons I could and showed them how to employ them. On one trip, I carried a small cache of RPG-7 rocket launchers to the Miskitos. They'd never used such weapons before, so I set up a target on a makeshift range, then put a piece of cardboard behind the launcher as I prepared to fire. I wanted them to see how dangerous the rocket's exhaust could be. I walked my audience through arming the rocket, then kneeling and aiming it.

I fired, and the RPG obliterated the target. The Miskitos cheered. It was a good moment. They could see this particular stranger knew what he was doing. They also saw what happened to the cardboard behind the launcher. It had been peppered with back blast and singed by the blast-furnace-hot exhaust coming from the tailpipe. Lesson learned. Don't stand behind the rocket launcher or fire it in an enclosed space. As obvious as it sounds, it was a common mistake made elsewhere that led to severe burns.

Traveling by Hilux on the pitted and rutted roads was rough on vehicles and drivers alike; the vehicles were tossed around. Tropical thunderstorms reduced the roads to rivers of mud, and frequently we bogged down. In fact, in the Mosquitia's outermost camps, like Auasbila, we traveled on the Coco River via dugout canoes. That made us vulnerable to potential Sandinista attack. Yet in those first months, I still managed to visit two camps a week, staying with each contingent to help provide basic training and establish rapport with the men and women there.

During one of my many trips between the camps, we came to a river filled with fleeing refugees. Hundreds of them, including many women carrying babies as small children clung to them as they waded across to the Honduran side of the river and the comparative safety of one of the UN-established refugee camps there. The trauma of their experiences was stamped on their faces.

These were haunting moments for me that I dwelled on for years afterward. Americans back home would never believe the suffering we witnessed down there in such moments. It was the same suffering triggered by the same ideology that the same type of people inflicted on my homeland in Cuba twenty-two years before.

In one camp run by "Commander Benito," I sensed the frustration of a force wanting to do something about the suffering but lacking the means to do it. The weapons they had were still inadequate for an offensive operation—plus, like every other group, they had no way to sustain a deep push into Nicaragua. Yet despite the shortcomings, the men in this camp possessed high morale and an aggressive spirit.

At one point, Benito's radio operator pulled me aside. His nom de guerre was Mike Lima, a former National Guard junior officer who'd done a year at West Point after being accepted into the Nicaraguan military academy at age seventeen.

Mike Lima's academy class graduated early in 1979 and was sent into a last-ditch fight to save the Somoza regime. During the fighting, he was wounded by shrapnel, captured, then escaped. He sought temporary asylum in a foreign embassy before escaping Nicaragua and joining Benito's band of Contras.

"I want to fight," he confided to me. "We need to go out there and get into combat."

Talking with Mike Lima, I recognized he was a capable young man. He understood the importance of winning over the local populations. He saw them as sources of assistance, pools from which to recruit. Within them, the Contras could build a network of informants to keep track of Sandinista military movements. He saw the connection between the people and the guerillas that had, time and time again in other insurgencies, created the framework for success.

Impressed by Mike, I went and met with Benito and talked him into giving Mike a field command instead of leaving him behind, chained to the camp's radios. Mike soon proved himself a dozen times over. He would rise to become one of the best combat leaders in the FDN on the northern front.

The days were long and exhausting, made longer since I was the only native Spanish-speaking member of the American team. In fact, I was handpicked because I could pass for a non-American, as the U.S. role in Honduras needed to be hidden. That would change in time, but for the first fourteen months of the program, I remained the only CIA officer allowed in the camps and the only soul representing the Agency's efforts to forge an effective fighting force out of this ragtag confederacy of rebels.

Despite the hardships, I never resented my three-year-long routine of fifty-two weekly visits per year to my beloved camps.

At the end of those long and rugged days, I would retire to a hut or a tent for the night, and my mind would dwell on my future. I thought about this life and these men clinging to the hope that more help would arrive so they could defy the odds and liberate their homeland. I loved being a part of this mission.

Their crusade became my crusade. Our enemy was the communists and communism. That particular -ism sparked not the utopia it so loudly proclaimed but instead visited horrors on average people. Everywhere communists gained control, people suffered. Pol Pot in Cambodia. Stalin. The staggering bloodshed of Mao Tse-tung's "Cultural Revolution" in China. The purges and violence in Yugoslavia and Cuba, North Korea, and now here in Nicaragua.

In Miami, I felt like I was drifting sideways. Angry and embittered, off my path. Every day I felt like Sisyphus pushing my damn rock up the muddy hill. When the chance to work with the Agency came up, I jumped at it solely to get me out of that limbo. Little did I know it was God's way of putting me on the path to my destiny.

I realized that now, pondering these things as I did at night in the jungle. I had been born to be out here, side by side with these dedicated warriors. It made me realize that deep inside, I was a man who had always wanted to make a difference in the world. Part of that difference included striking blows at the ideology that robbed these Contras of their land and heritage—just like it had stolen those things from my own family.

I was making a difference. And the meaning I found out there with the Contras led me to the path I was meant to take. Until then, I'd had no real life plan. I'd drifted from one thing to the next. I wasn't drifting now. The path I needed chose me. I realized my job was to stay on it no matter how difficult it became.

Among the most difficult things I would have to do in my first months out here would be to confront the Argentinians. The Miskitos needed weapons, money, and supplies. If we could get the supplies flowing, I knew I could earn the trust of all the Contras, not just the Miskitos. I thought through how I would take that next step. The Argentines were a nasty lot of gangsters. I'd have to recruit my bosses' help if we were going to play a strong hand to slap them into place.

# 9

## ON THE SPEARHEAD OF THE REAGAN DOCTRINE

*Honduras*

*1981*

Not long after I arrived in Honduras, our base commander, Joel, rotated home. In his place, the Agency sent "Colonel Ray." Ray had been a teenager during World War II who'd jumped with the 503rd Parachute Infantry Regiment onto Corregidor Island during the Philippines Campaign in 1945. I quickly learned Ray was an old-school gentleman who possessed both wit and charm. But underneath the patina of refinement was a man of great courage with a heart as tough as his World War II jump boots. He served in Vietnam and Laos, working behind the lines for the Agency. Ray's aura, conviction, dedication, and reputation inspired me for the rest of my career. As I rose through the ranks, "What would Ray do?" remained my sanity check. Those are the giants I grew up under—more than a few of them. I do my best to emulate them to this day. It would be his vision that set the stage for the expansion of the support effort to the Contras.

Ray quickly realized the Argentines were a major problem for us. They were taking American money and doing little to nothing in return. Yet at the same time, the Argentines were the original foreign support for the Contras. They reached out to the Sandinista opposition after discovering Daniel Ortega had been funneling aid to Argentina's own endemic pro-Soviet opposition.

Part of the way the CIA sold supporting the Contras back in the D.C. political swamp was by highlighting that we'd just be buying our way into the existing Argentinian effort. They'd lead the way; we'd support with a few training advisors and money.

It looked good on paper, but the Argentines were so corrupt and contentious, it was soon apparent we could never create an effective fighting force out of the Contras while going through these surrogates.

When Ray learned they were holding back supplies from the Miskito Indians, he saw it as an opportunity to put the Argentines in their place. He directed me to take care of that. I felt like a pit bull with a bone on this mission. I couldn't wait to confront the Argentines and get the Miskitos better situated.

I met with the Argentine general and a colonel in one of the Tegucigalpa safe houses used by the FDN's chief of staff. "General Villegas"—that was just his alias—was a soft, bucktoothed thug of a man in his midsixties. Imperious and arrogant, he validated our inside joke: What is the best investment you can make? Buy one of these Argentines for what they are worth and sell them for what they think they are worth!

In the field, I was Captain Alex, which presented a problem when dealing with the Argentinians, since the rank-conscious General Villegas considered me an underling in what had been his show.

Nevertheless, I was instructed to win the hearts and minds of the Contras, not of the Argentines. To this day, just thinking about the Argentines makes my blood boil. They were a stark contrast to the Honduran officers I met, all of whom were men I would end up admiring for life.

The meeting did not start well. I sat across from Villegas and his minion—a colonel who, as best as we Americans could figure, was in charge of the general's campaign of graft and thievery in Tegucigalpa.

They were running their own nest-feathering cons together with money supposed to be used to help these Nicaraguan patriots in the camp. Given the desperate conditions I witnessed, it was hard to conceal my disgust for these rank opportunists.

There were minimal introductions and small talk. Instead, I made it clear that we knew the Miskitos were not getting their share of the available supplies and that, per Colonel Ray, would change starting now. The general pushed back, throwing his rank around. He had no defense to his bald-faced racism, so he resorted to bombast and intimidation. It didn't work. When he pulled rank, I pulled logistics: "These are U.S. supplies, and *we* represent the United States' interests here. Those supplies will go to the Miskitos."

The general balked. This was his show, and he wasn't going to let a mere captain tell him how to run it. We went back and forth, the conversation growing heated. Finally, I'd had enough. I told him we'd cut the money and supplies off until the Miskitos were given their share.

Villegas grew so angry that he snapped a pencil in half. Knowing he could do nothing about this—I'd unmasked how little actual authority he had now—the general sat there and silently stewed while I finalized the logistics plan they would employ on behalf of the Contras.

Message delivered. His gravy train came from the United States, and no matter the stars on his shoulder board, he was no longer in a position to deny the will of the Agency.

After the meeting, he went to our Chief of Station (COS) in Tegucigalpa and complained about me. The COS offered a warm smile and said, "Alex is my man on this."

Translation from diplomatic speak: "Fuck you."

Much to General Villegas's outrage, I was then assigned to examine the Argentinian books to make sure every dime was accounted for and spent where it was supposed to go. That was arguably my first lesson about the CIA's strict accountability. Ray explained that all special programs were approved by Congress as "fenced funds."

This meant that any money allocated to a program—to the penny—had to be used for that particular program and nothing else. So much for the myth of "black, illegal funds."

From then on, I questioned every nickel and became such a thorn in their side that Villegas's senior aid, a colonel, once spat at me, "You are only a U.S. captain!"

I smiled back and replied, "Yes, but the important part is the 'U.S.'"

They had no choice. Under the new sheriff, Ray, the Argentines did indeed start sharing the available weapons, food, and ammunition with the Miskito Indians. When I returned to their camps, the reception I received was totally different. They knew I had gone to bat for them as I had promised, and that went a long way toward building trust with them.

The Miskitos quickly employed the new supplies of weapons and ammunition in cross-border raids against Sandinista Popular Army positions. They did not disappoint. In these actions, their bravery and ferocious fighting spirit shone, and I made sure that it was well documented. They were warriors without a nation, battling to reclaim their conquered homeland. They did so like men possessed. I had no doubt that with more support and training, they would be the most effective force in the FDN.

It was here I learned lesson number two from Ray: the Miskito were popular with several U.S. political sectors. Among Native Americans and some prominent liberals, the Miskito were considered to be the oppressed, indigenous forces untainted by association to Somoza. That political viability back in the States with elements often hostile to the Agency helped us enormously. Ray's insight on this helped GS-10 Alex to learn the bigger picture. It was also a mentoring lesson I would not forget and continue to this day to pay it forward.

While the cross-border raids on the Sandinista army's encampments improved morale and gave the Contras combat experience and a sense that they were in the fight, they were mere pinpricks to the regime. This was not the way to win their country back. To do that, the FDN needed staying power—the ability to conduct an offensive into Nicaragua and eventually hold ground. The only way that could happen was with a solid source of supplies and a means to deliver them deep into Nicaragua. There were few roads, fewer Contra vehicles, and no logistical tail to support such an operation. The overall Contra force was still barely a thousand men, though they were recruiting more every day.

Clearly, we needed airpower. A Contra offensive could only be sustained with air-dropped resupplies, but there was nothing like that available in the early days of 1981. Ray immediately went to work on that problem while I continued training and assisting in the camps, preparing the Contras for the day they could launch a larger operation.

Ray's next lesson to me: amateurs plan tactics, professionals plan logistics. We could assemble an enormous army, but if we couldn't find a way to keep them in beans and bullets, it would be a hollow force.

For the time being, the cross-border raids would be the best we could do. In the camps, while morale continued to slowly improve as the weapons and supplies trickled in, the conditions in the jungle never ceased to appall me. Malnutrition, malaria, dysentery, and parasitic infections were common problems in the camps in those days. I even saw cases of mountain leprosy (leishmaniasis).

Being a trained medic, I provided what medical care I could, but just as food was scarce, medical supplies were usually also unavailable. I saw open sores, men with hollowed cheeks from weeks of minimal rations and chronic diarrhea, and malaria. They were in bad shape. Yes, the training needs were great, but they couldn't fight if they couldn't even walk, so much of my time was spent coordinating their crucial logistical support. Again, Ray's lesson stuck with me as I saw the practical realities on the ground. More medical supplies were desperately needed.

Despite the harsh living, the Contra foot soldiers refused to give up. That kind of grit always inspired me. When I relayed stories highlighting their tenacity to Ray, he asked me to document as much of the reality as I could with a 35mm camera. From that point on, I took photos in every camp of the conditions and the people. At the end of my week, I would drive back to Tegucigalpa and drop the exposed rolls off at our base. They were developed in-house, and the prints were given to me. Unbeknownst to me, Ray asked for duplicate prints from those negatives, which he sent back to the task force. Little did I know, the photos ended up on the desk of CIA director William "Bill" Casey.

Bill Casey was a legend in clandestine circles. A brilliant manager, attorney, and businessman, he joined the OSS during World War II and rose to command the Secret Intelligence Branch in Europe, where he spearheaded the spy operations against Nazi Germany. With Ronald Reagan's election in 1980, Bill Casey became the head of the CIA. The Agency had suffered badly in the 1970s as a result of Vietnam, the Church Committee's discovery of its excesses in the '50s and '60s, plus the fiasco with the Iran hostage crisis. In the months after Casey took over, he quickly set a new agenda. The CIA would be engaged, aggressive, and daring, like the OSS of World War II. Instead of reporting information to the White House, Bill took the CIA job only on the condition that he could help shape foreign policy as well. Never had the CIA had this amount of influence before, and Casey intended to use it to stem what looked like a rising tide of pro-Soviet communist power then sweeping the globe from Afghanistan to Africa and Central America.

In March, after only two months in power, Casey put together a plan to support pro-U.S. factions in communist-ruled or American-hostile nations. His list included Afghanistan, Cambodia, Grenada, Laos, Iran, Cuba, and Nicaragua. That document served as the prototype for the Reagan Doctrine, which the president unveiled in his 1985 State of the Union speech.

William Casey became the architect of our late–Cold War counteroffensive against the Soviets in the developing world. After two decades of defeats from the Bay of Pigs to Vietnam and Iran, we would fight back through the black ops to stop the spread of Russian influence.

At the end of my career, I looked back and thanked God that I had the honor of working for the greatest DCI since Wild Bill Donovan: Wild Bill Casey!

Developing the Contras as a legitimate threat to the Sandinistas would become a central part of that aggressive strategy, as was supporting the mujahideen in Afghanistan, who were fighting the Red Army's occupation there. These two covert operations played crucial roles in the Cold War's final act.

To coordinate the covert war against the Sandinistas, Casey wanted a maverick CIA officer who could think unconventionally. He needed to be aggressive and willing to take risks. He found his man in Rome's Chief of Station: Duane "Dewey" Clarridge.

Five foot ten, gray-haired, and prone to wearing exceptionally tailored Italian silk suits, Clarridge was an Ivy League–educated Cold Warrior who joined the Agency in 1955. He'd earned a reputation for being an eccentric but brilliant officer. He was glib, a hip shooter who thought on his feet and never worried about the consequences. Over his career, he'd been viewed almost with awe by those who worked under him and as a major pain in the ass by his superiors. Loved or hated— there was no in-between—Clarridge got things done.

In the spring of 1981, Casey pulled him out of Rome and made him the head of the Latin American division in the Operations Directorate. This was the first major step toward creating the infrastructure at the top that could transform the Contras into a war-winning force with our covert support.

Of course, in the moment, I knew none of this. My worldview barely extended beyond the jungle on the Honduran border. With but a few weeks total in Langley, first as a contractor, then as a quick paramilitary hire, I knew little about the inner workings of the Agency or the complicated tangle of politics back in D.C. I'd heard stories about Dewey from Ray, who was a big admirer, but it was so far above my pay grade back then, I paid little attention. My world consisted of the day-to-day mechanics of trying to teach shoeless peasants how to shoot straight. Little did I know that the machinations above my head would put me at the tip of the spear of what evolved into the Reagan Doctrine.

Shortly after Clarridge settled into his new role, he and Casey flew into Honduras on a "black visit"—a top-secret trip—in order to be briefed directly by those on the ground. As usual, I was in one of the camps when I got a radio call asking me to return to our base of operations in the capital. When I arrived, Ray introduced me to Dewey Clarridge and Bill Casey.

"Mr. Director, this is Alex, your man in the camps."

Casey looked at me and said, "I love your photos. Keep sending them."

I had no idea they were even being sent to Washington. That they were in the hands of the director of the CIA left me doubly surprised.

"You know why I love them?" he asked.

"No, sir, I do not."

"I have them on my desk. I take your photos and I beat those Democrats over the head with them. These men are fighting for freedom. The photos show the Democrats what their needs are. Please keep those pictures coming."

"Thank you, sir."

After that, I most certainly did.

In the months ahead, Bill Casey returned to Honduras a couple of times on black visits to meet with senior Hondurans and the Contra leadership. He even met with the Argentines on occasion, and I served as his translator during those meetings—no pressure there! There I was, a GS-nothing interpreting for the DCI. His presence in Honduras signaled to everyone that the position of the United States was changing. The Contras mattered in Washington.

From the outset of the new administration, finding a way to drive the Sandinistas from power became a top priority. Not only would it curb Soviet power in the region, it would also deliver a blow to Castro's Cuba. With military aid flowing in from the Soviet Union and Cuba, the Sandinistas were furiously trying to undermine other regimes in Central

America by stoking pro-Soviet insurgencies. While we were just starting to get supplies into the Contra camps, there was another covert logistical operation running through Honduras at the same time. This one was controlled by the Sandinistas, who were using assets in country to help smuggle weapons to the communist insurgents in El Salvador. It was a dark and fluid situation, and it looked like the Soviets held the upper hand.

Much later, I learned that Reagan tried a carrot approach, offering millions of dollars in aid to the Ortega regime. For a short time, the infiltration of weapons and ammo to El Salvador stopped as the Sandinistas coveted that money. But the offer was soon withdrawn, and by June 1981, the gunrunning to the communist insurgents recommenced. From that point on, the covert war began to pick up steam.

On the other side of the border, Bulgarians, Russians, more Cubans, and other Warsaw Pact types arrived almost every week to train and equip Ortega's conscript army. By the fall of 1981, the struggle along the Honduran border was well on its way to becoming a proxy war between the superpowers.

While the Sandinistas were unified and well supplied by their allies, the Contras were in bad shape. The FDN leadership was splintered and remained riddled with intrigue. There were growing tensions between the field commanders and the senior leadership in Tegucigalpa. The Argentines continued to be the worst possible stewards of this complicated effort.

From our view in the jungle, we faced long odds as underdogs. It made me work that much harder for the Contra fighters I'd grown to respect so much. Fortunately, Ray was able to secure a helicopter from the Honduran military for me to use to get between the camps. The hours of driving from place to place wasted so much time and was substantially riskier. Now I could get to the camps in a fraction of the time.

The Agency pilot initially assigned to me was a Cuban refugee who had fought in the Bay of Pigs disaster, dragging home a badly shot-up aircraft. "Gustavo," as we called him, was a tough, resourceful aviator and a dedicated anticommunist, but the men lost in 1961 still haunted him at times. One evening, I found him in his room in Tegucigalpa with his sidearm out while sitting beside a mostly empty bottle of liquor. I was young and naive and bulletproof back then. Finding Gustavo like that was one of the first times I encountered how our work could scar a man's soul. Luckily, Gustavo was a patriot and a family man; in time, he pulled himself together.

He was a great pilot, and we worked well together through many difficult operations, both over the jungle and along the coast in the years to come.

Whenever we flew into the Miskito camps, I always studied the jungle landscape with particular attention. I'd heard stories of the lost "Ciudad Blanca" (White City) of the Monkey God, rumored to be somewhere along the Mosquito Coast, and I would try to see if I could find its outlines concealed somewhere below by the rain forest's canopy. I never did find it, but a team of scientists eventually did locate it not far from those flights I took. Most of those scientists later fell dreadfully ill from leishmaniasis, a parasitic infection that can cause massive skin ulcers and liver and spleen damage.

I knew the effects all too well. About a year after I first arrived in Honduras, I had dropped twenty pounds. Living week after week slowly took a toll on my own health. I refused to slow down, but my body finally couldn't take it anymore. One night, Ray called for a medevac flight to come get me out of one of the camps. My fever had spiked, I had the chills, diarrhea, and stomach cramps that left me weak as a kitten. I was flown to Miami, where an Agency-cleared doctor who didn't even ask my name drew blood and stool samples.

After running some tests, he came to me and said, "The good news is you haven't got anything that I haven't treated before. I just haven't ever seen it all in one person."

I had amoebic dysentery, giardia, and a handful of other tropical infections. To this day, I still have stomach issues as a result of that first year in Honduras. But the doctor said he could get me back on my feet. He gave me two treatment options: a slow, gentle course of antibiotics and other medication that would take a few weeks, or a more radical approach that would take half the time. "You'll hate me for two days, but you will get better."

I wanted to get back to my Contras, so I went with option two. He gave me the treatment, and boy, he was not kidding! For two days, I languished in his care, even more debilitated than I was when I first arrived in Miami. In fact, it was the sickest I've ever been in my life.

But at the end of that forty-eight-hour ordeal, I began to recover. My strength returned, and in a week, I hopped a flight back to Honduras, eager to get back to work.

When I returned to my duties, the situation between the FDN and the field commanders had grown even tenser. Then, an incident occurred that had long-term, unforeseen consequences. Comandante Suicida's romantic partner, and camp nurse, "la Negra," ran into a Sandinista ambush and was killed on a dirt road leading to one of Suicida's westernmost camps. This tragedy shook the men's morale to the core and further raised suspicion among the ranks regarding how the Sandinistas knew when and where to strike.

Whenever I visited, she would prepare gallo pinto—brown beans and rice—with fried eggs on top, just for me. She was a wonderful, devoted woman who not only materially assisted the men in the camps but kept Suicida grounded. She had a balancing effect on him. In return, he led his men with Zen-like calm and unmatched fearlessness.

One day, while driving back to the camp, La Negra's vehicle drove into a Sandinista ambush right along the border. She was killed in a hail of gunfire. Her death plunged the camp into despair. Suicida grew increasingly unstable and came to believe her death was orchestrated by somebody at FDN headquarters, purposely leaked so the Sandinistas would do the dirty work for them. We will never know.

While I was working in a different camp, I was told that the FDN leadership removed Suicida from command and brought him back to Tegucigalpa. I never saw him again. While rumors swirled for years about his eventual fate, subsequent historians concluded the Argentinians assassinated him as retaliation for supposed crimes he'd committed while raiding into Nicaragua. In truth, Suicida's real sin was being the most vociferous about his suspicions that the Argentines and some corrupt FDN lackeys were lining their pockets with U.S. money intended for the Contras in the camps.

Without La Negra and Suicida, the western camp fell into disarray. Two of Suicida's subordinates took over, but these two represented the worst of the Contras. During the 1980s, some parts of the American media tried to portray the Contras not as patriots but as nothing more than armed killers who plundered the countryside, committing all manners of atrocities. The entire effort has been painted with that brush by historians and writers ever since.

There was a kernel of truth there, but only a kernel. Occasionally, such atrocities did take place, but for the vast majority of the time I was there, the Contras fought for the people in the Nicaraguan countryside and tried their best to protect them from the Sandinistas. The peasants largely sided with the Contras as a result, especially after Ortega took a page from Joseph Stalin and started a forced collectivization program that stole farmland from its rightful owners.

That said, the two men who took over Suicida's force were the poster children for Contra excesses. They degenerated into banditry. Discipline broke down. A few of Suicida's men went all in with the new leadership, but most were disgusted by what they were seeing. Word leaked from the camp to FDN headquarters that the new leaders had gone rogue. With about three hundred men, they were raiding ranches to steal cattle and rob villagers. After a woman came forward and told the FDN senior leadership that one of the rogue leaders had raped her, it was clear they would need to be brought in to face justice. But how do you extract two thugs with a private army protecting them?

Ray asked me if I could get them out. A good plan and some support always goes a long way. Still, this would be a tricky operation for only a few men to try to execute. But I told Ray I figured we could pull it off—with a little luck and a lot of balls.

# 10

## FRIENDS IN LOW PLACES

*Suicida's Camp*
*1982*

The Huey swept low over the rugged mountain landscape, my newly assigned Honduran pilots deftly making minute corrections on the controls to keep us just off the treetops. We were going in fast and low, standard procedure since the Sandinistas acquired Soviet-made Mi-17 helicopters.[1] Staying low also gave the Sandinista troops below us as little time as possible to track and target us. Nevertheless, our Huey caught occasional bullet sprays, and we would hear them strike the bird like somebody was hammering on a tin roof. Shooting at a moving helicopter is difficult, even for the highly trained. Even if they aimed just in front of the pilot cabin, bullets would most likely hit the tail section . . . and hit they did. Twice the pilots found bullet holes in the tail, three feet behind where we passengers were sitting against the back wall—and always on my side.

Suicida's camp lay ahead on that remote hilltop. The place had

---

1. Subsequently, circa 1984, they upgraded to Mi-24 Hind—the same weapon that terrorized the mujahideen in Afghanistan.

changed significantly since his disappearance. He had been a real leader, devoted to his men and the cause, fearless in battle. He had led from the front on every mission.

On my previous trips, I had trained the men on mortars, machine guns, and sniper rifles. The latter they didn't think too much of, unfortunately. Even after I personally showed them how effective these weapons could be, Suicida and his men decided sniper rifles weren't macho enough. They wanted lots of firepower raining down on the Sandinistas, not a one-shot-one-kill system. So mortars and machine guns it was. Throughout that training, I spent a lot of time building respect with Suicida's three hundred or so men.

I hoped that relationship would pay off on this trip. Krill and Cara de Malo, the two subcommanders who took over after Suicida's disappearance, had gone way off the reservation. They were terrorizing a little village only a few miles from the camp by showing up with their weapons and throwing their weight around. Discipline had begun to break down as the new leaders spent most of their time drinking and whoring in the village.

Caro de Malo had a nom de guerre that suited his behavior. In English, that means "Bad Face" or "Face of a Bad Guy." He was one of the Contras involved in the rape, and it was particularly awful. Reports were that he'd tied the woman to a tree, then they murdered her husband.

The small Honduran military detachment in the village couldn't hope to stand against these two and their private army. Less than a dozen strong, they'd been the ones who alerted the Honduran command to the situation and they, in turn, sternly advised the FDN to clean up their act.

We had to get Krill and Cara de Malo out of the camp and then get Contras there back to fighting the Sandinistas. Not only was it a moral and legal imperative, but under Suicida, they had been some of our toughest fighters. Losing them to this banditry was a strategic blow to the effort.

In the helo with me that day were two FDN junior officers and "Captain L.," a Honduran army officer assigned as our day-to-day liaison. If the men were now loyal to Krill and Cara de Malo, things might get dicey very quickly.

There was no place to land directly in the camp. Instead, we used an open field about a fifteen-minute walk from it. The pilots circled once at higher altitude. We could see two men at the edge of the clearing, waiting for us. We'd radioed ahead we were coming, in part to ensure the Contras didn't mistake us for a marauding Sandinista helicopter.

We touched down, and the four of us dismounted. It turned out, Krill and his bodyguard were the two men we'd seen from the air. They came forward to greet us.

Krill's bodyguard was a gigantic beast of a man. Tall, shaggy-haired, bulging with muscles. But where he had brawn, he lacked brain. To put it mildly, he was no rocket scientist.

After the welcome, while still standing by the Huey, I said to his bodyguard, "Hey, my stomach is all screwed up. Can you run into town and get me some medicine from that little kiosk?"

I handed him some cash. He glanced at Krill, who nodded quickly. The bodyguard turned and walked out of the landing area, double-timing toward the little village a few minutes away.

Once he was out of sight, I said to Krill, "Listen, buddy, they need to talk to you back at headquarters."

He shook his head. "I can't leave the camp."

I knew this man. I'd helped train him. In the almost two years since I'd been in country, I'd worked hard to treat him and the others with respect while at the same time making it clear I was not a person to mess with. Building rapport like that was something I'd learned as a kid. Treat people well, but make it clear you're doing so from a position of strength.

I hoped that would pay off right then. "Krill," I told him, "you know me. I'm trying to give you an easy choice. I guarantee your safety if you get in the helicopter right now. If not, you're going to get hurt because either me or somebody else will come get you by force."

Captain L. added, "This is an official Honduran request, and I'm here officially to deliver it."

Krill could see he was in no position to resist. Alone, at least a mile from camp and the armed men there, all he could do was nod. We took his sidearm and put him aboard the helo. Captain L. climbed in to be his armed escort, and the pilots spun the bird up. It lifted off in a cloud of dust and headed back toward Tegucigalpa, leaving me with the two junior FDN officers.

Krill's bodyguard rushed back into the field a moment later, holding a packet of medicine and four Cokes. "Where's Krill?" he demanded anxiously.

"He's going back to headquarters. They've got something big planned, and they needed to talk to him," I said.

The bodyguard did not look mollified.

"He'll be back tomorrow," I said, unconcerned. The bodyguard stared at us suspiciously. "Take us to camp, would you, please?" I asked.

He complied, but it was a tense fifteen-minute walk. Once we arrived, he vanished, no doubt to go tell somebody Krill was gone. Word quickly spread through the camp, causing some alarm and confusion.

"Where is Krill?" one of his underlings asked me.

"He'll be back tomorrow. Right now, we need to talk to Cara de Malo," I answered.

The underling shrugged. "He's not here. He'll be back later."

"We'll wait for him."

That did nothing to mollify the underling.

We stayed through the afternoon, carrying out some of our routine duties around the camp while we waited for Cara de Malo to return. Toward evening, he still had not shown up. Had somebody warned him off? We didn't know.

Just before dinner, the three of us were walking around the camp, when a whispered "Psst," straight out of a Warner Brothers' cartoon got our attention. I turned around to find a Contra I knew, hunkered down inside a nearby bush. I walked over.

"Major, Major," the Contra whispered. I'd recently been "promoted" from captain to major to keep my cover authentic. Can't be a captain forever unless you're doing a crappy job, right?

The Contra showed his face, and I recognized him immediately. Two trips before this one, he'd come to me in desperation. His wife was ill and needed antibiotics, but he had no money to purchase them. I reached into a pocket and gave him the cash I had on hand—the equivalent of about twenty dollars. He thanked me profusely, and I learned later the antibiotics did the trick.

"What's going on?" I asked him.

"Some of these guys are scared you're here. They know you sent Krill back. They're talking about trying to kill you tonight while you sleep."

Our Huey was not scheduled to return until early tomorrow morning. We were stuck in camp for the night and could be vulnerable to an assassination attempt.

"Thank you," I said to the Contra. "Distance yourself from me. I won't forget this."

He nodded and disappeared into the brush.

At dinner, I watched those eating with us very carefully. I'd long ago learned to pick up little tells—quick eye movements, second glances between conspirators, changed mannerisms. I could see a few seated with us were behaving that way, all the while smiling and carrying on as if everything were normal.

My Contra ally was right. I could see it around the table.

These were not men who were going to openly try anything. I had an AR-15 that never left my side, and they knew me well enough to know if challenged, I would fight back and take some of them with me.

They were going to try something a bit more underhanded and with surprise.

We finished dinner, and one of the Contra subordinates said he'd show us to our quarters for the night. He led us to a remote hut at the base of a steep slope covered in pine trees.

This was what you would call a clue.

As soon as the FDN officers and I were alone inside, we discussed our situation. All three of us agreed it looked like they were setting us up for a midnight hit. With us on the outskirts of the camp, away from everyone else, they could blame our deaths on a Sandinista raid after the fact.

I had my AR-15 with four magazines. Hundred and twenty rounds. On my hip, I wore a 9mm pistol. I also had a last-ditch weapon, a Walther PPK pistol strapped to my ankle that *no one* knew I carried. An Agency friend who'd been a hostage in Iran during the crisis had warned me to always be as well armed as possible since it was known the camps had been infiltrated by Sandinista agents at times. He gave me a couple of mini grenades that I always pocketed before leaving Tegucigalpa. My two FDN companions carried their rifles, and one had a sidearm.

If the majority of the camp was against us, we wouldn't stand a chance, but I was confident that would not be the case. But to give ourselves the advantage, we climbed out a window facing the hillside and crept up the high ground shortly after dark. We found a good defensive position with clear fields of fire and hunkered down. I assigned the FDN guys sectors of fire, then we worked out a sleep schedule. One of us always had to be on watch.

We were about a couple of hundred yards up the slope in great positions among the pine trees. We would be tough to dig out, especially at night. But if they came in force, we'd be overwhelmed.

Okay. This was where we played Custer, but hopefully with better results.

I took first watch, wondering if this might be the last few hours of my life.

Sometime after midnight, I heard a commotion down by our hooch. I tapped my two allies to wake them up. "Hey, lock and load. They're here."

A few voices rose from below us. They certainly weren't the stealthiest assassins who ever lived. We were grateful for that.

A flashlight suddenly speared the darkness. Then another, outlining the hooch with their beams.

"Don't fire until I tell you," I said to the FDN guys.

My FDN colleagues lay on their bellies, and I got on one knee behind a sizable boulder, watching the scene below us. When they rushed inside our hooch and found nobody to kill, they lost momentum. Figuring to quickly kill us in our sleep was one thing. Finding us gone and obviously alert was another thing indeed.

This was why I always made it clear that if I got bit, I would always bite back.

They began arguing with each other over what to do next. They didn't have the stomach for a night firefight with us, especially if we were out there in the darkness, lying in ambush.

They melted away into the night, returning to the main part of the camp.

Unfortunately, we couldn't see how many or who they were; I guessed about four. They were there to commit murder, not for combat.

Dawn broke, and we decided to head back into camp to get some food. We acted as if nothing had happened. At breakfast, I studied the faces around us. Some looked relieved to see us alive. Others kept their distance. Was that out of hostility, or fear of association with us?

Amazing how quickly things could get this tense and fucked up after the loss of Suicida's leadership. Some of those looking at us with suspicion I'd known for two years.

After we ate, a couple of Suicida's loyalists approached us on the sly. They told us Cara de Malo was whoring in town. He'd "borrowed" a rancher's jeep for his personal use and had a couple of guys with him as protection.

We walked over to the camp's radio hut, where their simple but secure onetime pads and comms gear I'd helped get to them was kept under constant guard. This morning, I used it to call and confirm the arrival time of our Huey to the camp. As soon as our Huey arrived, I ordered them to land in the center of the little village in an oval-shaped park. We'd go down, get Cara de Malo, and get in the air without having to go back to camp.

As soon as we touched down, about a half dozen Honduran security types showed up to meet with us. They were the ones who'd reported Krill's and Cara de Mala's banditry, murder, and rape, so I knew they were on our side.

"Where's Cara de Malo?" I asked one.

"He's with two women in a house," said one of the Hondurans, pointing to the far side of town.

"Go tell him Major Alex wants to see him right now. Here."

Two of the Hondurans went off to find him. Our pilot kept the blades turning while we waited for Cara de Malo. Captain L., my two FDN officers, and I waited impatiently. Perhaps fifteen minutes later, a civilian jeep, top down, rolled up the street. Sitting beside his driver/bodyguard was Cara de Malo.

The jeep stopped a short distance away from us as we stood with our backs to the helicopter. Cara de Malo dismounted. I started walking forward toward him, my biggest and most disarming smile on my face. He stepped forward toward me, looking uncertain and fearful.

We shook hands, and then he stepped back. I could smell alcohol on his breath. His eyes were bloodshot, and he seemed a little unsteady on his feet. He'd probably been drinking all night.

"You need to come back with me to headquarters," I said. "There are some things you need to clear up."

"I can't leave. There will be nobody to run the camp," he replied.

"This is not a request," I said. "I'm here to escort you out."

Captain L. added, "This has the blessing of the Honduran government."

"I can't leave. They will kill me," he replied. He knew the score. He knew Krill was gone. He may have even been the one who'd ordered the attempted hit on us the night before.

He looked at me with trapped eyes, and then his gaze fell to the AR on my shoulder. I could tell he was sizing up his chances. They weren't good. Captain L. and the two FDN officers were standing with me, the helo crew behind us, and the local Honduran cops had formed a loose perimeter around us.

Drunk, scared, and outgunned, he decided to take his chances at first. He turned and made eye contact with his bodyguard, who immediately pulled out an Uzi from under the front seat. The second I saw the weapon, I grabbed my AR and swung it up until the barrel pointed directly at Cara de Malo's crotch. Nobody else moved.

I flicked the safety off.

That click brought Cara de Malo back to reality. My finger rested on the trigger guard, a half an inch and a split second away from killing him.

"I'm not looking for a fight. But I will give it to you if you want that. I am here to take you back to HQ. I can guarantee your safety."

He looked unsure. Behind him, his bodyguard held the Uzi, barrel pointed skyward as he stared intently at me.

"Caro de Malo, you've known me for how long now? I'm giving you my word that you will arrive safe. You'll have your chance to explain yourself. If you do not, the shit is going to hit the fan here."

He was wavering, I could see it in his eyes. I pushed him just a bit more. "If your bodyguard points that Uzi at us, I am going to stitch you up first."

That did it. His eyes filled with resignation. He nodded. The Uzi disappeared under the seat again, and the bodyguard sat like a stoic in the stolen jeep.

We led him to the helicopter as the pilots revved the engines back up. The blades chopped the air above us as I pulled Caro de Malo's sidearm from its holster. "You're a civilian on a Honduran Army helicopter," I told him. "There are no weapons allowed." The copilot reached back and secured Cara de Malo's handgun.

He rode back to Tegucigalpa in silence. When the helicopter landed,

a contingent from FDN headquarters was there to take him into custody. I walked away and never saw either him or Krill again.

The woman Cara de Malo and his minions raped testified in whatever passed for a trial for these two. It was damning evidence, and
much was supported from interviews of other camp guerrillas. The Contras were trying to fight a war of liberation. They could not tolerate this
sort of horrific barbarity, especially in Honduras, their host country.
Krill and Cara de Malo were made examples of. I much later heard they
were executed, and I also learned that Ray had hard-balled the FDN
command with the threat of pulling our support if they allowed things
like this to ever happen again.

Suicida's camp came around quickly after they were removed. Most
of the three hundred Contras there were like the one who warned me of
the impending hit. They wanted to fight the Sandinistas and get their
country back. The banditry and brutality the two subcommanders displayed was not the path to make that happen. With proper leadership,
those men became an effective fighting force once again.

These "renditions" (I did not know that term back then) were eye-
openers for me. Those were dangerous, volatile situations that could
have gone bad in multiple ways. In later years, when I taught young
officers how to interact with locals when working overseas, I would tell
them the story of the young Contra who tipped us off to the impending
attempt on our lives. In such environments, personal loyalty becomes
extremely important. You can only build that by showing respect and
consideration to everyone, no matter their position in the local hierarchy. That twenty dollars I gave him for medicine for his wife? It was the
best investment I've ever made, because when things get dicey, it never
hurts to have friends in low places.

# 11

## THE BARRACUDAS

*With the Contras*
*1983–1984*

The beginning of 1983 found me in the jungle with my beloved Contras, working hard to develop them into an offensive fighting force. Thanks to additional money and the full support of the Agency from Bill Casey through Dewey Clarridge on down to Ray, the Contras became one of the focal points of our renewed aggressive stance against the spread of Soviet-sponsored communism. From the failures of the 1970s Détente era, which only served to encourage Soviet adventurism without an American check, the Reagan administration ushered in a new era that reinvigorated our overall anti-Soviet efforts.

At the dawn of the 1980s, the Soviets seemed ascendant. They were making gains in Africa, South Asia, and Central and South America. To us in the West, it felt like a flood tide, rising to drown our allies and our interests in crucial corners of the world.

Simultaneously, the pro-Soviet movements in Western Europe and the United States continued to grow in strength, abetted by some in academia. To Cold Warriors, it felt like we were under siege from within and without simultaneously.

Supporting the Contras was my little piece of this strategic pie. Being away from the United States limited my worldview at the time, but I knew the campaign against the Sandinista regime was only one of many efforts to stop the Soviets. Years later, I learned the Cold War nearly boiled over in 1983, and the world moved closer to nuclear annihilation than at any other time since the 1962 Cuban Missile Crisis.

We struck back against the Soviets not just with our clandestine wars in Central America, Angola, and Afghanistan but with the conventional military in ways that revealed major gaps in the Soviet defense network. In the late summer of 1981, for instance, the NATO navies collaborated on a massive exercise in the North Atlantic involving eighty-three ships. The armada successfully dodged Soviet detection efforts, even avoiding a spy satellite specifically launched to locate the fleet. At the same time, U.S. warplanes surprised and launched simulated attacks on Russian long-range patrol planes. The fake attack proved a total surprise and caught the Russian planes while they refueled in midair during their searches for the NATO warships. It was a huge embarrassment for the Soviet military and contributed to a feeling of growing unease in Moscow that the resurgent American military power, defense spending, and new technology were fast eclipsing Soviet superiority.

The Soviet leadership had lived through the shock and surprise of the 1941 German invasion. All of them were obsessed with never allowing such a devastating blow to happen again. Under the Kremlin's direction, the KGB launched Operation RYAN, a full-court press to recruit assets and develop networks that could keep the pulse of the United States military and warn Moscow of any impending attack. Should news arrive that such a strike was coming, the Soviets planned to hit first.

The events of 1983 magnified Soviet unease into something bordering on paranoia. In the spring, the U.S. Pacific Fleet held one of its largest exercises of the postwar years.

Three carrier battle groups surged into the Northwest Pacific and took station less than 450 miles away from the Soviet Kamchatka Peninsula. While USN attack submarines surprised and chased Soviet nuclear ballistic subs under the Arctic Circle, the American carrier wings actually launched a simulated bombing raid against a remote Soviet outpost on Zelyony Island in the contested Kuril Islands.

In Europe, NATO aircraft consistently tested Soviet air defense, keeping the Warsaw Pact off balance with sudden squadron-level rushes toward their airspace. The aggressiveness netted a wealth of information on Soviet air defense systems, which we exploited. At the same time, such moves fueled the paranoia that Reagan was crazy enough to launch a nuclear first strike against them. Such fears seemed legitimate when the U.S. prepared to deploy Pershing II intermediate-range nuclear missiles to Germany—weapons that could reach Moscow in minutes.

On March 23, 1983, Reagan announced the Strategic Defense Initiative, quickly dubbed Star Wars. The plan called for developing a space-based missile defense shield using laser technology the Soviets were probably decades away from developing on their own. With nukes in Western Europe that could hit the Kremlin in minutes, plus an antimissile system that could neutralize any Soviet response, the Kremlin's leaders feared a 1941-esque surprise attack more than any other time in the Cold War.

On September 1, 1983, Soviet air defenses detected a single aircraft incursion into its airspace in the North Pacific. It turned out to be Korean Air Lines Flight 007, a civilian 747. The Soviets scrambled interceptors and shot the aircraft down, killing hundreds of innocents.

Tensions over the incident grew to a fever pitch. Recriminations echoed around the globe as Reagan called for boycotts of Soviet goods and Russian leader Yuri Andropov blamed the deaths of the 269 people aboard 007 on the United States military.

Two things happened in the weeks after that brought the world closer to nuclear war than any other time since 1962. On September 26, 1983, a new Soviet satellite-based nuclear missile warning system detected five missile launches from the United States. A Soviet Air Defence

Forces lieutenant colonel named Stanislav Petrov was on duty at the command center outside of Moscow when the launches were detected.

He had only minutes to decide what to do. Fortunately, he concluded this could not be an American first strike but the new system acting up. He disobeyed standing orders and procedures and did not sound the alarm. It turned out he was right; the satellites were fooled into thinking sunlight reflecting off clouds were Minuteman III launches, but that the fate of the world nearly came down to a lieutenant colonel's judgment demonstrated how humanity lived on a knife's edge into the twilight flare-up of the Cold War.

Two months later, a NATO exercise called Able Baker 83 set the Russians off again. This was an annual drill, but there were new features wrapped into it that caused the Soviets to fear it was a ruse masking an actual coming attack. Nuclear-armed aircraft in Eastern Europe were put on alert, and the world came within a hairbreadth of war as the Kremlin debated whether or not to strike first. Fortunately, cooler heads prevailed.

Of course, all this was above my pay grade at the time. From my foxhole view in Honduras, I only saw the upsurge in U.S. support for the Contras and our increasingly aggressive plans to help them reclaim their country from the Marxists who took it over. That surge included more supplies, specialized weaponry, and air support that we sorely needed for offensive operations.

We also needed more personnel, which we received that year. Our effort in Honduras was soon plussed up with staff for Ray, including Big Bill C, and program staff at base that included three women— Keggy, Nancy, and Brenda. For the field, we received trainers like former SEAL Big Hal, who focused on select FDN teams to build out the Contra's covert and commando skills. The reinforcements were most welcome and a great sign for us, the Nicas, and our loyal allies the Hondos, since it meant our campaign was being given a higher priority in Washington.

At the same time, the Sandinistas were getting equally aggressive in their efforts to counter the growing Contra threat to their regime. Soviet and Cuban arms shipments flowed in every week through Puerto Cabezas, Nicaragua's primary port in the Caribbean. Those weapons eventually included jet fighter-bombers and Mi-24 Hind D attack helicopter gunships, the same type that rained terror and death onto the mujahideen in Afghanistan.

The Sandinistas were also developing capabilities in Honduras. They trained about a hundred Honduran Marxists in Nicaragua to be the cadre of a series of pro-Sandinista communist cells. Fortunately, we got wind of this and tipped the Honduran army off as to when they were going to infiltrate across the border. The Hondurans wiped them out in an ambush.

Sandinista hit squads also operated throughout Honduras. In previous operations, they'd successfully kidnapped or killed Contra sub commanders, Honduran army officers, and even one of the Argentinians. It was one such hit squad that assassinated Somoza while he was in exile.

As the war escalated in Central America, I received word that the Sandinistas were on to me. One day back at base, Ray showed me some radio intercepts in which the Sandinistas described me quite accurately, though they thought I was a Puerto Rican because of my Caribbean accent. They even knew I had the number seventeen tattooed on my right arm. The number seventeen had long been my lucky number and was a reference to Saint Lazarus, my patron saint.

That the Sandinistas were on to my presence and role in the camps was not surprising. We knew they had agents who penetrated the camps. They also had operatives working in the shadows of Tegucigalpa and other Honduran towns. But the messages signaled a new reality for me: our enemy knew who I was and was trying to target me.

I tried to be an elusive target. I moved around, did not keep a fixed routine, and kept my head on a swivel. Even so, there are countless little choke points in life that determined assassins can detect and exploit.

For me, Puerto Lempira was one of those choke points. While visiting

Stedman Fagoth, the head of the Miskito Indian Contra component—called the MISURA—we would stay in Puerto Lempira for a few days at a time. There were only a few hostels in town—best described as Motel 0s—and a couple of "restaurants," one of which was on a barge in the harbor. During one meeting, Captain L., Stedman, a Miskito pastor, and an interpreter named Omar ate at the same restaurant three days in a row. Somebody in town was watching us and detected that pattern.

On day four, I finished up with our business and, with Captain L., flew out of town in the Huey. But that night, Stedman, the pastor, and the interpreter all returned to the same eatery. They were walking out of the restaurant when a Sandinista operative chucked a grenade in their path and opened fire. The blast slightly wounded Stedman. In the chaos after the explosion, several armed agents opened fire with handguns. Omar took a grazing wound to the neck, and the pastor was killed on the spot.

The hit team escaped unharmed.

Whether they were after me specifically, I don't know. It may have been an attempt to assassinate Stedman Fagoth, whose aggressive leadership plus our supplies had turned the MISURA into a major threat to the Sandinistas. Either way, the attack reminded us all of the Sandinista reach inside Honduras and underscored the fact they were stalking us.

We redoubled our precautions and took great care to minimize those choke points they could exploit. In the meantime, Ray and Dewey were cooking up ways to really hit the Sandinistas hard. The hit-and-run raids continued, and some of them were growing in size. The Contras were gaining capability, but the strategic equation remained tilted far in the Sandinistas' favor.

Ray was a product of the Second World War. So was Bill Casey. They saw the big picture, where I saw the fight in the jungle and grit of the day-to-day in the camps. It was a perfect marriage between vision and action. That year, Ray and Dewey crafted a plan to start attacking major targets that had either strategic or symbolic importance. They selected one for me that had both: the Puerto Cabezas pier.

Puerto Cabezas is the largest and most important port on the Caribbean side of Nicaragua. The docks there served as the primary means the Cubans and Soviets had to resupply the Sandinistas with weapons, ammunition, and fuel. The dock included an integrated fuel pipeline that allowed for faster transfer of oil from arriving tankers. If we could destroy this, we'd not only slow the resupply to the Sandinista forces, we'd make a big statement by blowing up the key link between the Sandinistas and their communist allies.

This would be a tricky operation, but Ray asked if it could be done. It could, with the right team. He gave me the green light, and off I went to recruit from within the Miskito ranks. I had just the guys in mind, too.

When I first started visiting Stedman Fagoth and the MISURA, one of the Miskito fighters I met noticed the SCUBA badge on my hat. He mentioned that some of the men were lobster divers. I took a great interest in this and went out of my way to meet them. They knew how to free dive without any gear and could stay underwater a hell of a lot longer than I could, but they also owned SCUBA gear and were quite good with it.

I assembled a small team from these expert divers. They were willing, eager, and very capable young men who, along with the other Miskito Contras, only wanted to see their homeland freed from the depredations of the Sandinista army. Contrary to much of the press coverage of the war back in the States, those depravations were real. The Miskito were often characterized as "right-wing rebels" by the U.S. media. In reality, they were just as anti-Somoza as the Sandinistas were. But after the 1979 revolution, the Sandinistas tried to suppress the Miskito movement for autonomy. Each wave of repression swelled the MISURA ranks in Honduras, and the Sandinistas quickly alienated the entire region with their brutal tactics.

The men I chose were the most ideologically committed to gaining independence from the Sandinistas. They were not mercenaries. They

weren't paid assassins. They were men fighting to liberate their villages
and reclaim their families.

Once I selected the men, we went to work training for our operation in an abandoned shrimp factory about seventy miles northeast of
Puerto Lempira. A hurricane had destroyed part of the building and
ripped the roof off, but the first and second floors were largely intact,
so we set up camp there. We did PT every day, and while they were already in good shape, they developed into physical specimens. After PT,
we worked on compass swims using attack boards (a simple device with
two handles that had a compass, depth gauge, and clock) and tactics.
I taught them underwater ops like screwing together metal pipes and
other underwater mental challenges. We worked through every problem
we could envision and came up with contingencies. In the late afternoon,
we hit the surf and went spear fishing to supplement protein for our
dinner.

While we trained, one key issue remained. The MISURA lacked
the type of explosives we would need to blow up the pier. Fortunately,
we received exactly what we needed: a specialized underwater demolition charge that combined compactness with tremendous blast power.

Later, we trained in another location near a Honduran pier of similar design. There, we practiced moving the explosive charge through
the water and emplacing it against the pier below the surface without
using any lights. During one of those night rehearsals, I swam right into
a Portuguese man-of-war jellyfish and got stung on the face. Let me tell
you, that is not something I ever want to go through again!

To help foster a sense of esprit de corps within our new team, we
called ourselves the Barracudas. And one night in late 1983, as the
world moved to the brink of nuclear war, we set out to prove that a half
dozen committed men could strike a blow at the heart of the communist effort against their families.

We used a hundred-foot boat to get us south along the coast in
what became a hellish twelve-hour stealth voyage in seas so heavy even

the boat's crew got seasick. We pushed on despite the conditions until, finally, we navigated to a point a few miles from the target area.

I got into the water as the crew lowered a panga—a motorized Miskito canoe alongside our mother boat. The Barracudas carefully climbed aboard, then wrestled the explosive device into the panga with them.

I greatly regretted not being able to go with them. After training them for so long, this was the moment where we had to part ways. I stayed with the boat and watched through an infrared scope as the panga headed for the coast. I had outfitted my Barracudas with IR light/strobes so we could always find them if they got lost.

The wait for their return seemed to last for hours. Later, I found out they had armed the device and set the timer in the panga just before they entered the water. Their captain was another bigger-than-life character named Sam Ignacio, who stayed in the panga with his binoculars to follow the men's flashing infrared lights. The rest of the team submerged in their SCUBA gear and swam through the underwater darkness to the pier. Sadly, a few months after this mission, Sam Ignacio drowned while on a maritime resupply mission. He was a dear friend, and I could not tolerate the sight of his bloated body recovered after some time in the sea.

We elected to make the attack at night to avoid civilian casualties, but that meant a lot of additional complications for the Barracudas. They needed to navigate underwater in near total darkness, then set the charge without using any sort of illumination. Fortunately, there were a few lights around the pier glowing above them as they made their way to the pilings and placed the explosive device. Nearby, a few guards patrolled but saw nothing.

The team escaped undetected and returned to the panga. Everyone climbed safely aboard, then headed for the rendezvous with the mother boat, which was just out of sight. We got them aboard, then turned north for Honduran waters, hoping to be clear of Nicaragua before dawn.

Two hours later, the charge exploded. The blast was so large it destroyed the fuel pipeline, splintered the pilings, and blew all the planks off the top of the pier. Later reports confirmed it was almost a total loss.

Six men had denied the Sandinistas several weeks' worth of weaponry and ammunition aboard Eastern Bloc ships steaming across the Caribbean to Puerto Cabezas. The Sandinistas shut down all reporting on the incident, an unusual thing since usually they howled to the world in protest after every Contra attack, accusing the freedom fighters of the savagest crimes against the population. It was pure propaganda, but the Sandinistas were adept at it. This time, the blow hurt, and the strategic implications were such that they stayed quiet.

The pier remained out of service for weeks. Meanwhile, the other two large Nicaraguan ports took up the slack. The other one on the Caribbean side, Bluefields, had a huge harbor area accessed only by a river. We decided to try to sink a vessel in the river channel with a rocket-propelled grenade ambush. There was one choke point that would have been perfect. The Barracudas tried to lay an ambush from both sides of the river but could never get a decent shot on the targeted vessel due to all the Sandinista patrols. Frustrated, we had to abandon that attack.

As the Barracudas operated on the east coast, other special Contra teams carried out other attacks on strategic infrastructure targets as well. The attacks left the Sandinistas reeling. Ray and the FDN kept them off balance with swift strikes from the sea and jungle. Our team of lobster divers turned saboteurs were just one puzzle piece in that overall plan, but some at HQS felt like we could make an impact on the war effort with the right target again.

Corinto, Nicaragua's third major port, opens on the Pacific Ocean on the country's west coast and played host to many Eastern Bloc ships, including North Korean cargo vessels bringing in more weapons and ammunition. Unbeknownst to me, in October 1983, the Contras launched a seaborne raid against the port using speedboats armed with light cannon and .50-caliber machine guns. The lightning-quick attack focused on the fuel storage tanks. The boats raked the target area, setting fires that ultimately—according to Sandinista sources—destroyed 1 percent of the country's yearly oil consumption. The fires spread to the port facilities and caused extensive damage, forcing the evacuation of part of the town. For good measure, the team strafed a North Korean freighter.

The port was a critical resupply point for the Sandinista military effort, and the FDN wanted to shut it down for months, if not permanently. In studying the target area, they detected a key choke point that could be exploited. A bridge spanned the harbor entrance that, if blown up, could foul the channel for the foreseeable future. Against my ardent advice—I knew that my Miskito team would not play well with the "Spaniards" on the west coast—my Barracudas received the mission. From the outset, things went very, very wrong.

# 12

## RISKS AND REWARDS

*Honduras*
*1983–1984*

Against my GS-11 objections, I was ordered to use my Barracudas to blow the bridge at Corinto. For the mission, I picked my four best Barracudas. We planned to attack it at night with two boats, each with a crew of Spanish Nicaraguans and a pair of Miskito divers. This was one of those cases where regional racism and ethnic acrimony went overlooked and the assumption at the top levels of command was that the mission and enemy would smooth over whatever differences existed locally.

That was a tough lesson to learn for all of us, but I could see issues developing right away. The Miskito Indians have spent generations being oppressed by other Nicaraguans, whom they referred to as the "Spaniards." To ask four of them to operate on the other side of the country, far away from the inlets and beaches they knew intimately, was already asking a lot. Asking them to work with non-Miskito boat crews was a bridge too far. Because of the racial dichotomy, the divers and boatmen never met until mission time. We picked an island off the coast of Honduras and worked out an attack plan with two other advisors, Leon, an up-and-coming SAD officer, and Jim W., a former U.S. Navy SEAL. Headquarters constructed a tabletop mock-up of the bridge that was almost as accurate as us being there. It was there that we would also train the divers on the use of the proper explosives.

The bridge was a much trickier target than the pier we'd destroyed. Long and built atop hundreds of pilings, from the outset, it would take a lot more blast power than our first effort to drop enough of the bridge to foul the harbor channel. To take it out, each team would need to emplace three charges on three different pilings. We acquired some non-U.S.-attributable explosives and trained our divers to secure them into position using bungee cords.

While we trained, we stayed at an abandoned resort called Spy Hill, of all things. The Miskitos worked like pros and were eager to learn. The days were long—water work is hard—and during downtime, there was no entertainment or escape. But we never heard a peep of complaint from my crew.

To get the divers to the bridge, fiberglass boats were imported from the States. They were extremely fast with open decks and a small bridge. For short periods, they could reach almost sixty miles an hour in good seas. Their speed would no doubt be an asset, but they proved mechanically unreliable and very finicky to operate. Each boat consisted of two boat crewmen and two Miskito divers.

I flew into a small Honduran island in the Gulf of Fonseca not far from Corinto, bringing the Miskitos with me in the Huey. It was there that the boat crews and divers finally met and received a full briefing on the target and mission. They would need to navigate through the gulf with full view of the extinct volcano that became the Cosigüina Lagoon, then turn south and run down the coast for about forty kilometers to reach the entrance to Corinto Harbor. This had to be done in darkness, so the margin for error was very thin. At a minimum, the attack teams were looking at a four-hour round trip to infil and exfil. Once they arrived in the target area, the boats would enter farther inland via the inlets, and when close enough, the dive teams would deploy and swim to the bridge, place the explosives, and then navigate back to the rendezvous area.

When the briefing ended, I could see nobody was happy. This would be a difficult operation in the best of circumstances, as getting to the bridge would require considerable stealth to avoid detection. The timeline was cutting it close, and if anything went wrong, they stood a chance of being out on the water at daylight, which would put them at the mercy of the Sandinista navy and air force if they were detected.

Nevertheless, we launched the mission as briefed, the boats speeding across the bay toward Corinto in the late afternoon so by the time they reached Nicaraguan waters, it would be nightfall. We'd need every minute of darkness to pull this off.

The rest of our team, including my good friend Leon, who was the senior officer in charge, and Jim, my two pilots, and I remained on our little island base with our Huey. I manned the radio all night, monitoring for any communications. Radio silence was in play with the boats, so the last thing I wanted was to hear them on the airwaves.

After sunset, they cleared the Gulf of Fonseca without incident. They swung south and hugged the coastline, but the closer they got to Corinto, the more shipping traffic they encountered. Dodging the boats out there slowed their progress and threw the schedule off. Truth was, the amount of activity totally surprised us; there was no indication of that in the pre-mission intelligence we'd received.

Using their speed and the darkness, the boats did manage to infiltrate to the drop-off point just outside the entrance to Corinto Harbor. That's when things started to go terribly wrong. The Miskitos, spooked by the number of patrols and civilian vessels about, feared the Spaniards would bail on them as soon as they hit the water. They refused to deploy. A furious argument broke out. Threats were exchanged, and lots of finger-pointing took place in the moment. Ultimately, they scrubbed the mission, and both boats started to exfiltrate. But to evade Sandinista naval patrols, they had to maneuver quickly. In the darkness, they became separated. One boat dodged the Nicaraguan vessels by hiding in mangroves, but the second suffered engine trouble and was bobbing like a cork in the Gulf of Fonseca. They radioed to me that they were trying to limp into the coastal mangrove swamps to hide and effect repairs when the engines died.

Although they carried suitable weapons to defend themselves, they would not survive long without propulsion. If a Sandinista patrol found them adrift in the gulf, they'd be killed for sure. Both our boats were out of action, and sunrise was only a few hours away.

It was time to improvise. I went to my Huey pilots, and along with Leon and Jim, I briefed them on my desperate plan. I resorted to my hard-earned pararescue training. After I explained what I wanted to do, Leon did not hesitate even one second and immediately approved my plan; no risk-averse leadership here!

I asked our base logistics guy, Papo, to find me some rope. I told Jim I needed some explosives. He rustled up a C-4 satchel for me, which I would strap to my chest. I threw together a couple of bags of spare parts, including spark plugs, for the boat engines. I also grabbed a couple of five-gallon cans of water and gasoline. I bundled the tools and parts into waterproof pouches that would float when they hit the sea.

While I worked, Papo came back with four lengths of rope, and said, "Major Alex, everyone's asking what you're doing."

"We're gonna go get 'em back!"

We tied four lines to the Huey's floor-anchor points, two to a side, then coiled them onto the Huey's deck. We then fashioned some home-made harnesses into makeshift STABO rigs. The STAbilized BOdy extraction harness was a device that allowed military personnel to be rescued by helicopter from field locations that prevented the conventional landing and boarding of a helicopter. Bowline knots and carabiners completed the rigs.

I figured if we could not get the boats restarted, we'd pull everyone off onto the Huey and use the C-4 charges to scuttle the boat. The mission may have failed, but at least we'd get our people back, and the damn Piricuacos would not be able to add a fast boat to their arsenal. Not on my watch!

I explained to my pilots what I needed them to do. We'd go out to the stranded boat in the gulf, do a low-and-slow pass toward it so I could jump out into the water with the gear. I'd swim to the boat, climb into it, and we'd see what the issues were before determining whether or not to evacuate the crew and destroy the vessel.

It was a classic PJ tactic, one that I'd practiced countless times. But outside that brotherhood, I am sure this sort of stuff sounded crazy to normal humans.

I climbed aboard the Huey equipped with a snorkel, mask, and fins, wearing jeans and a T-shirt. Two pounds of C-4 was strapped to my chest, while I made sure to secure my PPK in my ankle holster, mainly for good luck, as she never left my side. If we were caught and boarded by the Sandinistas, it would be my last-ditch weapon.

We took off and headed out over the water. It didn't take us long to find the first boat adrift in the Gulf of Fonseca, since the crew accurately reported their position. Our pilots swung around and made the low, slow pass at fifteen miles an hour at about thirty feet. On that first run, I kicked out the bags of gear, tools, fuel, and water. They splashed into the sea not too far from the boat.

We needed to do this quickly. A helicopter buzzing around in Nicaraguan waters surely would attract unwanted attention from Sandinista patrol boats. If they caught us out here, we'd be in serious trouble. The Huey had no door-mounted machine guns like the Vietnam-era birds. It would be us with a few AR-15s against machine guns.

The pilots reversed course and calmly set up the second pass. I stood in the Huey's doorway, back toward our line of direction, waiting for the word to jump. Though it had been years since I was in the air force, I'd done this so many times in training, all the steps returned to me in the moment. I went through my mental checklist, knowing that if I did this wrong, I could end up landing on my back or head. Hitting the water like that would be like falling onto concrete.

*Tuck in arms and head nice and tight. Mask on, hand over it.*

I took a final look over my shoulder. The boat was a short distance ahead. I could see the gear bags bobbing on the surface. Time to go.

*Lead with your butt, step backward out of the bird.*

I felt myself falling. The blue waters of the gulf sped toward me. I kept my body positioned so my heels and fins would hit first, then my ass, then my back. A split second later, the water engulfed me as I torpedoed into it with an enormous splash. My fins quickly slowed my descent, and I looked up at the surface and began swimming for it.

My head popped up. I gave the Huey crew my thumbs-up and kicked over to the supply bags. They were heavy, but fortunately not waterlogged. I grabbed a line from them and towed them over to the boat. It was slow going in moderate swells, and I really had to kick hard with the fins to make progress. I finally reached the boat, where I was greeted with four astonished looks.

Who jumps out of a helicopter almost thirty feet overhead? A former USAF PJ, of course. The Miskitos and boat crew had never seen anything like that before. Neither had the guys in the Huey, for that matter.

The men pulled the gear aboard, then helped me over the side. Meanwhile, our pilots flew the Huey over the horizon, but still in radio range so as to not attract unwanted attention. As the morning wore on, the crew swapped out spark plugs, filled the gas tank from the five-gallon jerry can I'd brought along, and monkeyed around with the engines until both fired up again.

We navigated back to our secret island base without incident. When we returned, we learned the second boat was still beached somewhere in the mangrove swamps north of Corinto. They'd been unable to get their engines started.

There was no way we were going to leave our guys behind. We

decided to use the recovered boat and go find our lost crew. If we couldn't get their boat running, we'd just tow them out. I took our Cuban Bay of Pigs veteran naval captain, plus another Agency officer adept at maritime operations. Beyond my 9mm, my PPK, and my AR-15s, we'd have little defense against a Sandinista patrol vessel armed with heavy machine guns.

I was now on my second day with no sleep. I recalled PJ Chief Master Sergeant Fisk's motto, "The only easy day was yesterday," accompanied by the usual: "Suck it up, Prado!"

Hooyah, Chief!

We hastily put together a plan for the rescue. Afterward, I climbed back aboard the boat wearing jeans, a T-shirt, and a sweatshirt. The Cuban and the other Agency officer we called "Speedy" climbed aboard with yellow rain slickers and hats, something I'd not even thought about for myself.

Big mistake. As we pushed out into the Gulf of Fonseca, we encountered heavy seas. By the time we broke out into the Pacific, the swells were running up to twelve feet high. Our small boat pitched and rocked, slammed down into the troughs between the swells to soak us with spray. By the time it got dark again, I was soaked to the bone and losing body heat.

Pounded by the seas, we pushed on, trying to find our lost men. The boat was equipped with HF and VHF comms, and I had brought a handheld Icom radio. As the boat slammed down on the back side of the swells, our main radios went out. We lost direct comms with our missing men on the stranded boat, but we could still relay messages to them with the Icom.

Suddenly, a flare shot up over the water a few miles away. Clearly, they'd heard the radio chatter and were out looking for us now. We pressed on, in total light discipline, pushing south as the waves hammered us, hoping to pinpoint the location of our lost boat.

More Sandinista patrol vessels appeared around us. We couldn't see them, but they popped more flares that arced through the night sky like comets. In the distance, a light machine gun opened fire, hoping to entice a response by their "recon by fire." Another one let loose a long stream farther out in the darkness.

They were either shooting at phantoms or trying to spook us into returning fire. We didn't have anything that could reach them; plus our only hope was stealth now that the heavy seas negated much of our speed advantage. After a while, the shooting and the flares stopped.

We continued on, the heavy seas masking our presence as well as we could, no lights and minimal radio use. Still no sign of our missing boat. By now, I was becoming hypothermic in my wet clothes as the seas lashed us with unrelenting fury, but adrenaline and my training were still kicking in: FIDO (F*** It and Drive On)!

A wave crashed into us, sending the boat reeling. A cascade of seawater drenched the bridge and threw me off my feet. My Icom went flying, hit the deck, and shattered. I followed it down, and the impact knocked the breath out of me.

Though by now we had a pretty good idea where the other boat was, based on our brief comms and related triangulations, we had to abort. Without comms, there would be no rescue that night.

As we turned for home, I noticed our Cuban captain and Speedy were both relatively dry, thanks to their slickers and hats. Momentary anger flared in me. *Why didn't anyone think to give me one of those bloody things?*

By the time we evaded the patrols and reached the Honduran end of the Gulf of Fonseca again, I was in bad shape. By this point, I'd been awake for two days straight. Now, the post-adrenaline dump robbed me of my remaining strength. I knew I had to figure out a way to warm up. I was shaking uncontrollably from hypothermia.

*Adapt, improvise, and overcome.*

My SERE school training kicked in, and I went below to search for anything that I could use to get my core temperature back up. In one of the boat's lockers below the small cabin, I found some flotation devices wrapped in plastic. I pulled them out, tore the plastic off, and stuffed the plastic up my shirt. It wasn't much, but it was something. Then I crawled inside the storage locker, closed the door, went into a fetal position, and stayed there until we made it back to our island. When we docked, I struggled to my feet and walked straight to a shower, shoes, pants—everything but my sidearm. I stayed under the warm stream, shivering like a leaf in a storm, for almost half an hour.

The next day, we went out heavily armed in six fast boats and recovered our lost team without incident. That was one piece of good news in an otherwise dismal mission. I was later awarded the Intelligence Medal of Merit for my actions to save the first boat and crew. At the time, it was small compensation for a failure I could see coming from the moment the plan was conceived back at Tegucigalpa.

Failure is always to be learned from, and the Corinto operation taught me a number of vital things I carried with me through the rest of my career. To execute any kind of black operation, you must go into it with a team built on trust and mutual respect. If that is not established, or if trust breaks down among the team members, nothing good will follow.

Having reliable, rugged, and simple equipment is equally as important as trust.

Those boats were unusually fast, but we knew they were fussy and required a lot of TLC to keep functional. In the heat of the moment, both of them failed, and it nearly cost the lives of eight good men.

███████

Fortunately, we scored a major success not long after this operation ended that balanced the failure with a much-needed Contra victory. Thanks to the arrival of massive logistical support and increased in-country air assets, we now possessed the capability to resupply our Contras camps more efficiently and more frequently. From where these reinforcements came, I never learned. I'd also learned never to ask questions—especially when it came to our new aircraft.

Of all the different components of the FDN, the Miskito were some of the most loyal and airtight. Their homeland had been taken over; their people forcibly removed from their villages. Torture, rape, and murder were common. The survivors of these depredations flowed into Honduras to tell their stories and redouble the Miskito Contras' sense of purpose.

While the Sandinistas had moles in every other camp, they were less successful in establishing a network within the MISURA—they were simply too detested, and the tightly knit communities knew who was who. As a result, the Miskito were picked to launch one of the earliest, major Contra offensives of the war.

In the waning weeks of 1983, while the world's situation grew ever tenser as the superpowers confronted each other, we stepped up our training effort with the Miskitos. More weapons and ammunition flowed to their ranks. We taught them basic logistics, then infiltrated across the border to pre-position supply caches in what would become their line of advance once the offensive began.

The FDN planned to use the MISURA to move south into Nicaragua to recapture the Miskito gold mines and cut the highways to Puerto Cabezas and Bluefields. Once established on the other side of the border, the Miskito were to conduct raids and ambushes against any Sandinista reinforcements sent by Managua.

In the days leading up to the start of the offensive, I ran myself ragged trying to handle a million last-minute details. We'd never attempted the size and scope before, so we were blazing new ground. The Sandys didn't make things any easier; as we flew over the area, we took fire, and our Huey's tail was hit by several bullets.

The morning the offensive began, a small force of Miskitos infiltrated across the Coco River—the frontier between Honduras and Nicaragua. They established a foothold on the south side, paving the way for several thousand Contras. I watched the main force cross the Coco River in everything from rafts and their native panga canoes to small boats. They looked like ants crossing on leaves. It reminded me of the stories from school of Washington's footsore, half-frozen army crossing the Delaware River to strike at the British in Trenton, New Jersey, during the darkest days of the American Revolution.

The Miskito made it across the Coco, then pushed on to their first objectives. They ran into entrenched Sandinista army units protecting outposts and critical road junctions. Hard fighting ensued, but the Miskito would not be denied. The Sandinistas buckled, then ran. The advance continued.

The early days consumed most of the supplies we'd forward-cached in the jungle. After those ran short, we used ratlines of men carrying supplies from Rus Rus and other points to where we could fly into and resupply the MISURA. In short order, the Miskito achieved all of the FDN's objectives. The highways were cut. The areas around the gold mines retaken.

The Sandinistas soon realized this was something different—far more than a hit-and-run raid. Alarmed, they struck back with their newly acquired Mi-24 Hind attack helicopters. Old Soviet MiGs made repeated strafing runs. Flying the Huey in the area became a dangerous game as a result of all the Sandinista air support sent to counter the Miskito operation.

Despite the weight thrown at them, the Miskito were there to stay. In the months that followed, the MISURA Contras reestablished themselves in their own liberated homeland. The Sandinistas tried to drive them back into Honduras with repeated counterattacks, but they failed to dislodge them from their positions inside Nicaragua.

It was a huge victory, one that took the pressure off the other Contra groups to the west, as the Sandys were forced to pull units out of their areas and use them to counter the Miskitos. Meanwhile, the FDN troops were also doing more than their part, fighting feverishly under the command of El Tigrillo (a legendary commander with loyal and devoted fighters), Mike Lima, Benito, and many others. It was clear that a new phase of the Contra war of liberation had begun. The Sandinistas had lost the initiative.

Yet even as we gained momentum, we experienced perilous moments and setbacks.

As the Miskito offensive continued, the Sandinistas deployed more troops to deal with the threat. They launched counterstrikes that consumed MISURA supplies and kept the Miskito fighters in near-constant contact. Their need for resupply slowly outstripped our capacities to deliver it.

Another Miskito leader, Brooklyn Rivera, decided to seize on the moment and generate internal dissent against Stedman Fagoth's leadership. Rumors swirled that Stedman was stealing funds meant for the troops and was siphoning supplies for his own personal gain. While this had happened earlier on with the Argentines and a few senior FDN ranks—something I made the camps aware of early on after my arrival in hopes of seeing it change—Stedman Fagoth was not among those doing such things.

Still, these were men who had seen the FDN leadership in Tegucigalpa confiscate their tiny monthly salaries for years. They'd seen the other camps get the lion's share of the supplies simply because of the racial animosity toward the MISURA. The rumors seemed plausible.

One afternoon, our base in Tegucigalpa received a distress call from our new surrogate—a retired SF sergeant—at the MISURA base camp in Rus Rus on the Honduran side of the border. "There are six commanders and six hundred men here to kill Stedman Fagoth." Our surrogate packed up all our crypto gear and made his way back to Tegu in haste.

I had met with Stedman that morning in Tegu and knew he had just boarded a light plane to take him to Puerto Lempira. From there, he would drive to the Rus Rus camp in a truck. He'd been in Tegucigalpa trying to secure more resupply for his men. Now, he was returning to them and walking into an ambush.

At our base in the capital, Ray was deeply concerned. A Miskito insurrection would take down the offensive and quite possibly neutralize the most effective Contra force as its leaders battled for control of it.

I knew these men. I knew I could talk to them and find a way to solve this before it devolved into chaos and murder.

"Chief, please let me go out there," I said.

We talked it over. The Chief of Station got on the phone with us and asked me, "Are you sure you can do this?"

I was pretty sure.

"Yes."

Ray looked at me with his wicked smile and said, "You're cleared hot, Alex." I could feel his confidence in me, and that steeled me for the task.

There was no time to spare. By then, we had a Hughes 500 Defender light reconnaissance helicopter at our disposal. I jumped into it with one of our pilots, and we raced to head off Stedman and get to the camp first.

We landed halfway at one of our forward bases to quickly refuel. The Chief of Base there asked me, "What the hell is going on, Alex? An insurrection?"

I wasn't sure. He asked me what I was carrying, weapon-wise. It would be me going to talk to six hundred armed Miskitos, so I thought the question was pretty irrelevant. "This isn't gonna be resolved with bullets."

He nodded. I smiled and added, "I'm good, but I'm not that good." We both shared a laugh, tinged with anxiety.

We pressed on and intercepted Stedman before he could get to the camp. "Alex, what are you doing here?" he asked when I found him.

I said, "What, you think I would leave you in a time of need?"

He lowered his head and then smiled; no further words were needed among the two of us. Stedman was a good man, and the trust between us was solid.

I explained the situation to him and told him to stay put. I'd go forward and talk to the mutineers.

We got to the base camp after dark. As soon as I arrived, I checked in with Ray to let him know I was at least alive for the moment. Then I went off to find out what was going on.

Most of the six hundred men who mutinied remained on the Nicaraguan side of the Coco River, but the six rebellious commanders and perhaps fifty or sixty men had entered the camp. I found them around a bonfire, their chests crisscrossed with bandoliers of ammunition. The six commanders had all sorts of gear dangling from chest rigs. They looked ready to fight.

They were not happy to see me.

I approached them without even my rifle and greeted them. I made a point of being cordial but cold. They regarded me with distrust. Some looked openly hostile.

For an instant, I wondered if I'd bitten off more than I could chew. These guys were pissed off, and they just might be stupid enough to take their anger out on me without thought of the consequences. If that happened, I'd have no chance. Moments like these in real life are not like those you see in action films like *True Lies*, where the good guy always faces insane odds and kicks everyone's ass. In real life, skill, courage, and determination can only go so far against weight of numbers.

Though uninvited, I sat down and got straight to the point. "What are your grievances?"

At first, nobody spoke. I suppose they were trying to size up my intent. I waited, patiently, my face a mask. This was the ultimate game of poker, and I was damned if I were going to tip my hand.

One of the leaders spoke first. When I listened without comment, others began to chime in. Each one leveled a torrent of accusations against Stedman. He was stealing their salaries. He was hoarding or selling their supplies. There was bitterness in their words that could only come from men who'd been fighting for weeks and beating their enemy, only to feel like their own leaders were subverting their efforts and not sharing their hardships.

The latter was ridiculous. Stedman led from the front more than most. He'd only gone back to Honduras to secure what his men needed in person since every other effort had failed.

When they finished, they looked even more resolved. With the grievances out in the open, the mutiny felt justified.

I'd have to change their mind on that. Teddy Roosevelt used to say, "Speak softly and carry a big stick." Wise words for such moments.

At length, I spoke. "You guys have known me for years. We have trained together. We have fought together."

The anger softened in some of the faces around me. Just a bit, but still noticeable.

I'd struck the right chord. Now I needed to exploit it.

"I'm going to make you three promises, and you know they are solid."

They listened expectantly in the firelight. Some of the men had been eating off banana leaves. Now, they stopped to watch me intently.

"First, Stedman has not been stealing from you. Our resources are limited, and the other camps still need supplies, too. They are all fighting right now to support you, and the Sandinistas are pressing everyone hard. We're stretched thin. But Stedman is doing everything he can to get more sent your way. He's not screwing you over."

I watched the reaction. Faces set, hard expressions. This was not what they wanted to hear.

"Second, you are part of a democratic effort. If you don't like how Stedman is running things, call a tribal council and vote him out of power. It is as simple as that."

No reaction. The anger returned in some of the faces. Others seemed to consider that point. There was some hesitation, perhaps confusion on what to do next.

It was time to use the stick. "Third, if you touch one hair on Stedman Fagoth's head, I will personally lead the troops who will hunt you down and kill you. All of you."

The men reacted as if I'd just slapped them. Shock registered through the firelight. Here was the payoff for the years of personal investment I'd made with these men. They understood I could be their biggest ally or their worst nightmare. I was not a man to be fucked with. They'd seen how I could fight through countless weeks of training and missions together. They knew if bitten, I would always bite back.

While they were off balance, I softened the message. "And I promise you one more thing. You'll get resupplied within twenty-four hours."

I got up and left to let them think it over. Nobody shot me in the back, so I figured that was a good sign. I walked over to the communications hut and called back to the base in the clear.

"Hey, Chief," I said to Ray, "I got a tough one for you, boss. I need resupply first light tomorrow. I gotta have lots of beans, bullets, and medical supplies."

The next morning, several World War II–era C-47 transports landed in Rus Rus and delivered everything I'd asked for. How the hell Ray managed that miracle overnight, I will never know. We made sure Stedman delivered the supplies to the mutineers. The rebellion died, and Stedman survived.

The mutineers returned to the fight in Nicaragua. I returned to base.

In March of 1984, my time with the Contras in Honduras came to an end. Ray had been a mentor to me through my many years in the jungle. I learned so much professionally from him that I would always be grateful. He had been my biggest supporter and advocate from the outset and had looked out for me professionally. In early '84, he approached our Chief of Station and discussed my future. "Prado doesn't have a college degree. We need to professionalize him and get him to the Farm."

The COS agreed. Ray contacted Dewey Clarridge and said the same thing. Two hours after that phone call, I was told I'd just been sponsored to go to George Mason University.

I'd been a paramilitary trainer for almost four years. Now, it was time for me to become a spy.

# PART III

# 13

## LIVING IN YELLOW

*Virginia*
*1984*

I returned to the United States after three plus years of fighting a secret war to find a new sense of normalcy and see what it would be like to be a family man living at home again. Just before I'd left for the CIA, I met a young woman named Carmen at a party back home in Miami. At the time, I was recently divorced and living in the same apartment complex as my cousin. We were two drinks into a bottle of vodka when this work friend of my cousin's wife showed up.

I was captivated by her from the first moment I saw her. I asked my cousin who she was. Carmen asked my cousin's wife who I was. It did not take long for an introduction. Sparks flew, and we saw each other a few times before I went off to Honduras.

We wrote each other frequently, and in those letters, we got to know each other in a way I'd never been connected to anyone else. Of course, she didn't know I was with the Agency then or that I was in the middle of a war. But the essentials of who we were as people? We shared a great deal of that in our geographical separation.

I went home briefly in 1982 and proposed to her. When she accepted,

I read her into my life with the CIA. Of course, the Agency had to do a background check on Carmen before we could actually get married. I returned to Miami for the wedding, just before we began training my Barracudas. Carmen planned the entire thing.

We returned to Honduras together. Carmen was also Cuban-born and had come to America via the Freedom Flights. Her father was college-educated and quite a strict gentleman. Until we married, she'd never left home.

Our marriage gave Carmen the E-ticket ride of her life. We soon moved into a Tegucigalpa neighborhood near other members of Ray's team. But for the first few weeks, while I was off training the Barracudas, I had to leave Carmen at the Hotel Alameda. Needless to say, my disappearance for almost a month right after we got married provided the first of many tests to our love.

After I got back, we saw each other usually only on the weekends. The rest of the time, I was in the jungle with the Contras. To fill her time, Carmen read books and started learning how to cook (talk about a marital challenge!). She'd worked in a bank in Miami when we met, living an average American life. Now, she was the wife of a CIA officer helping to orchestrate a covert war against a communist foe. To her, all of this was an incredible adventure. I loved that she loved it as much as I did.

Halfway through our tour in Honduras, Carmen became pregnant with our first child. Our first son was born nine months later.

Our return to the States gave us a chance to live a more normal married-couple kind of life. We rented a little house in Virginia, and I started the accelerated program at George Mason University. I had enough credits already for about two years' worth of a bachelor's degree. The other two years I crammed into one hell-bent-for-leather nine-month period. I studied harder, worked harder, than I ever had academically. I took classes on religion, geopolitics, geography, and history. Ultimately, I graduated after writing my senior thesis on counterterrorism.

None of my professors knew I was CIA. After graduation, my real education began.

With my fresh degree in hand, I received orders to attend the Agency's legendary Operations Course at what is popularly called the Farm. Here, career trainees, mostly young college graduates, are introduced to the dark world of espionage and intelligence gathering as part of their development into case officers. A case officer, or operations officer (OO), is a frontline warrior in the intelligence-gathering war. Their job is to work overseas to develop and run spies. Agency personnel are never *agents*. We are *operations officers*. The locals we develop to spy for us are called *agents*. Hollywood always gets this part wrong.

The case officer's job is to cultivate, maintain, and protect those agents, meeting with them when necessary or finding clandestine ways to exchange information. There are many ways to gather intelligence these days—via satellite, aerial reconnaissance, intercepted radio transmissions, cell phones, wiretaps, and so on. They all give us puzzle pieces of information, but none of those things are nearly as useful as human eyes and ears in key places. Human intelligence, or HUMINT, is the essence of our work. Because of that, the case officers play a significant role in defending America.

I'd already been a paramilitary officer (PM) for four years, working within the Special Activities Division (SAD, more recently, Special Activities Center), Ground Branch. To have a true career in the Agency, all PM officers needed to be fully operational case officers as well. In the early days, some went to the Farm just to punch that ticket, then returned to the paramilitary side of the house. Others developed into versatile operations officers with a full understanding of both intelligence gathering and covert operations. With the onset of what became the Global War on Terrorism (GWOT), SAD-homebased officers became very popular and successful. Many went on to fill key, senior positions in the Directorate of Operations.

A PM officer could blow things up and had an intimate knowledge of dozens of different weapons systems. However, these were cool tools for use only in extremis. Yes, like most PMers, I was a blunt object, and brute force was my stock-in-trade—at least training others to use it anyway. Now, at the Farm, I was introduced to a totally new world. One of intrigue and subtle danger. Blunt objects had no place here. In this new realm, finesse and subterfuge were the orders of the day. We quickly learned that if you had to revert to your martial expertise during an intelligence-gathering operation, you had already screwed up.

The Farm focused on teaching us new case officers the dark arts of tradecraft that would keep our agents and ourselves alive in incredibly dangerous, multi-threat environments. Most aspects of tradecraft are counterintuitive. To understand why those dark arts were so important, we were taught what we would face when up against rival intel agencies. For some of the young college students with little life experience, that was pure culture shock. Having lived in a communist country and witnessed the depravity of such a system, I had a better feel for what to expect from the opposition.

We Americans are generally raised to be law-abiding citizens with an ingrained sense of fair play. The world beyond our borders simply does not function that way. Our adversaries do not adhere to the same rules we enjoy and cherish, which sometimes puts us at a consistent disadvantage against ruthless, unscrupulous foes like the Chinese, Iranians, Cubans, and Russians.

Some of our first classroom lessons focused on the sort of tactics employed by our foes to compromise people and turn them into sources. There are two main ways of doing this: recruit from strengths, or recruit by exploiting weaknesses. Our Agency prefers to recruit from strengths, as those agents tended to be the most reliable sources. For example, say you're working in a country with a corrupt dictatorship. You find and cultivate a straight arrow inside the government who is seeking a way to change things for the better. The Agency provides him or her with that opportunity. We're recruiting from strength here, as we've developed an asset with a strong ideological commitment.

Some of them even refused our offers to pay them. Those agents weren't supplying us with information to get rich. They were doing so because they saw a wrong they thought we could help right.

That said, remuneration is an important part of the recruitment process. Being capitalists, we understand that everyone has dreams of a better life for their families, whether a college education for their children or a better roof over their heads. Some in the community joke that CIA stands for Cash in Advance; I say that moniker is raised out of jealousy.

That was our greatest advantage. The Agency, the United States, we were seen at the height of the Cold War as the "good guys." That sort of moral capital helped us a great deal in the field.

On the flip side, the Russians and the Chinese are not beyond recruiting in a very different way. Instead, they often recruited from weaknesses. They would observe people they were interested in and discover whatever their weaknesses were. Maybe they had a secret gambling problem, a concealed sexual proclivity, or a hidden drug problem. They would detect it and exploit it through blackmail, forcing their target to spy for them.

If they could not find a weakness, they could well manufacture one, which is just as good from their perspective. Many a young businessperson or foreign service officer from country X finds himself or herself inexplicably irresistible to beautiful partners and suddenly find themselves in a "honeypot trap."

Imagine this scenario: The Chinese, Russian, or Cuban intel service is eager to get economic or technological information out of a married, foreign businessman or diplomat overseas. They watch his patterns, note the bars and hotels he visits while he is overseas, then send this irresistible woman his way. She lures him upstairs to her room, where the target is videotaped or even drugged. The escort vanishes. The intelligence service takes over. The businessman wakes up with his entire life turned upside down. In some extreme cases, they put him in bed with a member of the same sex, often underage, and take photographs while he is out cold.

Whatever the case, the target is now owned by hostile intelligence because he knows if the photos or footage ever see the light of day, his life, family, career, and possibly his freedom will be taken from him.

It is a savage way to do business, but it is often par for the course for our rival agencies. The Farm taught us the nature of the threat—those rival agencies would be gunning for us.

Terror groups would be gunning for us as well. Middle Eastern groups such as Black September and the Palestine Liberation Organization were deadly effective at times against even the Israelis. Hezbollah, the Iranian terror group, successfully identified, stalked, and kidnapped our CIA station Chief in Lebanon in March of 1984. William Buckley was a highly regarded paramilitary officer in the Special Activities Division, a U.S. Army Green Beret veteran who fought in both Korea and Vietnam. As he left his apartment in Beirut on March 16, 1984, he was abducted at gunpoint. Buckley had been warned he was in danger but had not changed his routine, nor was he carrying his sidearm on his body. Instead, he'd put it in his briefcase.

After he was kidnapped, he was tortured for seven months by Hezbollah operatives. He was either murdered or died of a heart attack while under torture a year later.

Buckley's horrifying fate was a fresh wound for the CIA while we were at the Farm, a reminder that the tradecraft we were being taught was not an academic exercise; we were learning it so we could protect ourselves. Cold War rules were giving way to "Beirut Rules." The spy game was being changed forever.

One basic principle drilled into us for our survival in the shadow world was called *situational awareness*. A popular tool used to convey situational awareness and the different levels of it was a system called Cooper's Colors. A Stanford-educated, two-war Marine officer named John Dean "Jeff" Cooper developed Cooper's Colors; his intent was to create the mindset needed to survive in a world full of murky threats. Each color in his system represented a different level of awareness and readiness, ranging from white to red.

**WHITE:** You're unaware and unconcerned. You're not looking for threats. If you're attacked while in this mindset, you'll probably be overpowered or killed before you can get over your surprise. At the Farm, we were taught we should never be in White unless we were sleeping, or maybe making love to our spouse. An officer overseas in this level of cluelessness to their surroundings will almost certainly become a victim.

**YELLOW:** You are aware of what is going on around you. You're noticing things; your head is on a swivel. You're checking behind you for any potential threats or tails. You're looking at higher or lower elevations around you, but you are doing this all in an inconspicuous and relaxed manner. Essentially, you're taking in the environment around you and trying to discern any patterns or behavior that could indicate a threat.

Yellow was to be our permanent baseline mindset. If you have a pulse, you are always aware of your environment and the people in it. To relax from this standard invites a catastrophe. Like William Buckley did.

**ORANGE:** This is a more specific alert mindset, where scanning the surroundings has detected that something is not right. A car may appear to be following you. Or persons down the street appear to be nervously eyeballing you. Your job at this point is to identify the threat and formulate a plan of action to deal with it if necessary. Further complicating your decision is the kind of threat you are assessing. Is it criminal? Is it terrorism? Or is it a hostile intel service trying to surveil you? In each case, your decision to act will be very different.

If you conclude it is "only" a hostile service establishing surveillance on you, then you simply note their presence and proceed to bore them with your nonoperational behavior. You try to memorize vehicle makes, license plates, and even faces. We call this *tradecraft*. Then you have to do the thing you never see Bond or Bourne do in the movies: you write it all up.

However, if you determine the threat is physical—crime or terrorism—then your reaction had better be right and based on reality before you proceed to Red. Again, unlike the dime novels and action thrillers, the real formula is: Detect, Avoid, and only in last resort, Counter. Remember, you are in their turf; they have a plan of action to which you are reacting. Because of that, the odds are always in their favor. Your only hope is to somehow disrupt their attack plan.

**RED:** While Orange establishes your threshold for action, Red shifts into the mindset to execute that action. You Detected in Orange, now you hope to Avoid while in Red; the best defense when you are flying solo is to Avoid. We called it *getting off the X*. The attackers have formulated an ideal (for them) plan. Deciphering it and avoiding it altogether is the schoolhouse solution. This could involve surprising behavior like driving through a stop sign or turning onto a one-way road against traffic. Blowing your car horn might be all it takes, depending on the situation. It could be slamming the brakes, hitting reverse, doing a 180-degree turn, and blowing past them in the opposite direction. Something out of the ordinary and unpredictable is the best means to throw a monkey wrench into their operation.

But a car chase? *Forgetaboutit!* That is far too dangerous. Instead, you hightail it to the nearest police station, hospital, friendly embassy, or five-star hotel (these all have security and cameras).

In worst cases where it is impossible to avoid an attack, there are times when our officers have had to draw weapons and defend themselves. We have had officers shoot and kill assailants in a Pakistani street. Later on, you will see two such personal incidents: one in the Philippines and one in a hostile Muslim country in Africa. The bottom line is Red is where people die. Case officers either successfully defend themselves or become victims. Red is the last-ditch defense.

Within the context of Cooper's Colors, our instructors at the Farm taught us many techniques and tactics we could use to identify, avoid, or negate threats. When moving around a foreign capital, either by car or on foot, we learned to use surveillance detection routes (SDRs) to find anyone tailing us. An SDR is carefully planned series of stops, turns, and changes of direction designed to look totally natural and innocent. It is not. A well-designed SDR will send an officer to a series of errands—say, the store, post office, gym, and so on. At each stop, the officer will search for vehicles or faces he's seen at previous stops or while traveling between them. Sometimes, we may have the luxury of a second team that will follow the officer executing the SDR. The second team will observe and detect tails from their position behind the officer.

It is the same exact discipline that all other services use. Our own FBI has their hands full trying to identify foreign intelligence activities in our country. The secret to tradecraft is that it is not a secret; it is the showcasing of a benign existence while carrying out your intel collection mission.

We practiced these SDRs in local towns and cities, working with our instructors to spot the surveillance on us. Surveillants are often local police officers or other trained individuals who assist as adversaries during the training. It was intense training right in the middle of American life, just as we would be operating overseas. It was also a reminder that as case officers, our job was to be invisible to those around us. We lived in a dimension of everyday life that few even knew existed around them. We could be sitting at a stoplight surrounded by commuters heading home from work, a few moms taking their kids to soccer practice, and perhaps one KGB agent sitting in a red sedan four cars back who has been ordered to find out who we are and where we are going. If everyone does their job right, the people around will never have a clue of the cat-and-mouse game unfolding right under their noses.

We learned countersurveillance tactics, escape, and evasion. Students go through a mini-SERE school where we learned how to resist interrogation. Our instructors showed us how to identify potential threats from assassins to honeypot traps—beautiful women (or handsome men) intent on seducing us as a method of compromise.

As the basic building blocks of tradecraft were added to our toolboxes, our instructors ran us through exercises in the real world—everything from developing a relationship with a potential asset to finding dead-drop locations where information could safely be exchanged was done both at the Farm and in the towns and cities around us.

It was an intense program that kept us busy for almost fourteen hours a day. We had weekends off, but we often had so much work to do to prepare for the following week that I went home to Carmen and our infant son only twice a month. The other weekends, I would usually start with a couple of skydiving jumps around seven in the morning to get my blood going. Then I'd devote the rest of the weekend to writing reports, making maps, locating spots to exchange information with our role players in upcoming exercises, and so on.

All the school's teachings came together in a grand, ongoing exercise that had us simulating working out of a foreign location. All the things we'd do overseas as a case officer, we did at the Farm. We reported to our Chief of Station, we worked to cultivate and run agents. We conducted countersurveillance, planned our SDRs. All the while, our reports were being read right alongside the reports of the role players. If we missed anything we should have caught, the role players alerted our instructors.

In this intense operational training environment, I believe my life in the streets paid off big-time. Many of the fresh college grads in our class found themselves out of their depth when they were asked to steal secrets for the first time. In me, they were competing with a guy who had to steal hubcaps to pay for his dates. When they were planning a break-in to a target building to plant bugs, they were competing with a guy who had more than once broken into buildings to escape from the cops after a neighborhood brawl.

One particular incident boosted my confidence. We were taking turns performing our tasks in an auditorium in front of the rest of our class of spooks. One scenario had us carrying out a dead drop while under surveillance. Walking around the stage using props for screening and flow (meaning to move naturally, unnoticed, undetected), we were to drop a small object into a flower bed for a recruited "asset" to retrieve later. When my turn came, I ran through my movements, and the head instructor suddenly pulled me aside. A crusty veteran of "denied" operations in China, he said, "I'm reporting you to the FBI—you've had prior operational training." He was as serious as a heart attack. I was speechless.

Then he smiled. He said I was a natural and that my demeanor would carry me a long way. Perhaps the good Lord did have a plan for me during my misspent youth!

Ultimately, all of us who made the cut mastered the tradecraft. No matter how scientific our selection process was, every class had attrition. In mine, three failed to cut it. The Agency didn't like washing out career trainees (as we were called) after heavy investments were made in their development, but it did happen. Just to get into the door required a thorough screening process for the new recruits, starting with background checks, interviews, and even a full lifestyle polygraph test. A good case officer has to have a delicate balance of personality traits and skills. Finding those in young recruits is a lot like trying to find a Pro Bowl–caliber quarterback in the NFL draft. You never really know until they're tested. In our case, some of the best pedigreed career trainees who seemed to have all the right mix of charisma, charm, and physical strength couldn't hack it in the field.

A few of those were redirected into admin or analyst careers. A couple eventually graduated provisionally from the Farm at the bottom of our class. One did okay overseas. The other quit after his first tour. In many respects, it was a lot like being in harm's way: you never really know how you're going to react under fire until it happens. That level of danger and stress can never be truly modeled in a training environment, because everyone knows the danger is not real. Still, the course at the Farm threw as much stress and tension as possible into the equation to see how we would react to it.

We drank out of this fire hose for sixteen weeks, learning everything from codes and casing targets to photography and building concealment

devices for dead drops out of things like fallen tree limbs, within which
we could conceal exposed film or data. We learned how to use disguises
and aliases and how to cultivate an asset—all within the context of a
simulated fully functioning foreign operation. We did everything they
did overseas, right down to the paperwork and the forms used for our
case reports.

Toward the end of our time at the Farm, we were sent to a U.S.
city we'd never worked in before to undertake a series of final field exercises with another governmental agency. Both sides would know when
the exercises would start and the initial location, and our adversaries
would know who we were.

Our first assignment was to execute a dead drop. We didn't know
the city well, but we had maps and got creative. One of our trainees
was a triathlete and an exceptional runner. We decided to exploit that.

When the exercise commenced, our runner emerged from the
hotel dressed in jogging clothes. Our adversary's surveillance team had
parked outside the hotel in a black sedan, wearing suits and wing tip
dress shoes.

Big mistake. Our triathlete took off running, made a few turns,
and went up a one-way street. The surveillance team couldn't follow in
their sedan, so they bailed out and gave chase. In wing tips.

They never stood a chance.

Boy, were they pissed in the after-action review on that one!

As the training continued, we learned that the locals overseas consider every American a spy until proven otherwise. At the same time,
we would be operating right under the noses of foreign intelligence agencies doing everything they could to ferret out and compromise our case
officers. We would have to detect those watching us, shake them, and
never tip our hand that we had done so.

It was a guts game all the way. I couldn't wait to play it overseas.
I finished in the top 3 percent of my class and received my first assignment as a case officer: El Salvador. This was a perfect opportunity
for me, a country battling its own Marxist insurgency. I could assist

in the effort to defeat it before El Salvador went the way of Cuba and Nicaragua.

Our time in Virginia rapidly came to an end. We packed our things and shipped them to San Salvador. But at the last minute, everything changed when an Agency legend asked for me elsewhere by name.

# 14

## WASHINGTON TWO-STEP

*Central America*
*1986*

I arrived at my new station in Central America in the summer of 1986. I was initially disappointed that I would not be going to El Salvador after all; Carmen did not know any better. Soon she realized what a lucky break she'd gotten as far as living conditions. The fight against the FMLN—the Marxist insurgents ravaging the countryside—was one that I saw as a righteous cause. Instead, I was sent to support the southern front opposing the Sandinistas north of the San Juan River, which divides Nicaragua from Costa Rica.

From my years in Honduras, I'd heard a lot of chatter about the southern front. It was not well organized or coordinated, and the Sandinistas had penetrated the different Contra groups to a much greater degree than those on the northern front I knew so well. This would be virgin territory for me, and a supremely difficult assignment.

Joe Fernandez, the Chief of Station, had asked for me by name, which is what diverted me from my original posting in El Salvador. Joe was a legend within the Agency. A tough anticommunist Cold Warrior of red-Spaniard blood and temperament, Joe had been a South Florida police officer before joining the Agency. He was rugged and resource-ful, a demanding officer to work for, but was loyal to those under him.

He was also an unconventional thinker. He outworked everyone in the station, and his intensity matched his commitment to the mission. When something difficult needed to be done, he was always the man for the job. Joe was the quintessential CIA man: a shadow warrior with matching rugged good looks, cigarette elegantly poised in his hand, Montblanc pen scribbling on his ever-present yellow legal pad. Killer smile, but then there were the eyes; they were killer also and you knew they could pierce through bullshit like a laser.

The fact that he had asked for me by name was a huge compliment.

When I first sat down with him to get briefed on the situation, Joe was struggling to unite the various commanders running the southern front. He gave me a blunt assessment: Sandinista spies were everywhere inside the rebel movement here. Our host nation was hostile to the Contras and actively trying to ferret them out. This meant we would have to operate clandestinely to avoid getting arrested or worse by the country's security forces.

This wasn't like Honduras, where the Contras could rest and re-equip, then cross the border to get back into the fight. This southern front was another version of France in 1944. Joe was leading me into La Résistance.

To keep the Contras in the field inside Nicaragua required a lo-gistical tail that didn't exist here on the southern front. There were no supply bases in the host country, no roads and convoy routes that could be taken. They had to be sustained by airdrops. The problem was that the coordination of flights and ground crews was totally dysfunctional, and the Contras in the field were running out of ammunition and food. Ninety percent of our airdrops RTB (returned to base) with their pre-cious cargo. If we couldn't execute the aerial resupplies, the southern front would eventually collapse.

Joe *always* recapped his tutorials, and this was no exception: *Fix the f'ing airdrops.*

In Honduras, this would have been a moderate challenge. But in a hostile host country like Costa Rica? Totally different ball game. The Sandinista spies would frequently tip the Costa Rican police off to the location of Contra safe houses. The Contras themselves were undisciplined in the urban jungle and devoid of any tradecraft. Raids took place all the time, and many Contra subcommanders and support people were wrapped up, thrown over the border, or temporarily imprisoned. Trying to coordinate airdrops in Nicaragua while our contacts were getting raided and arrested presented an extraordinary challenge, especially since it was absolutely vital that we few gringos did not get wrapped up as collateral damage in any of these Costa Rican raids. Doing so would have created an international incident and damaged relations between the U.S. and Costa Rica.

Here, for the first time, I experienced the real-life importance of tradecraft. To help the Contras, we had to insulate ourselves from their leaks. As their safe houses were being taken down by the Costa Ricans, we had to figure out a way to meet with their support personnel in some other way.

We came up with a rolling office—a van specially equipped for such meetings. We would get word for our Contra contacts to meet us at a certain location. We'd have a car pick them up, run an SDR, then drop them at our van. While the meeting was underway, we'd have a lead car guide us through the city

Using these tactics, we successfully insulated ourselves from the leaks and Costa Rican security forces. That allowed us to work through the reasons for the resupply failures. We soon unraveled what was happening. The main problem stemmed from the Contra commanders and their inability to convert a drop location into eight-digit map coordinates.

We instructed the commanders to secure an area of our choosing, based on geographical features they could easily identify and triangulate. Then we provided the pilots with the accurate coordinates and related safety signals for the drops.

With the new tactics and procedures, the next ten drops had nine successful deliveries and one RTB due to inclement weather. Joe was happy—very happy!

Once we improved our security, we began to search for leaks among the Contras. For us to be able to function, we needed to plug those leaks. Here, Carmen stepped up and played a key role for us.

Through all the craziness of the past eight years, the one constant in my life was Carmen. When she signed on to be my life partner, I don't think either of us had any idea what that journey was going to look like. Young and in love, we went into it with a faith in each other that never wavered. Looking back, that seems amazing to me now.

Before she met me, Carmen lived a sheltered life. Sheltered, but hot-blooded. In the first moments after we met, I glimpsed a sense of adventure that had long gone unfulfilled. Our life in the CIA together unlocked that, and I watched her thrive as my career took us to nearly every continent together.

She used to say that through me, she lived the life she wished she could. This, even though for most of my career I couldn't tell her much about the things I did.

She didn't need to live vicariously through anyone; she had plenty of adventures of her own. During my second Contra tour, Carmen worked as an interpreter for one of the Agency's best polygraphers. "Craig," was a six-foot-three, former ████████████████████ who had been a state trooper before joining the CIA. He'd been sent down to us to polygraph some of the Contras we were working with in an effort to find some of the Sandinista moles who bedeviled the southern front.

Carmen was assigned to be his interpreter. She'd already gained a clearance and had worked various positions in this current station. However, this translator gig was a little more operational. To carry out these polygraph exams, Craig and Carmen had to move around, using different hotels and a limited number of safe houses. A six-foot-three African American being seen going into hotels with a five-foot-two white woman carrying a suitcase was sure to turn heads. Oh, and did I mention Carmen was pregnant and showing the "bump" with our second child at the time?

To pull this off, I put Carmen in disguise. Hair in a bun with plenty of talcum powder to give it gray tones and make her look older. Glasses. A shapeless coat to hide her baby bump. They still got plenty of looks in hotel lobbies. But they functioned superbly as a team, and Carmen thrived. It fed her own spirit of adventure, gave her a unique purpose, and made her feel like part of our team.

While Carmen worked to discover the leaks, we set up a new series of safe houses along the border with Nicaragua with the help of local ranchers. They were conservative people, devout anticommunists and sympathetic to the Contra cause. Working with them helped get our Contras in and out of Costa Rica without detection. We used this network to provide medical assistance to wounded fighters, as well as to get them out of Costa Rica to train in other locations before returning them to the fight. This pipeline became an important component sustaining the southern front.

One of the key members of our team was another Cuban refugee named Flaco. Flaco and his mother escaped from Castro's regime about the same time mine did. His father, like his son, was a natural charismatic leader. He originally fought on Castro's side, but soon became disillusioned with the Marxist direction the revolution took. Castro marginalized him and sent him off to be a military attaché in a low-priority Latin American post. From there, he defected to the U.S. and began working with clandestine forces to conduct reconnaissance and naval raids against Cuba. While on an ill-fated mission, his father was captured and executed, some say in the presence of Fidel himself.

Flaco grew up and became a successful businessman in Florida, but he burned to avenge his father's murder and the loss of his country. On his own, he sold his business in the early 1980s, traveled to a Contra camp, and joined the fight against the Sandinistas. He was the hardest of hard-core: ideologically committed, unshakable in combat, and willing to trade the good life back home for a muddy, mosquito-swarmed foxhole in a triple-canopy jungle to deal payback to the communists.

That was our kind of man. Before I arrived, he was removed from direct combat to serve as our logistical mastermind. The respect and admiration he had earned in combat made him even more effective in this new role. Plus, Flaco was the kind of businessman who developed contacts everywhere with ease. He became a vital component of the support effort in Costa Rica, thanks to his ability to find anything we needed to sustain our peasant warriors. Need a boat? Flaco would know the right guy to talk to and would know exactly how to talk to him to get what we needed.

Need a plane? Same thing. Go to Flaco. He ended up working a good ten years in support of these and other mutual efforts and developed incredible contracts all over the world. He was the best kind of warrior: loyal, a believer in our mission, and rock-solid in a crisis. If it had been up to him, he would have stayed at the pointy end, but his role became far more important running our mini-Maquis effort in Costa Rica.

As we implemented these changes, our aircraft started hitting the right drop zones. The Sandinistas couldn't penetrate our new security measures like before, and the Costa Ricans found it much more difficult to detect their presence. The additional medicine, clothes, weapons, and ammunition made a strategic impact on the war. The Sandinistas were now beset by two well-provisioned forces to their north and south. By mid-1986, the population, tired of their depredations and war on religion, turned increasingly against the Sandinistas. The Contras found safe havens and lots of support wherever they went in the countryside. If the war had continued unabated, the Sandys were looking at a total

defeat unless one of their allies intervened in some massive and destabilizing way.

As a field officer supporting the Contras' southern front, I was a
GS-12. Basically, that meant I was one of the low men on the totem
pole. I had an important role getting the airdrops properly scheduled
and delivered, but I was not privy to all the machinations going on far
above my head that orchestrated the acquisition of the supplies and
weapons. I had no idea where the aircraft came from or who owned
them. In Honduras, much of what we received for the Contras came
straight out of the Sears & Roebuck catalog. By 1986, the supplies were
coming from anywhere and everywhere, with most of the weapons being Eastern Bloc AK-47s and their derivatives.

I would get word that a specific kind of aircraft would be available with a specific cargo. My job was to help pick a place and time
to get those things to a particular Contra commander's force inside
Nicaragua. Everything else was compartmentalized. I never asked, and
nobody ever told me, anything beyond that.

So what unfolded only a few months after I arrived in Costa Rica
ensnared me in a much larger political battle I was totally unaware was
brewing back home.

It started with a phone call on October 5, 1986, from our local
clandestine communications center. A resupply drop had been scheduled for that evening for a northern front FDN force that had penetrated deep into Nicaragua. They were actually very close to some of
the southern front Contras we were supporting. The voice on the other
end of the phone line that day told me things had gone very wrong. The
bird was missing, presumed down. The nearest friendly forces to the
crash site belonged to the southern front.

Right away, we passed word for our Contras to get to the crash
at all costs, secure, and destroy it. Rescue any survivors. They made a
heroic effort to force march to the location, but the Sandinistas beat
them to it.

The wreckage revealed a lot of things, but far worse was the fact that the first Sandinista patrols on the scene discovered the crew's bundle kicker asleep in a hammock made from his own parachute. A bundle kicker is the person on a cargo flight who actually gets the supplies off the ramp.

In this case, the bundle kicker was Eugene Hasenfus, a Wisconsin-born former United States Marine. We later found out the aircraft, a civilian-owned C-123 that was charted from a holding company belonging to a cargo firm called Southern Air Transport, had been shot down by a shoulder-launched antiaircraft missile supplied by the Soviets. In this case, it was an SA-7, sort of the Eastern Bloc version of our Stinger missile that had cost the Red Army so many helicopters in Afghanistan.

I didn't know any of this at the time. Nor did I know that our aircrew generally did not fly with parachutes. Hasenfus did. When I found out the details long after the event, I learned that he'd been in the doorway when the missile impacted. He was able to get clear of the burning wreckage, open his chute, and come down into the jungle relatively unharmed. Everyone else died in the crash.

The crews had been instructed to head south if they ended up going down in that part of Nicaragua. The southern front Contras would do everything possible to make contact and rescue them. For whatever reason, Hasenfus didn't do that. Instead, he hunkered down not far from the crash site and was easily captured.

He became a case study of how crucial tradecraft can be in any clandestine operation. The crews—or Eugene, at least—had gotten sloppy with their operational security. When he boarded that C-123 that morning, he failed to empty his pockets of anything that could be useful to the Sandinistas. He turned out to be one of the biggest intelligence coups of the entire covert war. What came out of his pockets destroyed careers and embroiled the United States in a brutal political clash that ultimately tarnished the last years of the Reagan administration.

The Sandinistas quickly showcased him to the world. They produced photos and film footage of the intelligence gleaned from Hasenfus's pockets—phone numbers of contacts, business cards, notes. Receipts. It was a catastrophic reveal of our effort to covertly support the Contras.

As the storm brewed in Washington between the Democrats in Congress and the Republican administration, further resupply flights were scrubbed. The Contras would have to carry on in some other capacity, and my role in the operation was shut down. I soon became just another case officer in the station, meeting folks and partaking in the diplomatic life.

Meanwhile, the funding for the Contra war gradually came to light in D.C. A few years before, Congress had passed legislation in 1982 and 1984 called the Boland Amendment, which banned the United States from providing any military assistance, or funds to be used for weaponry, to the Contras. The Sandinistas had become a sort of a cause célèbre to the American left, and with the Democrats in control of both houses, they attempted to hamstring the Reagan administration's effort to depose them.

In 1984, Reagan ordered the National Security Council to "keep the Contras together, body and soul" despite what Congress had directed. At the heart of this policy conflict was which branch of the government had ultimate authority over foreign policy.

The Reagan administration believed the conduct of foreign policy lay entirely with the executive branch. The Democrats in Congress disagreed and pointed out that the authorization of funds was its responsibility. So the Contra controversy fell into a constitutional gray area of overlapping authority.

In October 1986, military aid for the Contras was reinstated with congressional assent.

After Hasenfus was captured, a Lebanese magazine reported that the United States government was trading weapons to Iran for seven hostages their terror proxy, Hezbollah, had kidnapped in the Middle East. The Iranians were in the middle of a bloody stalemated war against Iraq and were desperate for weapons. Originally, the arms exchanges were made through the Israelis, with U.S. stockpiles backfilling what the Israelis sent to Iran. Later, the NSC set up their own arms pipeline with an additional price markup that the Iranians paid. That added cash amount was subsequently funneled to support the Contras. Hasenfus's capture and the discovery of his aircraft's registry to Corporate Air Services (the holding company for Southern Air Transport) ultimately revealed the Contra component of the Iran arms sales.

In the moment, this was all above my pay grade. Nevertheless, I was caught up in the Washington tempest it set off. Dubbed Contragate at first by the press, then later Iran-Contra, the final years of the Cold War were dominated stateside by the many investigations the scandal spawned.

Joe Fernandez was one of the first to be ousted and destroyed by Iran-Contra. He was recalled as Chief of Station—a fact reported by *The New York Times* and several other sources. He was repeatedly interviewed by investigators, where he took full responsibility for orchestrating the airdrops, shielding Bill Casey and others from political blowback.

Falling on his sword like that came at a huge cost to him personally. Those who should have gone to his defense within the Agency did not. Whether that was fear for their own careers in the midst of the biggest political firestorm since the Church Committee hearings or for other reasons, I don't know. But from my perch looking up, it sure seemed he was hung out to dry. In June 1988, he was indicted on four counts of obstruction and making false statements. It was the first time in history a CIA Chief of Station was criminally charged. The case against him was eventually dismissed in November 1989, but by then, his life and career had been reduced to a shambles. He was cashiered from the CIA and lost his pension.

As all that unfolded, I had returned from Costa Rica shortly after Carmen and I had our second child. I was working a desk at Langley. From my perspective, we had been fighting a noble effort for almost a decade to topple an illegal, brutal, and murderous regime in Nicaragua.

Anyone who thought that was wrong should have seen the women and children I'd seen escaping the Sandinista reign of terror.

Years of eyewitness experience convinced me the press coverage here in the States was deliberately painting a nonsensical and false picture of what was going on in Honduras and Nicaragua. The coverage distorted the situation for the people back home, and the left rallied behind the assertions that the Contras were nothing more than "murderous right-wing death squads."

The Contras I met in the camps were anything but that. They were Nicaraguan farmers and peasants who suffered endless privation, escaped to Honduras, and rallied to the cause because the Sandinistas had wiped out their villages, killed their priests, or raped family members. The women and children I saw fleeing those depredations across the Coco River were burned into my memory forever. They literally had nothing left—most didn't even have shoes.

Iran-Contra was the first time I'd come in contact with the political piranha tank that is Washington, D.C. It was an ugly, despicable scene, a Democrat-versus-Republican brawl in the capital that destroyed the careers of good men and patriots who had devoted themselves to the CIA.

In the years to come, I often remembered that lesson and why I joined the Agency in the first place. I was there to make a difference, not make a career.

The Contra war ended with a cease-fire armistice and a Sandinista promise to hold free elections. They came to the negotiating table because they were in danger of losing everything, thanks to the covert effort Casey and Reagan ramped up in 1981. I just wished Bill Casey had seen the results, but he died of a brain tumor a short time after the Iran-Contra news broke.

But the greatest of our Cold Warriors had laid the foundations for the two biggest clandestine victories of the Cold War. The first came in 1989 when the mujahideen drove the Soviets out of Afghanistan. The following year, the Sandinistas indeed held free elections. Hollywood celebrities flocked to Managua to rub shoulders with their Marxist fellow travelers. They'd supported Danny Ortega for a decade and were there to see his regime's legitimacy finally enshrined by a vote of the people.

The opposition—spearheaded by many of the FDN's senior leaders—was marginalized by the government at every opportunity. Ortega used every means available to his regime to promote the Sandinista ticket—and his own official reelection. Nearly every observer on the scene predicted an overwhelming Sandy victory.

The next day, the smoking ruins of Ortega's legitimacy boiled up over Managua like a cloud. His opponent, the UNO party's Violeta Chamorro, had crushed him nearly 55 percent to 40 percent. The Sandinista slate was demolished, and they were thrown from power.

For us who'd given so much in support of the Contra war, this victory was one of the seminal moments of our lives. We could not have asked for a better result—a revolution triggered by tyranny that succeeded in bringing the tyrant down by the power of the people's vote.

███████████

██████████████████████████████████, after all this had played out, I took my son to a local bookstore one Saturday as a treat. While we stood in line, I heard somebody say, "Heard you were back."

I turned to see Dewey Clarridge regarding me, a wry smile on his face. He was immaculately dressed in a blue linen Brioni suit, a handkerchief carefully tucked in the breast pocket. He stepped from around a shelf of books and shook my hand. "Good to see you, Ric."

He'd long since moved on from his position in the Latin American Division, and I was quite surprised he even remembered me, let alone remembered my name. We made small talk for a few minutes before saying our goodbyes.

As he left, he turned slightly and added, "If you need anything, let me know."

Dewey was old-school. Such words were not idle talk. It was his way of telling me he was looking out for me. I had a legend in my corner.

As we left the shop that day, I realized ███████████████████ ███████. My work in the jungle had given me a level of visibility most GS-nothings never get. It was incidental to the cause I believed in, but knowing there were people far above in the chain of command looking out for me gave me a sense of profound reassurance. No matter what went on with the endless Washington two-step, I was on the right path with the right people quietly guiding my way.

# 15

## SWIMMING UP THE CHAIN

*Southern Hemisphere*

*June 1988*

While the Iran-Contra political circus ground on in Washington through 1988, I was eager to stretch my wings in a way that allowed me to continue the fight against communism while utilizing the knowledge I'd gained at George Mason University. I'd researched and written about different terrorist organizations during my time at GM, and I was particularly interested in the Marxist groups in Central and South America. There were endemic Marxist insurgencies all over the world, even as late as 1988, but the homegrown ones in the Southern Hemisphere were particularly brutal and vicious.

When a counterterrorism slot opened up in one of those countries, my then SAD Ground Branch Chief strongly suggested I apply, and I jumped at the chance. I was accepted for it immediately—turns out, I was the only person in the Agency to apply for it. That came as a surprise to me, but in the final years of the Cold War, counterterrorism (CT) was sort of a bastard stepchild within the Agency. That would change in the 1990s, of course.

I went down to my new station about a month ahead of the rest of the family to get the lay of the land, find a house, receive our HHE (household effects), and deal with a myriad of other mundane logistical details required to get a household up and running in a foreign country.

Right away, I could tell this assignment would be a challenge. The capital city was filthy, impoverished, and desperately overcrowded. The Marxist terror group operating in the country kept attacking the power transmission towers, which triggered widespread blackouts. There were times when the electricity failed for over sixteen hours at a stretch. This caused mayhem in the streets, as the stoplights would often be nonfunctional. Traffic was already the sort of *Mad Max* chaos I'd seen in other countries, but here, the locals took it to a new level of crazy. They ignored traffic signs and lanes, sped down sidewalks, sending pedestrians fleeing in their paths. Snarls and wrecks were common, as were road-rage brawls after fender benders. With the stoplights down, going through intersections was a wild free-for-all and not for the faint of heart.

On my first ride from the airport, I knew running surveillance detection routes in the labyrinth of streets here would be an extraordinary challenge. The city was cobbled together over centuries, with roads never designed for cars overlapping more modern, if poorly constructed, thoroughfares. It was a hodgepodge mess that sprawled for miles in every direction. Shanties and hovels stood shoulder to shoulder in the shadow of modern skyscrapers. People begged in the streets. Police were everywhere. Army tanks and soldiers armed with assault rifles stood guard in front of government buildings.

This was a country at war with itself. For eight years, the Marxist insurgency had raged, led by a cultish, almost mythical figure who'd once been a philosophy professor at a third-tier college. Let's call him "Tomas" because his true name would be recognizable and geolocational. When the country held its first-ever democratic elections in 1980, he saw that as the moment to strike and led his fanatical ideologues in a series of attacks on polling stations. They burned ballots and declared they were the people's army bent on establishing a dictatorship of the proletariat.

They were Maoist in orientation, supposedly devoted to the plight of the country's vast underclass, especially the rural poor. They took to the mountains to establish a base of operations, then built networks throughout the country with which they could launch attacks.

The professor's followers were fanatically loyal to him and the cause. They recruited from villages and college campuses, creating a blend of pseudo-intellectual diehards and hardy frontline fighters. Of the latter, most were younger—teenagers and twentysomethings, with almost half being female. For some, there was an intense allure of romance to the cause of revolution.

After those first attacks in 1980, it did not take long for the Marxists to turn on their own base of support. When villages balked at supporting them, they would murder the leaders. They were known for descending on a village with a captured local farmer in tow. They'd put their prisoner on public display, announcing he was a reactionary and had spoken out against communism. They'd whip him as the villagers looked on in horror, then execute him.

Those sorts of excesses turned many peasants against the peasant revolution. At times, when members of the terror group entered a village, the people would set upon them with stones and homemade spears. In one case, six teenage Marxists were tied to a town's "rock of justice" and slowly strangled to death by the locals.

The violence and brutality escalated and soon spun out of control. In 1983, the professor's adherents swept into a town and hacked to pieces men, pregnant women, and children with hatchets and axes. Almost a hundred people were murdered.

While they tried to terrorize the people in the countryside into submission, other cells launched attacks on economic targets. In one case, they took over a university's experimental farm that was being used to develop a line of cheeses that could be exported for desperately needed hard currency. To the Marxists, this was a capitalist enclave to be destroyed. They spent hours slaughtering the farm's dairy cows with machetes—and did such a poor job of it they started a stampede. Local peasants who worked on the farm rushed to the scene to find frenzied cows fleeing blood-covered, machete-wielding Marxists. The peasants pleaded with the terrorists to stop, but in a morning of haphazard violence, most of the farm's animals were killed.

Killing animals became one of the professor's go-to tactics. In towns that refused to submit to their authority, the Marxists would murder dogs and hang them from light poles as a warning to anyone who tried to oppose them.

As the violence escalated, the police and army deployed to the countryside. They proved almost equally brutal. Hatred for the Marxists burned hot in the security forces, as they'd seen both family and comrades captured and murdered by them. Summary executions, rape, and torture all took place, especially in the rural areas.

This was a war without good guys.

Trapped in the middle, the peasantry suffered horribly. Eventually, over seventy thousand people would die as a result of the rebellion spawned by the professor and his Marxist revolutionaries, but that number did not tell the full story of misery and anguish visited upon this already poverty-stricken nation.

When I arrived in 1988, the cycle of violence was reaching a climax. The Marxists had overrun many of the nation's mines in the mountains outside the capital, where they seized great stockpiles of dynamite and other explosives. The terrorists were always short of guns, but they had an abundance of bomb-making material that they used widely.

To fund the revolution and acquire more guns, the Marxists took over the drug trade, organizing the coca growers into a collective they controlled. They'd sell the coca to the drug cartels in exchange for AK-47s and cash. The Marxists became quite adept in the underground capitalist cocaine market.

The money and weapons fueled the cycle of violence. In the cities, the revolutionaries carried out bombings nearly every day. Initially, they attacked government institutions or economic targets, but by 1988, they had extended their bombing campaign to include leftist professors, intellectuals, and writers they deemed not "ideologically pure enough." They attacked rival communist guerrilla groups for the same reason. Eventually, they started attacks on innocent civilians with no other strategic reason than to inspire terror. They bombed buses and trains and set off explosives in crowded public spaces. They pulled off assassinations and kidnappings and cowed the press by murdering reporters not aligned with their cause.

The death toll mounted daily with little end in sight.

Not long after I arrived, the Marxists hit a very symbolic target.

███████████████████████████████████████████████████

████████████████████

███████████████████████████████████████████████████

████████████████████

The terrorists surveilled that target and discovered the bus that carried the elite soldiers who defended it used the same route at the same time every day from their barracks to their assigned post.

One morning, they blocked the bus with a VW bug. The bus driver laid on his horn, distracted by the obstructed path. Meanwhile, a "teenage-looking" girl (she was actually twenty-one) who seemed to be selling fruit from a small handcart suddenly rushed the bus and shoved the cart under it. A moment later, a bomb concealed in the cart detonated, which touched off the vehicle's gas tank in a sympathetic explosion. The bus was blown apart and consumed by flames, killing over a dozen of the elite dragoons.

A nearby policeman saw the girl fleeing the scene and rushed after her. But she had backup covering her escape route. One of the Marxists, dressed innocuously like everyone else on the street, stepped behind the cop, drew a pistol, and shot him in the back of the head. Both the shooter and the bomb planter escaped.

My job in the capital was to assist the local security forces wherever I could to thwart these attacks and take down the cells conducting them. This was very different from anything I'd ever done before, so I started from the basics.

First thing: if I was going to operate in the capital city, I needed to know its streets. Before the era of GPS and Waze, I spent hours driving through every neighborhood, map in hand, getting the lay of the land. It was a miserable place to navigate, but I slowly came up my learning curve. Later, because of this, I was asked to help out on other operations where my knowledge of the street layout was an asset.

As I learned the grid, I began meeting with the contacts my predecessors had developed. We had about a dozen. I read through their jackets and didn't see a whole lot to work with in those pages. After meeting with them in different locations around the city, I grew convinced that most of them simply couldn't offer us useful intelligence. In one case, a student asset sat down with me and handed a sheaf of flyers to me. They were Marxist recruiting notices left on his campus with a meeting time and place on them.

"Great," I said to the asset. "What happened at the meeting?"

He gave me a blank stare.

"Did you go to the meeting?"

"No. I just picked these off the floor afterward."

The Marxists were committed, dangerous and exceptionally hard to penetrate, so I understood the asset's reluctance to have direct contact with them. New recruits were tested for their ideological purity, then put through an acid test to see if they had the chops to be a terrorist. Usually, this meant they had to go kill somebody to prove their loyalty and commitment to the cause. Not a lot of people wanted to go through that to supply information to us for a couple of hundred dollars a week.

After the first few months, I had to cut all but four or five of our assets off the payroll. We weren't getting anything for our money, and the attacks were escalating. It did not take long to understand that the organization we were trying to penetrate was exceptionally cagey and well versed with tradecraft. They were flexible, cunning, and could tactically evolve. When the government tried to stop their attacks on the power grid by sowing the ground around the transmission towers with antipersonnel mines, the Marxists rounded up dogs and threw them over the warning fences. They would run around, panicked as their kin detonated the mines around them. With enough dogs, they could create a path to the towers, set charges, and blow them up.

The power outages continued unabated.

Finally, we caught a break. A young woman who was friendly to us tipped us that a group of Marxists routinely used her small home in the capital as a meeting point. They were tough, intimidating, and all veterans of violent actions. This was a potential gold mine of intelligence for us, but we needed to figure out a way to get it undetected.

Fortunately, we had a creative tech team at our base. They went out and bought a used table that matched the décor of the woman's very humble home. They hollowed out one leg and installed a microphone and radio transmitter. We delivered the table and taught her how to activate the system before the cell arrived.

We established a surveillance post that overlooked her house. There, the tech guys set up recording devices connected to a radio receiver, along with other gear. Soon, we were all set; we just needed to figure out what radio frequency would give us the best reception. To do this required something called a *path-loss test*. It meant sending somebody over to the house with a device sending out a signal at different frequencies so the techs in the listening post could divine the clearest one. Then we'd set the transmitter to that frequency.

We couldn't be seen around the house, of course. We could not do anything that could arouse suspicion in case the terror cell was surveilling their own safe house.

Neighbors tend to talk, too. A couple of American-looking nerds with a bunch of technology coming and going at the safe house would be what we call in the business a *clue*.

Instead, I dressed in rags like a poor urban *cholo* and concealed the transmitter in a shoulder bag. I looked like a drunken street derelict. I was dropped off a few blocks from the house by a former LA SWAT team member who had recently joined the Agency. He was a tall, tragically white American who would have stuck out in this neighborhood, so he stayed in the van, armed with a shotgun in case I needed backup.

After he dropped me off at the corner, he anxiously sat in the van where he'd have eyes on me.

I walked down the street mumbling to myself, and I held the shoulder bag's strap with one hand. Under it lay the transmitter's button. Within reach of my other hand was my trusty 9mm pistol with fifteen rounds of Silvertip ammo. I pressed the transmitter as I approached the house, sending the signals to the tech guys.

Just as I reached the front door, the five Marxist terrorists spilled out of it. I looked up to see them wearing shorts and T-shirts with one of them carrying a soccer ball. They literally ran right into me, then started giving me a ration of grief. I'm not used to being shoved around, but the moment you go kinetic in a situation like this, you lose the game. Finesse and acting are what see you through.

In the van, my backup man saw what was happening. He reached for the shotgun and racked it just in case things went sideways fast. I was perhaps two blocks away, but I can swear I still heard it. Fortunately, the terrorists did not.

They shoved me around for a bit, teased and mocked me, then lost interest. They headed into the street to kick the ball around. I went on my way, continuing the path-loss test. I so wanted to double-tap each of them, and have five rounds to spare. But this was a new realm, and the rules of the game demanded self-control. In clandestine operations, if you resort to firearms, your mission is already compromised.

We got the information we needed. The techs tuned the transmitter in the table leg to the best frequency, and we settled down to wait for their return. When they did, the woman of the house secretly turned the system on, and we were good to go. The information was going to pour in, I was sure of it.

Instead, we were thwarted by her chickens. They were so loud we couldn't hear a thing beyond their incessant clucking. In terms of terrorist OPSEC, those chickens produced the best organic white noise imaginable!

So the chickens had to go. We bought them and had them removed, then gave our asset a cover story for their disappearance. When our soccer-playing cell of revolutionaries next appeared at the house, they suspected nothing.

Our recorders captured every word of that meeting. Instead of being a gold mine of intelligence, though, the tapes were filled with five young men bragging and bullshitting for much of the time. But every now and again, we scored a nugget of useful information. They spoke of different attacks they'd conducted, supplies of explosives, and other details. On subsequent occasions, they started to kick around ways to attack the U.S. embassy in the capital. They talked through ways to bomb it, then considered an armed attack on American personnel as they were leaving or returning to the embassy. It was clear they were in the very early planning stages, so there was no immediate threat to the embassy. That gave us some latitude and allowed us to listen in for weeks longer.

The local security forces made a habit of bagging such cells quickly. They'd take these frontline terrorists—the shooters and the bomb planters—and parade them on television as a sign of the government's success against the revolutionaries. Truth was that the shooters and the bomb placers were a dime a dozen. They were the foot soldiers of the organization who were not very intelligent and were easily replaceable. Going after the small fish made no sense to us. Instead, we convinced our allies in their security forces to have some tactical patience.

We put tails on the five members of the cell to see where they went and who they spoke to. Gradually, we began to fill in a hierarchy within this cell and the links to higher levels of command and control.

We weren't after the subcommanders, either. In any terror organization, there's always somebody else ready to fill in for any commander who gets killed or compromised. Who we wanted were the support people: the ones providing the funding, the resources, and the logistical assistance to the cells operating in the capital. They were the weak point in a terrorist organization since the majority of them lived aboveground lives and could not be easily replaced.

We called this process *swimming up the chain*. Once we had our eyes on one link, we'd follow and watch, learning everything we could. That careful patience netted us another link in the organization chain, then another. We assisted our allies as they worked our way up and developed more leads, more targets to watch.

It was a remarkable process that Hollywood never gets right. Counterterrorism never yields the complete picture. You never find an asset who will give you the full scope of what a terror group is doing or planning, because any capable organization insulates its members from each other. They only know what they need to know to carry out their missions. Everything else is beyond their scope. That means our intelligence comes in dribs and drabs like disparate puzzle pieces. We never get the complete puzzle, but sometimes we get enough pieces to fill in the blanks and make some intuitive leaps. Those pieces come from a wide range of sources and methods, much of which may seem at first glance to be unrelated. There will always be considerable chaff and misdirection that needs to be weeded out. In time, with enough pieces and patient work, we can start to assemble a picture that looks like the actual situation on the ground.

The transmitter in the table leg gave us our first significant access to a chain in their network. In the months ahead, we swam up that chain and started to build the first cell of agents inside the professor's own organization. That's when we started doing real damage to the revolution.

# 16

## EXPLOITING THE CHAIN

*Southern Hemisphere*
*1988–1990*
In the months after we first bugged the safe house, our intel provided our host allies some excellent opportunities to wrap up more revolutionaries. They didn't squander those chances by scooping up the little fish. Instead, they learned to be patient and wait for opportunities. Eventually, the five revolutionaries we'd been listening to were arrested by our host nation's security forces. They were all picked up individually at vulnerable moments in the midst of their daily routines by teams that moved swiftly.

There was no bloodshed as a result. Our local allies interrogated and imprisoned them, which in this corner of the world was a very harsh fate.

Prison could be exceptionally hard on the revolutionaries. A few years before, the professor announced that the prisons were legitimate fronts in the peasant war against the government. There were numerous jailbreaks, riots, and attacks on the prisons as a result. Then, during a week in which an international conference was held in the capital, simultaneous uprisings by incarcerated revolutionaries took place in three prisons. The country's president ordered the army in to deal with the crisis. They showed no mercy.

Thirty prisoners died in a hail of gunfire as the army stormed the prison. The soldiers summarily executed 130 more in the aftermath.

One day a few months after those first five went down, one of my friendly contacts inside the local security forces tipped me off on an opportunity. They had been surveilling another cell for several weeks. They'd learned their routines, contacts, and habits. One of the men in the cell had a weakness that, had his terrorist buddies known about, would have gotten him executed. He smoked pot.

As ironic as this sounds, the professor's movement did not tolerate drug use. For the true believers, even as they were moving mountains of cocaine out of the country, using any drugs was an immediate death sentence.

The other cell members underwent harsh interrogation by our hosts within hearing distance of the pot smoker, Miguel. By the time my contact brought him to me, he was wide-eyed and terrified of what he would soon face.

My counterpart in the security force told Miguel he was in for a rough time. But he may have a way out of his predicament. He introduced Miguel to me in a car pickup meeting. I sat behind my counterpart, who was driving, and Miguel, who was riding shotgun. We made sure to strap his seat belt in place, and we'd scooted his bucket seat all the way forward. I patted him down, even though I knew my counterpart was sure he was clean. This was SOP, but it also delivered the message: you are under *our* control. You never make assumptions.

"Look," I told him, "I don't care what your politics are. I don't care about democracy or communism. I am a businessman."

My cover for action (CFA) in this case was a phony passport for flash purposes only. It supported my background that I was a Costa Rican who owned a security company.

"All I care about is getting information that I can use to help my clients who do business here keep their people safe."

Miguel was perhaps twenty-one or twenty-two. He'd been a student recruited out of one of the universities. His decision to cast his lot with the ideologues now looked like a dreadful decision that had destroyed his life. He was looking at years of imprisonment in a system known for its cruelty.

"You help me with that, and I'll make sure you're released, well paid, and taken care of—provided you tell me the truth. But if you ever lie to me even once or provide me with bullshit information, my colleague here will make sure you end up back in prison . . . permanently!"

His saucer eyes stared into mine. He knew I was giving him his only chance at some semblance of a normal life. Or at least one not defined by bars.

He started talking. He was a treasure trove of information and provided great insight into their modus operandi (MO), cell structure, compartmentation discipline, and even as much of who is who to which he was privy. That turned out to be only a few people, as this Marxist group practiced very thorough compartmentalization, tradecraft, and operational security. Miguel knew his immediate handlers, and that was about it.

He served the professor's bandits as one of the countless "bomb mules" in the capital. His job was to pick up a prepared and assembled bomb from another cell and receive orders where to leave it. He'd take it to the designated spot and hide it in some concealed location. Once he delivered it, the actual attack team would retrieve it, then arm and emplace it at the designated target. He was sort of a low-level terror middleman, the link between two chains in the organization. He gave us valuable insight into how that system worked and how the attacks were carried out.

The revolution's foot soldiers were not very bright or trustworthy to the higher-ups in the organization. Their fieldcraft wasn't very good compared to the higher levels of the organization. In the early years of the war, the government's forces scooped them up or killed them pretty regularly. To minimize those operational weaknesses, Miguel would leave the bombs within about a mile of the target area. That way, the attack teams were not on the street for very long, carrying compromising materials. They would get the explosives, emplace them at the target area, and clear out.

In 1988, there were dozens if not scores of such teams operating all over the capital. Their support came from the revolutionaries fighting in the mountains outside of the urban areas. Ratlines moved the dynamite from the mines to the cities, where bomb makers cut their fuses, often split the dynamite sticks up, and prepared them for an operation.

There were perhaps fifteen thousand revolutionaries devoted to their Maoist cause in 1988. Most of the fighters lived wretched lives in the jungle or in mountain caves. The support people lived better lives in the cities, laundering money, arranging for safe houses, providing medical and legal support, and carrying out a myriad of tasks that kept the revolutionary nodes in the cities functioning.

A bomb mule like Miguel possessed only a fraction of the chain that ran from the professor to the mountains and into the cities, but the puzzle pieces he did give us turned out to be important ones in the fight against the bombing attacks.

I gave him a pager and taught him a simple number code to use when he wanted to meet with me. He would call my pager, and that code would be displayed, telling me where and when he wanted to meet. The technology was brand-new, and it was the first time I used it operationally. It proved to be so much easier than the dead drops and street-side signals we'd used up until then. It was also much less vulnerable to interception and deciphering than a cryptic phone call initiating an emergency meeting.

After that, we turned him loose. A few of his buddies ended up in the prison system, and a few others were also released to obfuscate Miguel's new role, so the revolutionaries were none the wiser. He picked up where he'd left off, running his deadly errands between the bomb makers and the attack teams. We had a few routine meetings to further debrief him on his knowledge of the group and its players, and to reinforce our "sacrosanct" agreement.

My pager beeped one afternoon a couple of months later. I looked down at the text display and knew at once it was Miguel, wanting to meet. The code he used indicated extreme urgency, and he had picked a site near his home—a particularly bad and dangerous neighborhood. My counterpart in the security service would normally come with me as backup, but he was out of the capital at the moment. Taking anyone else was a breach in operational security, so this meeting I would have to do alone.

Miguel's rendezvous point was an area of the city where foreigners dared not tread. Fortunately, my native Spanish and my penchant for disguises afforded better odds, as I could blend in. Hopefully, both of us would survive the encounter without compromise. My older, battered, white Toyota operational rental would also fit in the 'hood and allow for an inconspicuous pickup, using the pre-cased location with great cover and flow. No Jason Bourne red Mini Cooper or Bond's Aston Martin for this gig.

On the Cooper scale, I was in Orange; then again, in this place, I was always in Orange. As meticulous as I was about running great SDRs to the meetings, I was even more anal-retentive about my post-meeting SDRs back home. No way I could afford to have someone follow me back to my sanctuary.

Other than the well-received debriefings, Miguel had yet to provide us with anything that truly justified the risk of meeting alone with a terrorist. I had no idea if he was trustworthy yet, or if he'd double-cross me and set me up. I ran through scenarios I could face. His terrorist buddies might ambush and try to kill me. They might try to kidnap me. I'd have to be ready to take whatever action necessary, from avoidance to taking lethal force to protect myself. The great lesson from the Buckley kidnapping in Beirut was a CIA officer can never be kidnapped. You've got to do everything to evade being snatched and thrown in a car.

I kitted up, starting with soft body armor and two radios (in ops comms, two is one and one is none). These days, the PPK was enjoying a well-deserved retirement. In its place, I holstered a Colt 1911 A-1 on the hip, a 1911 Officer's model in a shoulder holster, and my stainless five-shot .38 caliber "Lady Smith" (no macho ego here) on my left ankle. I studied the neighborhood on the local maps, devised my SDR, then picked up my white Toy-motor and set out to the rendezvous point.

That night, I headed out, head on a swivel. I reached the meeting point. Miguel slipped into the car. We kept the exchange short and to the point. He explained he'd been ordered to pick up a bomb and deliver it to a drop-off site in a section of town near the international quarter. An attack within a mile or so of that X would take place within hours of his delivery.

He proved to be no threat. There was no terrorist countermove. His pot smoking combined with the leverage we had made him compliant—and ultimately a very good asset. As quickly as he'd come, I dropped him off at his preferred location. Like a ghost, he slipped away and blended into the ghetto.

I went back to base and studied his intended dead-drop area on a map. We looked over every building and potential target within a one-mile radius and came up empty.

Finally, one of our team noticed that there was a property owned by the Chinese, less than a mile away. It was part of the ambassador's residence or at least that of his entourage.

Would the Maoists bomb a Chinese communist diplomatic property? At first blush, this made no sense. In the past, some of their cadre had allegedly trained in China and received some logistical support. Why would they attack an erstwhile ally?

I typed up my report and sent it up the chain of command. Word came back that nobody thought the revolutionaries would attack a Chinese target.

There comes a tipping point in most revolutionary organizations where the ideologically impure are purged. This happened with our own domestic terror groups like the Weather Underground in the 1970s. It happened during the French Revolution and in the aftermath of Lenin's takeover of Russia. Marxist revolutionaries always go through this phase where loyal members are driven out or killed simply because somebody within the ranks does not believe they showed enough commitment to the cause.

That was happening with the professor's terrorists at this point in the uprising's history. Instead of seeking out allies, they sought to destroy anyone on the left they considered traitors to the cause because they were not radical enough. Already, they'd attacked socialist journalists, kidnapped or killed fellow communists from other terror groups and revolutionary fronts. They purged their own ranks of the less ideologically pure and shamed some of their subcommanders into suicidal attacks to prove their loyalty.

Set into that context, a Chinese target made perfect sense. Through the late 1980s, the Communist Party of China turned increasingly toward free market capitalism. To the ideologues, that was a betrayal of Chairman Mao's teachings. They were traitors to the cause, not fellow travelers.

The revolutionaries blew up several vehicles parked outside of the Chinese residence just a few days later.

The attack confirmed two things. First, the terrorists were spiraling out of control. They were losing support from even the most left-wing adherents in their country. The majority of the population had turned against them and the very people they claimed to represent; the workers and peasants had formed militias in their rural villages to fight off their depredations. They were flailing and killing people senselessly now.

Most importantly, it also confirmed that Miguel told the truth with his first tip to us. That was a harsh way to confirm the intel, but there is no more undeniable proof of intel than proven by events. This is actual verbiage used in our intel cables when an asset's predictions pan out in open-source documentation.

We worked with him for many months, and while he never gave

us the sort of scoop to rival the Chinese attack, his information helped develop our understanding of the opponent we faced. Ultimately, he vanished without any warning or notice. It was one of those sad loose ends from my tenure in the Agency that I wish I could tie up. Was he compromised and killed by his revolutionary comrades? Or was he simply transferred to the countryside to continue the fighting there? That was a standard thing the revolutionaries did. To be a true devotee of the cause, the city dwellers had to do their time in the countryside, living like primitives in the caves and jungle shelters as they fought the army and the increasingly hostile population.

When I think about Miguel, I hope he survived his immature naïveté. He was a kid who fell victim to the siren song of a terrorist group's efforts against a corrupt and failing government. He was a young fool caught up in the emotion, romance, and excitement the revolution supposedly offered. He was not unlike a young Ric Prado, mesmerized by the attraction of rebellious bad boys from the streets of Miami . . . and the girls who loved them.

Those are the worst days to come home. An agent disappears. Somebody dies.

You return to your house emotionally spent, unable to share the details of what happened with those who love you most. The hardest part for me was finding a balance on what I could, or should, tell Carmen and what to compartmentalize for her sanity's sake.

First off, you cannot share operational details of who you met where, or for what.

That mandatory secrecy can cause friction and doubts. If you share too much of your "adventures," you risk making your family members paranoid and apprehensive. After all, it is not their world. If you keep them completely in the dark, then there is little sympathy or understanding for the stresses you cope with on a daily basis. When "Johnny's" dad has a bad day, it is because a business opportunity fell through or the stock market took a dip. When a CIA officer has a bad day, an operation was compromised, or people got killed.

Every CIA family had to find the balance that worked for them. For us, balance sometimes included using Carmen operationally. Carmen had been a translator for us in Central America and had done other things for our station as well. While she was compartmentalized from the daily bruising work we did in the street, she had her own security clearance and was always part of the team. But in this tour, Carmen rose to the occasion and smacked one out of the park for our team. I'd never been prouder of her.

When I had first arrived in country, I'd found a beautiful house to rent that belonged to a prominent doctor. It was absolutely palatial, with an enormous office for me and plenty of room for Carmen and the kids. It was U-shaped, built around a beautiful patio that could be accessed through many sliding doors.

Given that security was always a concern, the house's twelve-foot-high concrete walls that defined its perimeter fit the bill for what we needed. It was an incredible place, one that we'd have never been able to afford anywhere else. But in this desperate, impoverished nation, the rent was well within the housing allowance. The constant violence, the bombings, and the military's crackdowns created so much instability that everything remained cheap—especially the value of human life. And we paid our rent in U.S. dollars!

The situation was so tenuous that we were under what was called a "fifteen-minute burn notice." After the Iranian embassy was overrun, stations and bases in hot spots overseas had to be able to burn all their paperwork in fifteen minutes or less, just in case the situation quickly went to hell.

The international community in the capital city existed in sort of an isolated world of its own, complete with its own rules. The Soviet and Chinese diplomats rarely crossed paths with Americans or other Westerners. Same with the Warsaw Pact types from Bulgaria or Hungary. They'd have their own diplomatic events, we'd have ours. The overlap was few and far between. Even then, the overlap usually occurred at sterile events hosted by the local government.

Diplomatic functions make for great places to identify and develop contacts.

Those parties are important for intelligence agencies, so restricting access to them was equally important. In this country especially, we rarely saw our adversaries as a result.

That changed, thanks to Carmen and our house. After we first arrived, I asked Carmen to join the Women's Diplomatic Association. With her native Spanish and background in bookkeeping, the group quickly made her its treasurer. Every other year, the association hosted a massive party for all the diplomatic missions in country. It was the social event of the season, and everyone was invited.

In 1989, I asked Carmen to offer hosting the party at our house. It was perfect for a large social gathering, and the association quickly agreed. I went to the Chief of Station, explained the coup, and asked for the Agency to help sponsor the party beyond what the Dip Association could normally afford. Here was our clandestine angle: Carmen, being a native Spanish speaker, was never associated with the U.S. mission in country. Our place was owned by a local doctor. There was no obvious connection to the United States, much less to the Agency. Because of that, I hoped we'd get a chance to mingle with our Cold War adversaries and hopefully make some unique contacts.

Our COS agreed. He secured funds for plenty of alcohol and great food. Carmen was put in charge of making the entire thing happen. She did an amazing job, setting up a dinner party and reception for over 150 people. And no one had any clue this was an all-American operation.

The night of the party, the crowd began to show up, dressed in their Sunday best. It was a dapper, semiformal affair with all the protocol associated with such events. As the night wore on, the music, the great food, and the flowing alcohol took effect, and so everyone relaxed and became far more informal. Laughter echoed through the patio, and men who'd never met before held drinks and swapped stories in every language imaginable.

The Hungarians were there. So were the Chinese and Soviets. All our rivals and adversaries packed into my patio, drinking American-funded booze. I couldn't help but smile with pride at Carmen for pulling this off.

And believe me, our handpicked officers were like sharks that night, swimming through the small talk, making contacts, trying to learn who was who in the missions where we never had the chance to meet. Carmen was a rock star, the perfect hostess as she circulated through the crowd, charming the socks off everyone. One of the most important parts of tradecraft that often goes overlooked by Hollywood is rapport.

Usually, to develop an asset, you've got to be patient, have charisma, and build a connection. It takes time—sometimes it takes years. But those moments at social gatherings like that one sometimes pay off.

Everyone changes stations and assignments as they progress through their careers. A contact made in South America may end up in a significant post somewhere else in the world and may subsequently be willing to share information with us. That was the beauty of Carmen's night, and I loved how we made a great team.

There were other husband-and-wife teams in our office that year as well. "Mary Beth" was a first-tour case officer. A beautiful young brunette with a razor-sharp intellect who proved utterly fearless in the field, she'd met her husband at the farm. "Bob" and Mary Beth were frequent guests at our house and were beloved by our sons. Bob taught our oldest boy to wiggle his ears, a trick he can do to this day.

One day in early 1990, Mary Beth came to me with an issue. She had been running one of our base's most productive agents for months. His intel was absolute gold, material we could never get from any other source. Yet a policy change in Washington caused havoc in our corner of the world. Word came down from Langley that we had to cut ties with this asset. It was a ludicrous order, and our COS protested it. The response was firm and nonnegotiable: do it.

The reason? In the year after Iran-Contra, the legal cases and investigations revealed the Agency ran agents with sketchy moral backgrounds.

Congress wanted that cleaned up. No more morally questionable foreign agents on the payroll.

This looks great on paper. The good guys making sure they only work with good guys overseas, right? Well, take a look around your town. If you want to identify and bring down a local drug ring, do you think the well-behaved Boy Scouts in your area will be able to help? Of course not. Genuinely good people rarely know who the local criminals are. The dark world is a seedy place, the human underbelly. To find out who is trying to do what to our fellow Americans and allies, we are at our most successful when we realize that reality and exploit the contacts we can make within the shadow world.

The change in policy hamstrung us and forced us to give up one of our most productive agents. Since Mary Beth was his case officer, she had to break the news that the Agency was cutting him loose. He'd be losing a significant chunk of his income, so this was news that would not go over well.

Granted, the agent worked for a pretty rough organization. He had a violent past, but in countries like this one where terrorist violence was rampant, George Orwell's quote comes to mind: "We sleep safely in our beds, because rough men stand ready in the night to visit violence on those who would do us harm." So for those effete bureaucrats demanding we fight a ruthless enemy while abiding by Queensberry rules, this priceless asset was a natural to cut from the Agency payroll. Yet for those of us on the ground, all we could think of was the loss of the information he provided. He gave us insight that nobody else could deliver.

When the COS told Mary Beth to fire the agent, they discussed the dangers that might arise. His violent past made this a legitimate concern. He was powerfully built and muscular. Should he lose his temper, Mary Beth could face real danger. The COS told her to come talk to me and work out a plan to deal with this termination.

Mary Beth and her husband were, and to this day are, personal friends of mine.

There was no way anything was going to happen to her on my watch. I told her I'd be her backup. We worked through the details. She set the meeting up.

On the appointed day, Mary Beth began her SDR. I was waiting in a second car at a predesignated point. After she made the rendezvous and picked up her agent, she drove past me. I slipped behind her and followed a few cars back. She pulled over a few minutes later and parked on a street we'd agreed on. I parked behind them, a car length away and at a forty-five-degree angle to the asset's rear.

If the agent looked to get violent and Mary Beth feared for her life, she would signal me by stepping on and holding the brake pedal. The brake lights would be my cue to intervene, even if it meant putting a bullet in the back of the guy's head. I sat behind the driver's seat, watching them talk, my M1911 Colt in easy reach in my cross-draw holster. "Whatever you do, don't accidentally tap the brakes. And wear your disguise glasses so you don't get any blood or brain matter in your eyes," I told her in our final briefing, only half in jest.

That last suggestion didn't even faze Mary Beth. She nodded, then selected a set of fake prescription glasses. I was in complete awe of my young colleague; she had more cojones than most men who brag at being mucho macho.

The asset was no fool. He glanced over one shoulder and saw me. I deliberately did not make eye contact. That would have been too obvious. Instead, I looked away, staring off at the street scene around us.

Of course, he didn't buy it, and that was the point. Every few minutes, he'd look back and check me out. I'd play dumb. But we both knew why I was there.

Mary Beth went through her speech, telling the agent that due to budget cuts, we had to break contact for a while. We were hoping that in a year or so, things would improve so we could bring him back on the payroll. She gave him a nice "termination bonus," but for now, the Agency had to let him go.

Nobody takes getting fired easily. When the CIA does it with a foreign agent, we are very careful not to burn our bridges; even more so in cases like this one where this asset had always kept his end of the bargain. You never know when things might be different down the road and that agent might be of use again. In this case, it would have taken a policy change from Washington, but those happened all the time anyway. Even if they are never brought back on the payroll, we made a point of making every split amicable. Nobody wanted pissed-off former agents with axes to grind against us running around doing damage. That served no purpose.

So Mary Beth's speech was as gentle and hopeful as the situation allowed. The agent took it surprisingly well. When she finished, and they said goodbye to each other, the agent glanced back at me, then smiled at her. "By the way," he said, "please tell your pit bull back there everything is okay."

How many short, slender, beautiful brunettes do you know who are willing to get into a car with a man so notorious for his violent streak that it alarmed official Washington? How many would be willing to sit in that car alone with that person and fire him? Mary Beth had only been in country for a few months, yet she had a veteran case officer's courage.

When I look back at my career, working with people like Mary Beth was the best part of it. Nowhere else outside of the Agency could I have had such a privilege.

███████████

There were times, of course, that I had to cut somebody loose, too. During the final stages of my time in country, I had a particularly rough one that turned into the exception that proved the rule.

We had professional colleagues from another U.S. government agency who'd been running an agent of theirs for almost five years. He'd been giving them exceptional intelligence in their realm of responsibility. "Pedro" had been their golden rock star, but that eventually changed, and he stopped delivering on his usual topics. Instead, he started giving them details about the professor's organization and their imminent plans to attack our U.S. ambassador. They passed the information along to the embassy's regional security officer (RSO), who immediately started a massive security personnel buildup. At our ambassador's request, I was brought into the case because of my now-proven expertise in the local CT account.

Remember, like most hard-target intelligence work, the counterterrorism game is one of gathering tiny, disconnected pieces of information. The professor's organization was well insulated and highly compartmentalized. Each link in the chain knew only what they needed to know to carry out their role. Unless you turned a senior leader, you were never going to get the full picture, just a keyhole glance from here or there that makes no sense until you match it up with other sources via different methods.

Pedro painted the biggest intelligence picture and the deepest knowledge of anyone inside the professor's organization. He was a gold mine again, and as our colleagues laid out the details, I was at once surprised and suspicious. To me, this seemed too good to be true, yet the guy was a battle-tested confidential informant whose intelligence reporting had produced dozens of operational successes for many years.

Additionally, he reported just enough credible nuggets of CT information that jibed with what we already knew that we could not dismiss him offhand, especially with the ambo's life as target.

In consultation with the COS, the ambassador tasked me with personally meeting the CI and doing a sniff test.

Rapport and building a personal connection are everything in this aspect of the intelligence world. We talked over how best to do this. We settled on me playing the role of a higher-up from Washington who had come into the country to meet our rock star informant personally.

My colleague "Vince" set up a meeting. I rode in the back seat of the car, strategically behind the driver and the front passenger seat, dressed in a suit and tie, shades over my eyes. The asset climbed into the car, and Vince made introductions.

I started out by thanking him for all the great threat information he'd been providing and told him I had flown down to personally thank him for his efforts.

He was smiling and very happy to know we were happy.

Elicitation and rapport building go hand in hand, so while complimenting him on his spectacular new access, I asked him to review the information he'd already provided. Having read all of his previous reporting, I would be looking for discrepancies in the regurgitation of his "facts." Additionally, the best interrogation question is the one you already know the answer to! I had a few of those on tap as well.

I asked him, "So please tell me about these guys you have managed to get so close to. Who are they? What are their plans? In your expert opinion, how disciplined and determined are they?"

He started talking. The cell he was working with had begun planning an attack on the U.S. embassy. He gave us names, weapons they possessed, and details of the plot they were working up. He told us about meetings they'd already had and what happened at them.

"This is great stuff, and we appreciate it a lot. But we need you to let us know when they are planning to meet next. That way we can wrap them up." I also added that if we could disrupt this terrorist cell, his payoff would ensure he could retire and be set for life.

"I understand," the informant said.

A few weeks went by before Vince called to tell me that Pedro wanted to meet again. We set it up, and the guy told us about another meeting that had just taken place.

"They showed up so fast, I had no time to call you," he explained.

This time, I was not shoveling praise on him. I was polite, but clearly disappointed. I leaned on him. "We need you to give us something we can exploit. Not just things that have already happened." I also explained that if we could not get to the bottom of this soon, we would have to pull the ambassador out of the country. Unstated, but surely obvious to him, this also meant that the cell would grow suspicious of a leak and they would dissolve and disappear. Either way, this would be the end of his lucrative meal ticket.

A few days later, Pedro called Vince right at five o'clock and tipped him off to a meeting. It would start in an hour. He gave the address. Vince hung up and immediately called me. What no one but the ambo and COS knew was that through their local contacts, we had arranged to have a unit on standby for just this event. I made a call, and a special squad raided the target house.

After breaking through the door, they found an elderly couple inside. The woman was knitting. The old man had no clue what was going on. There was no meeting, and they certainly were not running a safe house for the professor's minions.

Vince's agent had fed us bad intel. Why?

To find out, I suggested an easy trap. Nothing apparently would change—at least at first for Pedro. I was again dressed as a headquarters executive when I got into the back of Vince's car. Vince drove the predesigned SDR, then met up with his CI for a rolling-car meeting. Pedro slipped into the passenger seat in front of me. I did all the talking. "We appreciated the call. But it was too late to set up a raid, so we missed them. So please tell us what happened."

The CI began to talk. The meeting went well, he said, and laid out once again in great detail who said what and how things unfolded.

As we already knew, this was all bullshit. Vince grew furious as we listened to this made-up tale, but as a true professional, he kept cool and never tipped his hand.

Stealthily, I reached between the seats and popped Pedro's seat belt. Right then, Vince hit the brakes and sent him flying into the dashboard. Stunned, he had no time to react as Vince reached over and grabbed him.

"You lyin' motherfucker!" he screamed at his asset. "We hit the house, and nobody was there!"

Terrified, Pedro broke down in tears. He began wailing, swearing he was sorry.

Gradually, the entire story came out.

The intel he'd been providing for five years came from connections that, for whatever reason, were severed a few months before. The end of those relationships dried up his useful information. His paycheck from Vince was on the line, and he had no other source of income.

Out of desperation, he'd conceived the plan to give Vince intel on the professor's terror group. Of course, the RSO's piqued interest further fueled Pedro's confidence and made it impossible for the whole embassy, including Vince, to ignore. The trust so carefully cultivated through those five years was shattered in an instant.

Now, Vince was not CIA, yet parting ways with an agent/informant was usually done with the same sort of care Mary Beth displayed in her pink-slip moment. This guy was the exception. Vince bounced him out of the car with a stern "Don't ever call us again!"

The guy had wasted a great deal of our time and limited resources, as there was genuine concern the embassy would be attacked. Then there was the elderly couple whose door had been kicked in. They'd been terrified by the arrival of our friends in the security forces. We compensated them for the damage, but we were not in the business of traumatizing the elderly. All of this pissed us off and ensured this particular agent would not get a gentle send-off.

As disappointing as it was, the incident taught me a couple of valuable lessons. First, it confirmed that trusting my instincts would usually be the right way to go. The intel smelled too good from the outset. That was the key. When somebody comes to us with a bucketload of information and no way to verify it, chances are it is bogus. From that point on, if a source gave us too much, my BS meter would go off. Intelligence is a game of scraps and pieces. A bit here, a bit there. Somebody comes in with a whole puzzle put together and delivered in a nice, tidy package is going to be full of crap.

I got a lot of mileage out of that lesson in the years ahead.

We did our best to assist our allies in this dark and terrible time. The country continued to writhe in the agonies of civil war. Such wars are always the most merciless. Brother against brother, neighbor against neighbor. Passions run hot, and fury-filled atrocities mark the passage of the fighting. Bombs destroyed buses, trains, and neighborhoods. The army's counterterrorism commandos descended on mountain villages whose people had been traumatized into supporting the revolutionaries.

As the war reached its bloody climax, the professor and the senior revolutionary commanders, including his wife, lived a life of luxury unbeknownst to all but a few close confidants. He was always a middle-class man with a taste for the good life. Living in caves was not for him. Instead of fighting in the countryside along with the rank and file, he cowered in mansions rented for him by engineers, doctors, and other academics who supported his cause. The homeowners had no idea their properties harbored one of the worst mass murderers in modern South American history. If ever there was a Marxist revolutionary who proved George Orwell's point in *Animal Farm,* it was the professor.

*And the pigs had become men.*

After Miguel's disappearance, we stepped up our efforts. Getting an asset inside the revolutionary cells proved an exceptionally difficult challenge, and foibles like drug use that could be leveraged into a recruitment proved few and far between. Nevertheless, our work with the local security teams on the network we'd uncovered helped take down some significant support personnel whose role in the city simply could not be replaced. Subsequent efforts ultimately did penetrate the professor's organization again, this time at a higher level. We made a big impact, as did my handpicked replacement, Bob. A first-tour officer, Bob showed the grit and groin to handle these kinds of assets. When I rotated home in 1990 in preparation for a fourth high-threat tour, this time in the Philippines, Bob worked with singular devotion to expand that penetration. He succeeded brilliantly, and those efforts materially aided in ending the civil war.

Ultimately, one of the professor's safe houses, an apartment above a ballet studio, was discovered and staked out by government forces. He was wrapped up in a raid a short time later, a frail, aging man devoted to a cause that had long since proven totally bankrupt. By the time he was captured in late 1992 and subsequently imprisoned in a cell on a remote island, the Chinese had gone full capitalist, the Soviet Union had collapsed, and the adherents of Marx had spent a century murdering millions in the failed pursuit of their workers' utopia.

The professor, like the ideology he embodied, was swept off the world stage at last. His revolution collapsed in most areas and barely survived in some inconsequential and distant strongholds, and the country spent the next three decades trying to heal the wounds the civil war he started had inflicted on the population he so ardently claimed to represent.

# 17

## THE SPARROWS

*Philippines*
*1992*

Victor Corpus graduated from the Philippine Military Academy in 1967 and was commissioned a second lieutenant in the army. He was young, idealistic, a devoted patriot. In three years of service, the corruption of the Ferdinand Marcos regime left him morally repelled. The rot was so bad it extended through the ranks of the army. In 1970, he was assigned to the Philippine Military Academy as an instructor.

He grew disillusioned. Convinced he could not effect change from within, he emptied the armory at the academy and drove off into the Luzon countryside, where he joined the Marxist revolutionary New People's Army (NPA). The weapons and ammunition were sorely needed for a guerrilla force founded only a few years earlier with sixty firearms—all of which the Philippine Army quickly captured.

Maoist in orientation, the NPA sought to bring down Marcos with a three-phased revolution centered around armed conflict in the countryside. The first phase was a defensive one, where the NPA would keep the regime off balance with lightning-quick attacks in rural areas throughout the archipelago. Phase two envisioned a strategic stalemate where

Marcos's power would slowly erode as the NPA's attacks grew more punishing and powerful. Phase three would see the NPA launch massive conventional offensives into the cities, where they would wrest control of the country and set up a dictatorship of the proletariat.

Ferdinand Marcos used the NPA's threat of a communist takeover as leverage to remain in power and shake down the United States for more aid money. The truth was, the NPA was a tiny force in those days, unable to do much real damage. Yet after its operatives threw grenades onto the stage of a political rally in 1971, killing or wounding a number of key liberal opposition figures to the Marcos regime, the blowback that followed helped spur the NPA's growth.

Marcos declared martial law. He suspended the writ of habeas corpus and used the crisis to remain in power despite the Philippine constitution's two-term limit for its presidents.

What followed became the longest-running Marxist guerrilla war in history.

Victor Corpus rose to power within the NPA, earning a seat on the Communist Party of the Philippines' Central Committee. Yet in the field, he witnessed corruption and brutality that equaled or exceeded what prompted him to desert from the Marcos regime. He concluded that they were two sides of a corrupt, evil coin. In 1976, he recognized casting his lot with the Marxists had been a terrible mistake. He surrendered to the Marcos regime, where he and his wife were thrown in prison.

They languished there for the next eleven years as the NPA's strength steadily grew. From the insignificant force founded in 1969, by the mid-'80s, the NPA counted almost thirty thousand fighters in its ranks. They carried out bombings in the cities as well as assassinations and raids on outposts, and they blackmailed corporations through protection rackets to raise funds.

In 1986, the Yellow Revolution swept Marcos from power. Cory Aquino replaced him and was determined to rebuild a democracy in the Philippines. She pardoned and released thousands of political prisoners, including the NPA's founder, Jose Maria Sison, who went into exile in the Netherlands. Victor Corpus and his wife were also released.

For a short time, it looked like Aquino might secure peace in the archipelago. A cease-fire took effect between the NPA and the army. But it only lasted a year. Political instability—army officers attempted multiple coups from 1987 to 1989—led the NPA to believe they could return to the fight and destroy the nascent democracy.

Open warfare broke out again. Aquino turned to Victor Corpus for help. He was reinstated in the army with the rank of lieutenant colonel. By this point, he was a national figure, a man whose principals and moral compass were so widely admired that a movie was made on his life. *Operation: Get Victor Corpus* opened throughout the Philippines in 1987. In it, he accused the NPA of orchestrating the 1971 bombing and also fingered key members of the military for plotting against Cory Aquino.

When I arrived in Manila after my South American tour in the summer of 1990, I worked under a legendary officer named "Dave," who became a lifelong friend. Dave was my kind of guy, rugged and capable, loyal, fearless in the moment. He was whip-smart, a man at ease on a Harley as much as in a senior planning meeting with generals and diplomats. He played hard, worked harder, and always took the toughest assignments. From the first day in Manila, I loved working with him.

We worked closely with Lieutenant Colonel Victor Corpus. He was the assistant GZ (intelligence officer) for the Philippine Army at the time and was tasked with hunting the NPA down. His knowledge of its organization, leaders, and tactics may have dated back more than a decade but remained relevant in a land writhing in near-perpetual conflict.

He was a man of principle, a person I would later call a "warrior of the light." He despised corruption and sought to bring peace to the Philippines with his loyalty to Cory Aquino. He played an important role in helping the army track down and destroy the company-size NPA cells raiding through the countryside.

Yet the NPA's strength and capabilities continued to grow. By the late '80s, they had their own wing of the NPA that operated in urban areas. Later on, it broke off from the NPA and became its own Marxist organization called the Alex Boncayao Brigade.

This urban guerrilla force quickly flexed its capabilities. The year before I arrived, a hit squad ambushed and killed legendary Green Beret Nick Rowe. He was one of only a handful of Americans to escape from a North Vietnam prison during the war, after which, he set up the army's Survival, Evasion, Resistance and Escape school in 1981.

Nick had come to the archipelago as part of the Philippine's Joint U.S. Military Assistance Group (JUSMAG) to assist in the effort against the NPA. The Marxists detected his presence, surveilled him, then executed an ambush that killed him with a lucky shot as he drove in an armored limousine through Quezon City. He'd reported only a few days before that the NPA was about to execute a major attack and that his name had been found on a hit list.

Though the intelligence war Vic and his comrades waged against the NPA was paying dividends—the army was really taking it to the cells in the countryside when I arrived—the urban cells and assassination teams were still capable and extremely dangerous.

A few weeks before I arrived in Manila, NPA hit teams murdered three American servicemen in hopes of derailing the negotiations between the U.S. and Aquino's government on extending American base leases in the Philippines. Those dramatic attacks made international headlines.

███████████████████████████████████████████

███████████████████

Dave and I developed a thorough understanding of the threat facing both the government and Americans in the islands. They were the most dangerous insurgency I'd seen yet.

We provided the Philippine Army with electronic SIGINT (signal intelligence) systems that could listen in on NPA radio chatter. This always proved useful, and the systems picked up great nuggets of information. The trick was these electronic devices had to be deployed all over the country, usually in hostile NPA territory. Working with the good guys required helicoptering out to these remote posts, usually on some forsaken mountaintop with a tiny landing zone. The SIGINT gear would be protected ██████████████ with razor wire, sandbags, and trenches.

During the week, Dave handled most of the local meetings and oversaw the logistical coordination from Manila, while I flew around to the SIGINT sites helping to coordinate delivery of equipment and making sure everything functioned well. I'd come home for a few days to be with the family in Manila, then back in the field by Monday morning.

Threats were plentiful out in the field in those days. The rural NPA companies routinely launched attacks on these remote outposts, and not a few were overrun. The cities saw their share of NPA operations, too, conducted by the ABB wing. They would carry out bombings or surprise attacks on governmental targets. Flying around the ██████████ ████████████████████████████████████ required exceptional discipline and situational awareness. Hell, if an unbeatable badass like Nick Rowe could be killed, we were all mortals.

Then there were the communist hit squads, known as the Sparrows. They added a different dimension to the carnage, one that was intensely personal and exceptionally effective.

Sparrow Teams usually consisted of three men who carried out lightning-quick assassinations inside major cities. In Davao, on the southern island of Mindanao, the Sparrows honed their skills by assassinating police as they walked their beats. One man would pull the trigger, the others would grab the cop's weapon and ammunition, then vanish into the city. Very few got caught.

Legend had it, the ABB used three men for a special reason. The assassin would be given one bullet to carry out his mission. If he failed, the other two would kill the assassin. It was a very Marxist way of ensuring complete obedience and dedication to the mission.

To maximize surprise, the Sparrows developed a quick-draw method second to none in the world. They wore loose sweatpants and T-shirts to conceal a 1911 Colt .45 in their crotches. With one hand in their pockets, the other hitched at their waists, they looked benign to most observers. But a quick push upward from the pocket hand sent the pistol right into the assassin's gun hand ready and waiting at his waist. The move was so fast, they could draw and shoot in a third of a second.

The ABB kept a tight control on the Sparrow Teams, developing target lists based on their own intelligence network. If they suspected an NPA member of being a double agent and supplying information to the Philippine Army, the ABB would target them.

They would carry out preoperational surveillance, get to know the targets' routines, then send the Sparrows in to take care of business. Check out their legendary move in this YouTube clip: https://www .youtube.com/watch?v=cPMEVzv0AO4

Their success paid dividends all over the Philippines. By the late 1980s in Davao and Cebu City, cops often refused to walk the streets. Nobody wanted to encounter these stone-cold killers.

As these teams and others operated around us, we continued our mission to develop SIGINT on their activities. Dave usually remained chained to a desk in Manila while I went into the field, but on one occasion, he came with me to Cebu Island in the Central Philippines to meet with a particularly aggressive and successful captain I'd come to respect a great deal.

The captain was a stud. He ran a tight ship, disciplined, capable, and very effective against the NPA. We spent the day in meetings with him and his subordinates, visiting sites and getting information on what they needed from us. At the end of the day, the captain invited us to go grab some drinks in Cebu City and then go to dinner. Dave, the captain, one of his lieutenants, two other tech guys—"Ernie" and "Bernie"—and I climbed into a pair of cars and headed into town.

At the bar, we drank beer and told stories, bonding with our allies. The drivers remained outside with the rigs. When we finished a final round, we settled up and left to go find a dinner spot.

Our Filipino friends Ernie and Bernie exited first. They hit the street shoulder to shoulder, chatting happily. Dave went next, lagging a bit from the main group. I was slightly behind Dave and to his left, last to leave. As I went through the door, I looked around quickly to get a handle on the situation in the street. Orange on the Cooper's Color scale was a way of life in the Philippines.

Immediately, I spotted three guys not far away, chatting with each other. The middle one saw us and locked on like a predator. The other two stopped talking. They glanced at each other, the middle one made a gesture, and they began walking three abreast, straight for Dave and me. The middle one had his hands in the classic Sparrow position. One in a pocket, shooting hand on his waistband ready to grip the pistol hidden in his crotch. The other two had hands in their left pockets.

Everything happened so fast after that. Adrenaline surged through my body. My heart rate spiked; I got tunnel vision. Dave was in front and just to the right of me, yet I lost sight of him. All I could see were the three men coming at us.

Instinctively, I went from Orange to Red. Under my tan vest, I kept a holstered, chrome M1911 Colt .45 Officer's model. I grabbed it and pulled it clear.

They kept coming. Eyes boring into ours.

I pointed the .45 at the middle one and dropped the safety with what sounded to me as an ominous *click*.

*You quick on the draw, pal? My Colt is already pointed at you. Checkmate.*

That got their attention. The chrome .45 looked menacing as

hell. They knew the jig was up. If they tried anything, I'd fire first before they'd even be able to get their weapons out. My expression said
just that.

They made no attempt to hide their intention. Their steely-eyed
predator look remained and they sneered as if to say, *Next time, Yan-
quis!*

They kept walking, seemingly without concern, but their eyes never
left ours even as they went by. I held my .45 on them until they vanished
down the street.

"Holy shit, did you see that?" Dave exclaimed.

I turned around to see him standing nearby, his own pistol out and
still trained down the street. I had such tunnel vision that I never even
saw him draw his weapon.

"Fuckin' A, I did," I said. "The question is, why didn't our other
guys?"

We both looked up the street. The rest of our group was several
feet ahead of us, totally unaware of what had just gone down. The Filipinos we couldn't do anything about, but our own guys were going to
get an earful about situational awareness.

Dave pulled out a cigarette and tried to light it. His hands were
shaking badly. He was a decorated Vietnam vet. Nothing usually fazed
him, and this was not fear; it was "the juice"—full adrenaline rush.

My hands were shaking, too. "Holy shit," I muttered.

We didn't even give thought to going after them. Any assassination
team would have established a perimeter. No telling who that might
have been. Had we given chase, we may have been ambushed ourselves.
I remembered the cop in South America who tried to stop the female
bomber after she had blown up the palace guard. Fixated on chasing
her, he never saw her backup and paid for that mistake with his life.
Surely those three would have had backup lurking nearby. Not worth
the risk.

We cleared the area fast. Later that night, we had a long, loud discussion with Ernie and Bernie for being in the White in the middle of a city well known for its NPA presence.

To this day, I am convinced that if Dave and I had not seen those guys and pulled our weapons first, both of us would have died. Lesson learned. There is no downtime in the field. There are no after-work hours where you can relax. You've got to be alert and aware of your surroundings at all times. It was our way of life in the clandestine world if you wanted to survive. I never forgot that lesson. Those who did rarely got a second chance.

It was heady stuff, tailor-made for types who loved to live on the edge and prove themselves day after day doing meaningful work to curb the violence. But even sometimes the best of us let our guards down. No human can be at Orange twenty-four hours a day, week after week. The assassins only have to be lucky once. Their targets have to be lucky every time. It was a game stacked against us, and the near misses drove that point home. To better prepare us, the Agency created a new three-week course called the CODA—Case Officer Operations in Dangerous Areas—which was designed to teach counterterror techniques for officers in foreign posts where insurgencies raged. It was a great class, filled with new techniques and countermoves against a variety of threat scenarios. Staying alive in Indian country was becoming more and more a science and less seat of the pants.

One day, after I'd returned to Manila from another inspection run to the countryside, Dave and I met with ████████████████, another important figure in the war against the NPA. As we were talking, I mentioned some of the tactics I'd learned while attending the CODA. ████████████ was very interested in it, especially since there had been many threats on his life over the years. "Ric, you gotta teach me some of this stuff."

We were always up for a range day, so Dave and I agreed to run through some of the things I'd learned. ████████████ said, "I'm going to bring my new Glock 18."

After the meeting, Dave looked at me and asked, "What's a Glock 18?"

"Hell if I know," I replied.

"Well, we have Glock 19s, so ours must be better," Dave said.

The Agency had just made the switch to Glock pistols. As we came to find out, there was a big difference between the 18 and 19.

The next day, ███████████████████ joined us on the range with his new Glock. I started teaching a short-range, quick-draw scenario based on a meeting that had gone badly.

Dave went first. Cigarette dangling from his mouth, he drew and fired at two point-blank targets with his pistol. He had good shot groupings, and he hit both targets with a few rounds.

Then ████████ turn came. He flipped a selector switch on his Glock 18.

"You understand what to do?" I asked him.

"Yeah," he said casually, "I think I got it."

The scenario began. ███████████████ drew his Glock, aimed, and fired in one fluid movement. A hail of bullets streamed out of the pistol's barrel, raking the first target. He switched to the second and laced it as well. When he was done, both target silhouettes had bullet holes from crotch to forehead.

Dave's cigarette fell out of his mouth. I gaped. We had no idea the Glock 18 could be fired fully automatic.

████████ turned around with a cat-ate-the-canary grin on his face.

He was our kind of guy.

It was good training for all of us, especially since the threats remained significant.

████████████████████████████████████

██████████████████

██████████████████████████████████████

██████████████

████████████████████████████████████████████

██████████████████████████

████████████████████████████████████████████

██████████████████████

That last Friday night before he was forced to abandon his house, Dave, Carmen, and I went over for a final dinner party. We gunned up for this affair. Beside the MP5K machine pistols we carried daily in the Philippines, each of us had our pistols, plus a backup. In my case, the holster on my ankle housed that Lady Smith five-shot revolver. That stainless revolver was a prized possession, call it what you may. Thanks to my good friend "Ed L.," I learned the utility of wheel guns.

We left the MP5s in our vehicle under the care of our designated bodyguard, Howie, a former professional football player and one of the most capable security operators in country. Upon entering ██████'s lovely home, we placed our primary pistols on a high shelf in the entryway to the house, away from the reach of the kids playing around the house. The dinner was a smash hit, even if an aura of sadness at its purpose hung over it. At the end of the evening, we retrieved our weapons and headed home.

The next day, ██████████ moved out of his house.

████████████████████████████████████████████

██████████████████████

Two days later:

"Where is he?

"Where is the target?"

The terrorists were watching the house.

██████████████ sent a team back to investigate. The property included a plaster-covered cinder-block wall about ten feet high. In the far back of his wooded lot, we found a four-foot hole carefully chipped out of the wall. Only the plaster on the inner side remained. The NPA hit squad had left that intact to arouse no suspicion. They were days, perhaps even hours away from launching an assault on ████████'s home.

Had it happened during the party, Carmen would have come under fire. The thought of that kept me up late for weeks after the discovery.

████'s house was well protected, but the assigned guards did not patrol outside the walls into the brush; otherwise, they would have detected this long before. The NPA assassins discovered this weakness and conceived a brilliant means to exploit it.

████████████ With the security team on-site, a surprise assault on a target like this would have probably taken a good-size force, perhaps a half dozen men. The house would have become a free-fire zone with women and children inside.

Including my wife. We'd gotten lucky. Again.

Not long after this, a father was kidnapped while dropping his kids off at the same school our boys attended. It was a reminder that in places like Manila, the whole family could be a target, not just me. There were moments in South America where I lost sleep worrying about an attack on Carmen and the boys by the professor's cultish adherents. There would be no mercy for them. In Manila, the same threat from the NPA and ABB existed, plus a new dimension. That dad who was kidnapped in front of the international school was snatched by a criminal syndicate, seeking only to leverage his life for a payout. The ransom was paid. He survived. The political kidnappings the ABB carried out never ended well. They routinely killed whomever they snatched.

As we worked to manage and minimize the dangers we faced as a family in Manila, a totally new threat of unimaginable power emerged that took everyone by complete surprise: Mother Nature.

# 18

## THE AFTERNOON OF DARKNESS

*Manila*
*Saturday Night, June 15, 1991*
Weekends at our home in Manila combined much-needed family time with a chance for Carmen and me to socialize with friends and neighbors. During the week, I'd be wearing field gear, jumping in and out of helicopters with Bernie and Ernie to get SIGINT gear where it was most needed. On the weekends, the fatigues and combat boots went in the closet, traded for a pair of khaki pants and a sports shirt. These were the best moments, coming back from all the chaos in the countryside to find a little oasis of peace and family in our little neighborhood of expats and diplomats. Playing with my boys or heading out for a nice evening with Carmen on my arm—this was the way I unwound and found a little balance to the pressure of always being "switched on Orange."

By the late spring, we were getting ready to head back to the United States. After four straight overseas tours in exceptionally dangerous places, I think we were all ready for a break. A short one, for me, as without the good fight to be fought, I knew myself well enough to know I would get restless.

The good fight was being won at last here in the Philippines. The pressure the Philippine Army put on the NPA was growing daily. Raids were taking down entire cells.

Leaders were defecting the ranks and trying to set up their own rival movements. The ABB even split off to become their own urban Marxist insurgency. The ranks—once almost thirty thousand strong— dwindled as the less committed walked away from the revolution. Throughout the world, Marxism had collapsed. The ideology seemed morally and practically bankrupt to an increasing number of its former devotees.

The Philippine Army was finally winning. We'd be leaving the country on a high note. Even better, our country made the long trek back from its post-Vietnam weakness to a place of strength and success once again. The Gulf War ended in a hundred hours in February, our Cold War adversaries were throwing in the towel, and it appeared the world stood poised on the brink of a new era where the threat of nuclear war no longer lingered over our heads.

It was a heady time for sure.

So on one of our last weekends in Manila, Carmen and I headed out to celebrate and enjoy life a little. Along with some other friends, we hit a party in our neighborhood that went late into the night. At the end of it, Carmen and I said our goodbyes, then started walking to our car.

The whole neighborhood lay under a dusting of grayish powder. The cars, parked only a few hours before, were covered with the stuff. I watched as a friend walked over to a car to write "Wash Me" on the trunk with one finger.

Doing so permanently etched the words into the paint.

Unsure but unconcerned about what was going on, we walked the few blocks home within our gated neighborhood. Shortly after we arrived back at the house, our embassy radio net started crackling with a mandatory radio check. Then came the formal announcement: a volcano was erupting north of Manila. Clark Air Base lay less than nine miles from it. Our largest naval base in Southeast Asia, Subic Bay, had been deluged with ash and debris. Clark Air Base had been evacuated. The last people there were just pulling out.

This started back in April when 4,800-foot Mount Pinatubo began venting steam. Until then, the heavily eroded, jungle-covered mountain peak in the Zambales Mountains was not even recognized as a volcano. Several thousand Aeta indigenous people lived on its slopes, and when it began to vent steam, they reported the phenomenon to a Catholic nun, who passed the information along to some governmental officials. A joint American-Filipino team of geologists went and investigated Mount Pinatubo and discovered evidence of a massive eruption some five hundred years before. Deeply concerned, they emplaced sensors around the volcano and set up shop in a building at Clark Air Base to keep watch over this restless giant.

Earthquakes followed through April and May, and the geologists grew alarmed. They gained the ear of the base commander and warned him that a major eruption was probably imminent. The air force stood by and made plans to evacuate the base should it become necessary.

On Monday, June 10, the volcano blew clouds of ash into the air. Magma boiled to the surface. The writing was on the wall: Clark Air Base needed to be evacuated. At 0500, the call went out to get nearly fifteen thousand people—servicemen and -women, their dependents, civilian employees, and so on—out of harm's way. Long columns of vehicles slowly moved south for Subic Bay while every flyable aircraft took off and redeployed to bases outside the volcano's reach.

Two days later, the volcano erupted with inconceivable power and ferocity. In a matter of seconds, millions of tons of ash boiled skyward, creating a mushroom cloud twelve miles high. Clark had been abandoned just in time. The ash swirled into the atmosphere, dusting most of Luzon through the rest of the week.

On Saturday, June 15, Typhoon Yunya made landfall on Luzon's east coast and swept across the island with winds peaking at 120 miles an hour. The heavy downpours triggered flash floods, drowning families as rivers suddenly jumped their banks and swept buildings away. Some 320 people died.

At the same time, Mount Pinatubo exploded with the force of two hundred atomic bombs, proving the eruption on June 12 was just a preshow. The main event blasted volcanic ash and pumice twenty-four miles into the atmosphere. The mushroom cloud created in seconds looked positively apocalyptic.

It continued to erupt throughout the day—six times, in fact. As more ash and ejecta were flung skyward, the eye of Typhoon Yunya passed right by the volcano. The swirling winds flung the ash even farther into the atmosphere, spinning it in all directions. Clouds of ash were blown clear into the Indian Ocean, where unsuspecting airliners flew into them, choking their engines. At least sixteen jetliners suffered a total of $100 million in damage from those unexpected encounters thousands of miles from Luzon. The ash cloud ultimately circled the globe several times, creating a barrier in the atmosphere that not only damaged the earth's ozone layer but cooled global temperatures by more than a degree for three years.

Simultaneously, the rain soaked the ash still blowing out of the volcano, creating balls of pumice-ash-mud that plunged down on Luzon for miles in every direction. As the storm raged, the wet ash acted almost like wet falling concrete, crushing rooftops and buildings and destroying vehicles. Later estimates concluded that a cubic foot of this stuff weighed thirty-six pounds. In some places, it accumulated so quickly on rooftops that the people below had no chance to get out when their structure collapsed under the sudden weight.

The rain poured down in biblical torrents, creating titanic walls of volcanic mud known as *lahars*. Sliding down Pinatubo and other peaks at over forty miles an hour, some of these lahars were at least six hundred feet high. They mowed down anything in their path, filling entire river valleys while killing hundreds of villagers. The lahars acted almost like chain saws, slicing through bridges and buildings, tearing apart anything made by man. When the rains ended, the lahars hardened, just like concrete, burying entire stretches of fertile farmland for decades to come.

All the while, earthquake swarms by the thousands rocked Luzon, causing even more damage and misery.

Dave and I counted many friends among the SEAL team stationed at Subic. We made some phone calls over to the base to see what the situation was over there. Our friends reported a sky darkened by ash, widespread destruction, and few supplies on hand. They had no power, no access to cash, and no place functioning where they could cash a check. To compound things, the typhoon slammed into Subic with incredible force.

Things were getting desperate for them.

A few days went by with no relief. Our best friend, "Master Chief Bailey," called me that morning and said, "Hey, man, we're really screwed here. We still have no electricity, every business is closed or destroyed. Half the base is evacuated. We're almost out of groceries."

"Okay, we'll take care of it," I told him.

We put $500 in cash into envelopes for each of the guys, then went around to all the bars and restaurants in Manila that the SEALs liked to frequent, asking for donations. The Filipinos jumped at the chance to help. They gave us cases of beer, canned food, Cokes, and contributed more cash, meat, and other supplies. By the time we were done, both trucks were piled with stuff. We convinced two young policemen to ride shotgun to ensure their safety. We got them on their way to Subic by the end of the afternoon.

At the same time, we received disturbing news that widespread looting had broken out in the towns around Clark Air Base. We used Clark to store our gear. We could not let that fall into the hands of a desperate mob. Sooner or later, it would be sold to the NPA.

I volunteered to take a crew to recover the gear. We used armored vehicles with diplomatic plates, which we kitted up with weapons, ammo, and fuel. With Ernie and one other Agency officer, we again joined forces with a unit friendly to us (I'd been made an honorary member).

We used armored vehicles with ████████████████████████
with weapons, ammo, and fuel. With Ernie and one other Agency officer, we set off for Clark.

We drove into a monochromatic, apocalyptic landscape of gray
ash. It covered everything, including the palm trees, which were bent
and squashed under the weight of the stuff. Bandits raided the remaining roads, robbing those just trying to escape. Entire villages had been
scraped away by tsunamis of volcanic mud. The roads were torn up,
and we had to divert around destroyed bridges. We found one that
looked like it had been perfectly cut by a gigantic pair of scissors. A
chunk remained on our bank, entirely intact. On the opposite bank, we
could see another chunk, equally unharmed. It was bizarre.

The Philippines is a verdant, colorful country. Outside of the cities,
the jungles are emerald green, the farmers' fields striped and lush. The
eruption smothered all those colors with layers of grim, gray ash several
feet deep in places.

We used to drive to Clark a couple of times a month to shop at the
USAF Base Exchange (BX). Carmen and I had become very familiar
with the route up. Now, I couldn't recognize anything. This was an
alien place, filled with ruined, abandoned towns, flattened jungle, destroyed vehicles—all coated by that sickly gray "cement."

We drove through this hellscape for hours until we finally reached
Clark Air Base. As we entered the post through the base housing area,
we peered through our dirty windshield at a community totally destroyed by looting. Every single house had been stripped down to the
studs. Window frames had been pulled out. Drywall yanked out.

Refrigerators dragged off, furniture gone, plywood torn out and
hauled away. In places, the houses were little more than skeletons—a
few support beams, a wall or two, and part of the roof. We stopped to
investigate and discovered that even the copper wiring had been ripped
out and taken.

We passed hangars squashed by piles of ash. They looked like giant Coke cans smashed by Thor's boot. A few aircraft that could not

be moved remained. One DC-10 transport jet had been tipped off its nosewheel onto its tail by the accumulation of ash on its horizontal stabilizers. A couple of Vietnam-era F-4 Phantom fighters stood derelict beside an equally ancient F-105 Thunderchief attack bomber. They were sheathed in volcanic mud and ash.

This was a scene straight out of an end-of-the-world Hollywood epic. Not a soul remained on post. The looters evidently had cleared out before our arrival without getting to the warehouses yet. When we reached ours, we found it buried in hardened ash. To open its roll-up door, we had to dig it out with axes, picks, and shovels. It took hard work to clear enough to access the door and roll it up. Inside, we found our gear and truck miraculously intact.

We started loading everything onto the flatbed sometime around noon. As the guys got a handle on that, I decided to recce the area and take some photos for the embassy to document the extent of the damage.

I took one of the armored trucks and drove around, snapping photos. When I came to the base's auto dealership, I discovered a lahar wave had pulverized it. Cars lay on their sides, thrown atop one another in a violent jumble. Others were simply crushed and smashed, and all of them trapped like giant dead ants in dried ash as hard as concrete.

Similar scenes of destruction existed everywhere. Clark Air Base had simply ceased to exist. There was no way this level of damage could ever be practically repaired. I returned to the warehouse to find two-thirds of the gear loaded onto the truck.

I'd just joined back into the effort when a sound like rolling cannon fire thundered in the distance. We looked around. "What the bloody hell was that?" somebody asked.

A colossal spout of ash rose over Pinatubo. It had erupted again. We stood watching the plume rise higher and higher, spreading out into another mushroom cloud. The awesome power of Mother Nature was never clearer to me than in that moment. It made us feel insignificant, like fleas on an angry elephant.

We humans like to think we're in control. We're not. All our creations, our technology, and our firepower paled in comparison to the destructive force of that one volcano.

I made a command decision. "Guys," I said as the mushroom cloud towered over us and started to block out the sun, "whatever's on the truck, button it down. We've got to get out of here. Now."

Nobody protested. We didn't get all our gear, but we got most of it. Now we had to save ourselves. The team piled into the armored trucks. I climbed into the flatbed's driver's seat and took station in the middle of our convoy.

We rolled out through the ruined base, racing for the main gate even as ash balls and pumice fell around us. Ash piled up on the windshield so quickly I had to turn the wipers on to see enough to drive. They grated and scraped across the glass and screeched in protest like a wounded animal. We kept going, but even as we made it through the gate and onto the main road for Manila, the ash cloud above us blotted out the daylight. We were bathed in eerie darkness, gray pumice and black, snow-like ash falling all around us. Our headlights guided us south through the demolished countryside.

Somehow, we got back to Manila unscathed. When we returned, my spirits were soaring. Here I was, the orphan kid from Cuba, rolling through what became the second-most powerful volcanic eruption of the twentieth century. I'd dreamed of adventures from my meager bunk in the Colorado orphanage. Those fantasies were my escape. I never stopped dreaming as I grew up in Miami. The horizon always looked better than the ground I stood on. Yet in all my daydreams of world travel, my imagination never took me into the teeth of an exploding volcano.

As we reached the safety of the Philippine capital, which besides an ash-dusting was unaffected by the disaster, I realized I'd just done something only a handful of Americans would ever experience. I knew I'd never experience anything like it again.

The best part of that crazy adventure? Dave didn't go along. He remained behind in Manila and missed all the fun. I got to rub that in for years.

Clark Air Base was never reoccupied by the USAF, which deemed it too expensive to rebuild. The aircraft and personnel stationed there redeployed to Guam. The U.S. Navy decided to rebuild Subic Bay, investing millions of American taxpayer dollars to return it to functional status by September 1991. Two weeks later, the Philippine senate refused to ratify the treaty that included the extension of the leases for Clark and Subic. At the end of December, Cory Aquino formally ordered the U.S. military to leave by the end of 1992.

It was a tense, sad end to a close working relationship that ultimately broke down over money. The Filipinos wanted $825 million a year for the base leases. Washington wouldn't budge from $360 million. Tensions ran high, and when the navy completed its pullout, the economy in the area around Subic collapsed.

The NPA continues to fight the Philippine government to this day, making it history's longest-running Marxist insurgency. It is a fraction of its former self and poses no substantial threat to the Philippine government anymore. In 1992, its leaders embarked on what became known as "the Second Great Rectification Movement." In the previous five years, the NPA had been crushed, driven deeper into the countryside, its leaders captured or exiled. The Second Great Rectification Movement was designed to recommit the movement to its founding principles and learn the lessons from its recent defeats to pave the way to victory.

Instead of leading the NPA to victory, the rectification served only to further fragment the Marxists into competing groups that began attacking each other, assassinating or executing their leaders. This Marxist civil war within its revolutionary insurgency demolished the NPA. From its peak of nearly thirty thousand members, it could barely count a few thousand by the mid-1990s. A decade later, the Islamic radical groups creating chaos on Mindanao overshadowed the Marxists and became the focus of the Philippine government.

The Prado family left the Philippines in the summer of 1991, not long after my encounter with the volcano. From out of Mount Pinatubo's fire, I landed back home right in the proverbial frying pan. After years of dedicated service to a cause and country I believed in with all my heart, my past welled up to put my career in temporary stasis right as the Cold War came to an end and a new world order, complete with new threats, began to emerge.

# 19

## A STRANGER'S LOYALTY

*Washington, D.C.*
*1991*

One of the great challenges for Agency families are the transitions between overseas tours and coming home.

███████████████████████████████████████████████

████████████████████████

███████████████████████████████████████████████

████████████████████████

    Going into a foreign post, there are all sorts of resources there to help you with the chore of setting up a new household. The Agency will provide the support, so you never have to do that alone. It makes the transition much smoother and a lot less stressful—though they can still be very hard on families.

    Going home is a different story. Nobody's there to help you. It falls on either the husband or the wife to find housing, get furniture out of storage. Then waiting for all our household belongings to arrive from our overseas post frequently turns into a headache. Things get lost, stolen, broken. Each trip overseas requires replacing a lot of things or leaving them behind in the States. Ultimately, you end up with half a household in storage, half a household in transit. Trying to find a house, sort through your things, and figure out what needs to be replaced or repaired, all while trying to settle into a new job at HQS (CIA HQ in Langley), causes tension, frustration, and considerable angst. The best CIA families handled it like military families. The moves become examples of discipline and organization.

The return from the Philippines proved to be the worst transition our family endured. Finding a place to live in the D.C. area and turning it into a home was never easy. The town house we owned had been rented out. When we got back, we discovered our tenants had left it in a shambles—a parting fuck-you gift to us after they'd ceased paying rent for months.

In the middle of dealing with that, our boxes from Manila finally began arriving. We quickly discovered our belongings had been looted, the boxes torn open somewhere along the way. Much of what was left to us was broken beyond repair. It was as heartbreaking as returning home after a house fire. Carmen took it particularly hard.

If the homecoming was bad, things at HQ in Langley got worse. Way worse.

In the years since I'd left Miami, a lot of developments had taken place with my old friends from school. Some became cops. Some stayed on the street and accrued increasingly serious rap sheets. One, "Big Al," allegedly became a major player in the local organized crime scene.

In the early 1970s, Al was convicted on a murder-conspiracy charge and sentenced to three years' probation. According to newspaper accounts, he'd been offered money to rob a couple of local drug dealers—except the drug dealers turned out to be undercover cops.

Five years later, somebody tried to kill Al outside his mansion in our old hometown. He took two bullets but survived and continued to thrive. He had political aspirations and made connections all over Florida. But that 1971 conviction stood in his way when he began to think about running for office. He appealed to the governor for a pardon and reached out to others in office for help.

According to subsequent court records and news reports—none of which I saw until years later—South Florida police officers compiled over a thousand hours of recorded conversations between Al and his friends and business colleagues.

As the tape recorders captured every conversation, the police grew convinced they were dealing with a major organized crime figure. Al bragged about having judges, city councilors, district attorneys, and even state officials in his pocket. Al always talked a good game, and eventually some of the cops on his case realized that the vast majority of what he was saying was just idle boasting.

Still, the cops (and later the press) dubbed him "the Great Corruptor." This was saying something, as South Florida back then was awash in graft and corruption.

Except for years the authorities couldn't catch him doing anything wrong. Then in 1986, Al was caught illegally trying to obtain the documents of his early '70s conviction. The police lowered the boom. They arrested him and charged him with bribery, then squeezed everyone they could find to add charges. A month after he was thrown in jail, the district attorney added thirty-nine more counts against him.

It wasn't until the spring of 1988 that Al's trial finally wrapped up. He was found guilty of seven of the thirty-nine counts, most of which had to do with bribery or drug trafficking. The DA wanted sixty years. The judge gave him ten, out in five with good behavior. It cost the police system $3.5 million to prosecute Al. The fallout was felt around Miami, and several prominent politicians were destroyed by their association with him.

Yet that didn't end Al's legal issues. The investigations continued and a select few of the police officers involved started to level threats against his associates if they didn't start talking. They wanted to keep Al in prison and did everything they could to get something further to stick.

All this had gone down while I was overseas serving my country, and I knew little of it until I got home in late 1991. Within weeks of returning, a couple of Miami officers showed up to interview me about my association with Albert. It became clear that they'd been squeezing people to get them to talk—to say anything. People talked to save their own skins, but all too often they would tell the cops whatever they wanted to hear, not the truth. When somebody has your nuts in a vise, it is very, very hard to tell them to fuck off.

As these particular cops played hardball with Al's known acquaintances, someone mentioned that I'd been Albert's friend from way back in high school and a few years beyond graduation. That much was true.

When they came to see me, these officers played the same game. They made it clear that if I didn't cooperate, they would destroy my CIA career. They pressured me to rat out my old friends so they could secure a conviction. It didn't matter than I had nothing with which to rat them out. They just wanted names and a means to continue to prosecute the investigation in an effort ultimately intended to lengthen Al's prison sentence.

I wasn't a saint as a kid. Neither was Albert, but these cops were accusing him of things I know he never did—at least not around me when I knew him. When I couldn't give them what they wanted, they spent the next year making good on their threats. In the months ahead, these officers tried very hard to destroy my career. Ultimately, they triggered a full investigation into me and my childhood back in Florida.

They accused me of committing violent crimes I could not possibly have done because I was not only outside the Miami area, I was out of the country deployed with the Agency.

The investigation brought my CIA career to a crashing halt. I was sidelined from further overseas tours until it was completed. For a year, I lived in a state of anguished suspended animation, taking language lessons and working a desk at Langley while the FBI and CIA went through my past with an ultra-fine-tooth comb. The lead FBI agent on the investigation was a former airborne soldier with combat experience. He was fair, thorough, and dogged at ferreting out the truth. I got the sense that he knew what was going on and being done to me.

This was the worst and most stressful time of my life. I'd seen careers destroyed over politics, over ops gone wrong. I'd seen good officers ruined over even the whiff of scandal. Though the Church Committee hearings were almost a decade and a half in the past, their specter hung over the CIA like a sword of Damocles.

Keeping the house in order was the highest priority at Langley.

Every night, I went home dreading what would become of my career. I had no worries that there would be any sort of criminal charges against me—I'd done none of the things the Miami-Dade cops "suggested" I had to the FBI—but I feared this would taint me in the CIA and tank my career anyway. I loved what I did. My entire identity, my purpose and meaning, all flowed from my role in the CIA. It was my life.

When the full weight of the two greatest investigative agencies in the world are directed at your past, you can be sure they will turn up anything and everything. I cooperated fully—I volunteered for multiple polygraph tests, I offered blood and DNA samples. When the police said they'd found a boot print at the scene of the decades-old crime, I gave them a cast of my own feet and boot size. It was not a match. Neither did my blood or DNA match any of the evidence gathered at the crime scenes relevant to their accusations against me.

In the middle of the investigation, the police revealed they had found a palm print they tried to link to me. I offered up my palms. Not a match, of course.

I cooperated in every way I could. I even handed over all my financial records, as well as everything the FBI asked for from me. Ultimately, I was polygraphed six separate times—and "no deception" indicated on all of them.

While the internal investigation continued, a judge in South Florida threw out the DA's entire case. In a rare moment of judicial outrage, from the bench he expressed his fury for the strong-arm tactics the police were caught using to try to coerce witnesses in testifying against Albert.

That should have been the end of it for me, but the CIA and FBI are nothing if not thorough. The electron microscope pointed my way stayed fixed for months. In the end, they found nothing, because there was nothing to find.

Yet rumors swirled around Langley about me. The whiff of scandal is career cancer, especially in a secret organization like the CIA. They would have dumped me in a heartbeat if any of this were true.

In the end, my future at the Agency came down to a review board meeting between all the Division Chiefs and the security team that worked with the FBI to investigate me. I was not allowed to attend; all of them had read my file, they read the internal investigation's report, plus they read what happened to the criminal cases in South Florida, that they were thrown out.

Dick Holm was one of the Division Chiefs in the room that day. I'd never met him, but he was another legendary officer with a storied career. He'd come up through the paramilitary ranks during the 1960s, serving in Laos and Southeast Asia before being posted to the Congo. There, he was nearly killed in a plane crash. He was burned over a third of his body, and local villagers found him and saved his life. He was one of the few men in the Agency in 1991 who wore the CIA's highest award for bravery, the Distinguished Intelligence Medal. Around Langley, Holm's word was solid gold.

The Deputy Director of Operations, Jack Downing, headed the review board that day. As he started, Dick raised his hand and told Jack, "Sir, I've got stuff to do. Can I make my determination now? Because I need to leave."

Jack replied, "Yes, of course."

Dick said, "Sir, I have read this young man's file. I say he stays."

All eyes in the room stayed on him as he stood up, tossed his copy of the investigation and my file onto the table, and walked out.

Every Division Chief agreed.

Though I was cleared of any wrongdoing, that whiff, the very fact there'd been an investigation, can still put the stake in the heart of a career. What Dick did that day was not only ensure I remained with the CIA, his reaction in the meeting showed everyone he knew what this was: revenge for refusing to play ball with the Miami-Dade cops. The whiff of scandal evaporated even before the other Division Chiefs left the room. My career would not be harmed after all.

When I found out what happened in that meeting, I was blown away. The last year had been devastating to me and to my family. Carmen, who loved the Agency as much as I did, fell apart over it. In truth, that was the worst aspect: seeing what those South Florida cops had done to my wife and family simply out of their fury against Albert.

Coming home every day knowing that the nightmare would be waiting in the morning was corrosive. Eviscerating. To this day, the pain from that time is like a half-healed wound. Even writing about it dredges the old anguish back up.

A few weeks later, I was in the language center working on a ███████████ language test.

I'd been working to get more fluent in it while my career was in stasis in preparation for my next overseas tour.

Somebody came into the room. I looked up to see a distinguished older gentleman with burn marks on his hands. Some of his hair was gone, and he had burn scars on part of his face as well.

He sat down in front of me and started working on a test of his own. I got up to use the restroom, and when I passed by him, I glanced down to see *Richard H*. written at the top of his page.

This was the man who had gone to bat for me. A total stranger, but my loyalty to him was instant the minute I heard what he had done. I knew I had to say something to him.

I finished my test and waited outside in the hall for him. Thirty minutes passed before he came through the door.

"Sir," I said. He turned his eyes to me. "Are you Dick Holm?"

"I am."

"Sir, you don't know me, but you did me a great right not too long ago. I'm Ric Prado."

For a long moment, he looked me square in the eye. Then he slowly came to attention and saluted me. "Son, it is an honor to meet you."

He offered his hand. I shook it in silence as I struggled to find words for the moment. I still couldn't believe he'd been my advocate. He had no investment in me. But he did have a big investment in the truth, and doing what was best not just for the Agency but the people who gave everything to it.

He asked me how I was getting along. That broke the ice. I found my voice, and we chatted for a few minutes, but I don't remember what we said.

Alone afterward, I couldn't choke the tears back any longer. The nightmare was over, thanks largely to a hero's loyalty and trust in a man he'd never met but knew everything about.

# 20

## THE OUTCAST KINGDOM

*Against North Korea*
*1990s*

After fourteen months of ███████ language lessons, plus a monthlong immersion, I looked forward to taking the family to an overseas tour in a peaceful, friendly nation. ████████████████████████████ we were all eager to explore the country. Our family library included three volumes of ████████████████████ histories of the country, multiple tomes, and biographies of historic figures ████████████████

One day, shortly before our scheduled departure, the Chief of the East Asia Division called me into his office. When I sat down, he dropped a bomb on me.

"The Chief of the Koreas asked for you by name. He wants you to come work for him on a special project."

I'd never met the Chief there, but his reputation was well known throughout the Agency. Hard-nosed, demanding—sometimes bordering on mayhem—he ran his station with an iron fist, which earned him the nickname "King Ralph." He spoke two Asian languages—Chinese and Korean—and was highly educated and hyperintelligent.

This would be a big change ████████████████, especially after

the past fourteen months. I couldn't do that to the kids and Carmen
███████████████
███████████████.

"Can you tell me about the program?" I asked the Division Chief.

"No, I can't."

"No information at all?" I asked, intrigued.

"No."

"I'll take it," I said.

If he couldn't explain the program to someone with my security clearance, I figured whatever this was had to be good.

It was.

King Ralph did not disappoint. His reputation was spot-on—a man harder than woodpecker lips, who squeezed the last ounce of effort out of everyone under his leadership. I arrived with my own reputation for being an ultra-aggressive case officer. The two of us quickly butted heads. ██████████████████████████████████.
████████████████ After a particularly salty email exchange, I confronted him and pushed back hard. It turned out, he respected that and eased up. Overnight, we went from constant conflict to working exceptionally well together. I suppose that was his way of testing me, seeing the mettle I possessed. Once I passed the test, we were solid. In the years to come, we became close friends.

In Korea, the Agency faced a unique challenge. The Cold War was over. The Soviet Union had collapsed, and the United States now reigned as the only global superpower left. Back home, Congress talked about a "peace dividend" and began to downsize the military and the defense industry. It seemed like a golden era was upon us, one in which we could trade freely with our overseas partners and enjoy a level of security our nation had not known since before the Great Depression.

Except, not.

North Korea in the 1990s was one of the strangest and most dangerous rogue nations history had ever seen. Born in the fires of World War II's final days when the Soviets invaded Manchuria, North and

South Korea declared themselves separate nations a few months apart in 1948. Two years later, North Korea invaded South Korea, intending to unite the peninsula under one Marxist dictator, Kim Il-sung. That invasion triggered UN involvement, led by the United States. In three years of horrific fighting, almost three million people died. North Korea was almost totally destroyed by the time the cease-fire took effect in 1953. Every building, road, bridge, and rail line had been bombed, shelled, or riddled with gunfire. It remained a desolate, impoverished nation thanks to Kim Il-sung's bizarre and oppressive leadership.

It limped along, propped up by manipulated economic statistics, plus its Chinese and Soviet allies, whom Kim Il-sung sometimes set against each other to shake loose more aid from them. They obliged, since he was unafraid of confronting the Americans and South Koreans defending the other half of the peninsula. Through the next several decades, the North Koreans fought one of the bloodiest and most ruthless shadow wars in the world. They kidnapped average citizens in both South Korea and Japan, forcing them to teach their agents the cultural nuances of both countries. They were kept in appalling conditions for years until their usefulness had run its course. Reportedly, they were then brutally murdered.

North Korean operatives carried out political assassinations, bombings, and commando raids along the South Korean coast. Of its twenty-five million people, almost 40 percent served in the military or in the reserves. By the 1980s, this tiny, isolated nation possessed the fourth-largest army in the world behind China, Russia, and the United States. Kim Il-sung also developed a nuclear weapons program that looked to be on the verge of success by the mid-1990s.

Meanwhile, a series of floods combined with inept central management of its economy led to a famine. Thousands of North Koreans died every month of starvation; estimates later put the death toll at over four hundred thousand.

By the time I became involved in the Koreas, Kim Il-sung was in poor health. His son Kim Jong-il increasingly made decisions and was clearly the designated successor for when his father died. The North Koreans achieved something no other nation ever had: a hereditary Marxist monarchy, one that continues today.

In July 1994, Kim Il-sung finally died of heart failure. As expected, his son took over, declaring a three-year period of national mourning for his dad, even as the famine's death toll mounted. What followed was a semi-thaw in relations with the South Koreans known as "the Sunshine Policy." It proved short-lived. At the same time, Kim Jong-il implemented a "military first" policy that diverted food and other re-sources to the army. There was speculation that this was designed to discourage coup attempts, and Kim Jong-il may have been in a more precarious position politically than we'd first thought.

Operating against North Korea is not like it is portrayed in the movies. James Bond may be able to slip in and out of Pyongyang, but in the real world, that simply doesn't happen. North Korea is the most locked-down police state on the planet. Every aspect of life there is controlled, including movement and travel. The entire environment is simply alien to anyone who grew up in a free nation.

Still, we found ways to counter some of the worst dark-world op-erations the North Koreans carried out. ▮▮▮▮▮▮▮▮▮▮▮▮▮▮▮▮▮ ▮▮▮▮▮▮▮▮▮▮

▮▮▮▮▮▮▮▮▮▮▮▮ I received a promotion to GS-15. We did some good.

On a global playing field, things were a little more even. As the North Korean economy collapsed through the 1990s, and the state became dependent on aid from China and the United Nations, it began using its overseas embassies as centers for criminal activity. The North Koreans would do anything to raise cash. They'd smuggle goods, run drugs, sell arms. Their cyber operations took root around this time, too, and in later years, they were quite successful in hacking into for-eign banks and stealing money. By the late 1990s, these criminal oper-ations formed their primary source of foreign currency outside of the aid they received from China.

North Korea is so broke that each embassy is not only expected to funnel currency home but to sustain itself as well through whatever criminal opportunities present themselves. They are essentially a country held together by a government-sanctioned criminal syndicate. There is nothing they won't do. We've found their operatives neck-deep in human trafficking, prostitution, drugs, guns, and even counterfeiting. Of the latter, in the early 2000s, they created the most perfect counterfeit U.S. hundred-dollar bill ever seen. It was so impressive, the Secret Service named it the Super Note. The Super Note was so good that it forced the U.S. Mint to change the design of the bill.

Bottom line: for all their country's many dysfunctions, North Korean operators excel in the sketchiest corners of the globe. I wonder if they note the irony that the most Marxist of the few remaining Marxist states survives by exploiting its talents in the most laissez-faire of marketplaces—the black one.

The North Koreans assigned to these embassies are chosen largely on their loyalty to the regime. Understandably, Pyongyang has always feared defections—I mean, let's be honest: *Who* would actually want to live in such a place? So only the most ideologically committed members of the regime are sent to these foreign postings. As double insurance against defections, Pyongyang keeps at least one close family member back in North Korea as additional insurance. Basically, they are hostages, and the diplomats know that if they defect or are caught working for a foreign government, their people back home will die. Horribly. This makes them exceptionally difficult to penetrate or turn. On the rare occasion we had an opportunity to approach one of their embassy types, the results were usually the same: they'd tell us to go to hell.

Later on in my career, I got the chance to play hardball with these types. With the help of a veteran U.S. Army operator detailed to us, "K-B," we dreamed up several schemes that I found myself in a position to personally carry out in spite of having recently been promoted to

Senior Intelligence Service ranks—our equivalent of a general in the U.S. Army and Air Force. It gave me the opportunity to strike back against these thugs face-to-face, and I relished the chance.

By this point in my career, I served as one of King Ralph's deputies. It was the highest "conventional" job I ever held at the CIA. It gave me responsibility for all of our worldwide programs targeting North Korea, as well as our robust liaison programs. I was also the Agency's senior representative on Korean matters to the National Security Council (NSC) and its hard targets board. Hard targets for intelligence operations were plentiful, thanks to the Hermit Kingdom's many tentacles. The job took me all over the world. In each case, we worked to counter the growing malignant criminal threat these North Korean embassies posed to their host nations.

For the most part, senior officers like me usually crewed a desk and let the younger guys do all the fieldwork. Besides, I had about 130 people working for me at the time. Managing them required most of my attention.

But I will always be my father's son. He led by example, and I needed to do that, too. Plus, fieldwork was always where my heart lay. I couldn't be chained to a windowless office forever. Instead, I took point on a couple of the schemes we cooked up. The key was again my ability to pose as something other than an American citizen. One idea in particular ██████████████████████████████ raised eyebrows with the local Chief of Station, as it contained both a measure of danger and risk. He contacted King Ralph and asked, "How do you feel about this?"

"If Prado wants to do it, let him do it. I'll back him," came my boss's reply.

With the green light, we went ahead with our operation. It was simple.

██████████████████████████████████████████

█████████████████████████████

████████████████████████████████████████████

██████████████████████

███████████████████████████████████████████████

██████████

The North Koreans smelled money. ███████████████████

██████████████████

███████████████████████████████████████

█████████████████                                    █████████

███████████████████████████████████████████████

██████████████████

███████████████████████████████████████████████

█████████████████

█████████████████████████████████████████████

████████████████████

The deal was consummated, and a North Korean intelligence officer was assigned to be my contact. We worked out a time and place █████████████████████████████████. But of course, when it did arrive, we'd coordinated with the local authorities to raid and capture the material—and the North Koreans with it. █████████████████████████

████████████████████████████████████████████

████████████████

                              ████████████████████████████████████████████ This sort of black mark was looked upon very unfavorably in Pyongyang, so it probably would mean the end of his overseas career. At the very least. The NK regime made a habit of punishing failure with extreme measures.

As he was waiting at the airport for his flight out, I approached him.

"Remember me?" I asked.

He glowered.

"I can make your life really good right now," I said. "You've been disgraced; your career is over. Why don't you come with us? We'll debrief you and you'll make some good money."

His face turned beet red as he realized he'd been played the entire time.

Sputtering with anger, he spat out, "Fuck you! I'm North Korean!"

Instead of a new start in America, he boarded the plane home, where he was consigned to the worst backwater posts in a country full of misery.

I slept like a baby that night.

Around this time, the collective American intel community discovered the North Koreans had just begun a new program that exploited legal and undocumented immigrants from Latin America and turned them into sleeper agents. They recruited them before they came to the United States using a combination of cash and coercion.

Those agents infiltrated into the United States, where the North Koreans used them sort of like first-world proxy shoppers. They bought high-tech items like computers and radios and sent them overseas, where they were smuggled to North Korea. This network, as it developed, proved to be yet another way around the economic and technology embargoes placed by so many nations against the Hermit Kingdom.

On a darker note, we also discovered that these agents served a dual purpose for their North Korean masters. ███████████████████ ███████████████ ████████████████████████████████ ██████████████ ████████████████████████████████████ ████████████ ████████████████████████████████████ ██████████████████

████████████ In one nation, we identified the North Korean intelligence officer.

████████████████████████████████████████████ He was an ugly, squat, arrogant son of a bitch, █████████████████████. We cooked up a scheme, and I told my people that'd I'd take point on it.

Using one of our local assets who was already in contact with the North Korean, we arranged an introduction ████████████████████ ████████████

████████████████████████ I arrived at our meeting point carrying a bottle of Johnnie Walker Black in one hand, a briefcase in the other.

Little did he know that the meeting location was wired and under surveillance. We had cameras secreted inside the room to capture all the action.

We sat down and started talking. He kept eyeing my briefcase. I made not-so-subtle references that conveyed to my pudgy mark that the "goods" inside were of exceptional value to his country. We knocked back a double Johnnie Walker. Then another. One thing about North Koreans—they are heavy drinkers. This guy was in his midsixties and in poor health; his liver was probably already on the way out.

We'd finished a third round. The bottle was almost empty. He was excited and jovial—as jovial as North Koreans get; they're usually pretty sour humans.

He'd lowered his guard. I could see in his eyes that his mind was racing with thoughts of promotions and accolades in his future. It was time to spring the trap.

"You know what I have here," I said. I put my left hand on the briefcase and slid it across the table toward him. Then I reached over and clasped his hand with my right.

He took my hand, and we shook. His eyes lit up. I said to him again, "You know what I have here."

He nodded and smiled.

I flipped the briefcase latch. The lip popped open just as I said, "Thank you for working with the United States government."

It took a second for him to process what I'd just said. Then he glanced down at the briefcase's contents. ██████████████████████████ his eyes fell on stacks and stacks of cash.

"Thank you for agreeing to work with me in helping the U.S. to overthrow the corrupt North Korean government."

He tried to yank his hand away. I was far stronger and held on to him. Panic seized him. He recoiled. I yanked him close.

Eye to eye, six inches apart, I said to him, "Either you work with me, or I'll destroy you."

My measured, controlled words sank in. He'd been totally conned. A single photo of him shaking hands with me with a backdrop of a cash-filled briefcase was enough to earn him a ticket to a North Korean gulag if the wrong people were to see it.

I let go of him. He slumped back into his chair, sweating and tugging at his shirt. I stared at him. "Think it over."

He refused to work with us. ███████████████

██████████████

████████████████████

██████████████████

███████████

The night I learned that news, I went home and cracked a bottle of champagne. I sat in our backyard and drank it, enjoying the moment. In a world filled with dirtbags and murderers who want to do harm to Americans, sometimes you have to play hardball. I was okay with that, especially when the good guys win and a dirtbag gets his due.

Don't fuck with my country.

# PART IV

# 21

## THE JIHAD FACTORY

*1995 Overseas Location*
Sandwiched between my two tours with the East Asia Division, a unique opportunity came my way that sent me back to what I loved doing most: counterterrorism. Don't get me wrong—fewer things in life are more gratifying than sticking it to the North Korean intelligence service, but chasing down radical ideologues who think nothing of slaughtering innocents in the pursuit of whatever political objective they have is what I'd learned to do best.

King Ralph broke the news to me in mid-1995. I'd been working for him for two years when he called me into his office one day. By then, we had long since developed a great relationship and mutual respect. He'd also become a trusted friend. The Agency's insularity and need for secrecy lead to close bonds between officers, especially when we're stationed overseas together. It is very similar to the way military units will bond. In the past year, King Ralph and I had laid the foundations of a friendship that would last the rest of our lives.

I sat down across from him at his old-school, massive wooden desk. He greeted me and said, "Ric, I have good news and I have bad news."

"Okay. What's the good news?" I asked.

"You're being promoted to GS-15. Congratulations."

"Thank you, Sir."

I'd reached the top of the general service pay grade within the CIA. This was great news. The next step up would be the Senior Intelligence Service rank—the senior-level management track—but that was never of any interest to me . . . little did I know.

"With the promotion, you're being reassigned."

"Where?" I asked.

"You're going to be named a branch chief in a new component of the CTC."

The CTC was the Counterterrorist Center, established in 1986 during the wave of radical Islamic attacks on U.S. targets that included the hijacking of TWA Flight 847 and the subsequent murder of U.S. Navy diver Robert Stethem on the tarmac at Beirut-Rafic Hariri International Airport along with the Palestine Liberation Front's takeover of the *Achille Lauro* cruise ship off Egypt a few months later.

By the mid-1990s, the CTC included hundreds of officers and analysts who worked to uncover the machinations of such diverse groups as Japan's Red Brigade, Iran-sponsored Hezbollah, along with a branch dedicated to Islamic extremist groups like the Palestine Liberation Front and Sunni-sponsored groups operating in Algeria.

Since the end of the Cold War, counterterrorism was where the action had moved. Fighting North Korean agents was a remnant of the CIA's glory years when we battled the Soviet threat and their vassals. The future looked to be a lot more asymmetrical, and the number of terror threats seemed to multiply by the month.

Try telling the politicians that. They were so obsessed with the "peace dividend" that collectively they failed to see the 1993 World Trade Center bombing as anything more than an aberration, not a portent. Instead of beefing up our counterterrorism capability, the Clinton administration cut the CTC's funding. Worse, after Iran-Contra, the CTC went from being operations-oriented to more of an analytical intelligence clearinghouse.

It was a difficult time. Yet that would soon change, and those of us who specialized in counterterrorism could see the storms on the horizon. For that reason, this transfer seemed like a plum assignment for me. I was going where the juice was again. My heart rate picked up just thinking about it.

Then I remembered King Ralph said there was bad news. "What's the bad news?" I asked.

He smiled and said, "The East Asia Division is losing you."

I arrived back in Virginia in the fall of 1995, eager to find out what this new assignment would entail. It did not disappoint. The CTC was an organizational experiment of sorts within the Agency. My old mentor Dewey Clarridge was the original CTC's Chief. He designed it to be flexible and operate on a global level at a time when the CIA was organized along geographic divisions. Terrorism was a worldwide issue, with different groups operating on many different continents simultaneously, so Dewey's vision for the CTC made a lot of sense. It allowed each branch within the CTC to chase bad guys wherever they went in coordination with the Area Divisions.

Since its inception, the CTC focused on state-sponsored terrorism. Groups like Hezbollah were supported by rogue regimes whose training and funding made them deadly effective. Nobody at the Agency could forget about Hezbollah's attacks in Beirut in the early '80s when they hit our embassy, blew up 241 Marines (including my first karate student, Billy San Pedro), and kidnapped CIA Chief of Station William Buckley.

By 1995, Dewey had long since moved on into retirement. The center was in the strong hands of "Winston W.," an exemplary DI analyst, and his pit bull Chief of Operations, "Jeff O." Jeff was another legendary ops officer whose unorthodox thinking and relentless demand for results made him perfect for the C/OPS job. At our first introduction, I found him to be smart, no-bullshit, and ultra mission-focused. At times, he bordered on gruff. Like most leaders at the CTC, Jeff was the antithesis of every bad joke about government work. Motivated by a profound sense of duty to protect the country we all loved, he worked late into the night, every night doing his absolute best to stop those intending to do our people harm.

If there was one person who could outwork Jeff, it was Mike Scheuer. Mike led the Islamic Extremist Branch within the CTC. He was an analyst, cold, calculating, with an ability to weigh multiple sources and find the balance between them. He'd dedicated virtually his entire career to understanding the Middle East and Islamic radicalism. By 1995, he knew more about the subject than anyone else in the building. His mind was an encyclopedia, a veritable who's who of jihadists bent on doing the West harm.

It turned out Mike would be my new boss.

Jeff laid it all out for me in his office after only a couple of months back at Langley. At Mike's urging, a new task force was being formed within the CTC, dedicated to one mission. It would be based outside the Agency's main facility and would have no geographical limits. A building had already been leased and outfitted for us, complete with a SCIF (sensitive compartmented information facility) where we could safely read, process, and transmit classified information without it being electronically intercepted from outside the building.

This would be the Agency's first "virtual station," meaning we weren't chained to a particular ██████████ location or geographical boundary. It took Dewey's original vision of the CTC and applied to it one specific task. Jeff had selected me to be Mike's Deputy Chief of Station and its senior operations officer.

"What are we going after?" I asked Jeff as he briefed me.

"Not a what. Who. Osama bin Laden."

"Who?" I said, before realizing how stupid I probably sounded.

Jeff smiled as if I'd just walked into a trap, and said, "Exactly."

As it was for most Americans in late 1995, that name meant nothing to me. I'd spent much of my career working different CT targets in South America and East Asia, but this was a guy who'd never crossed my radar.

Given we'd be standing up a special task force dedicated to one man and his organization, it was clear the CTC considered Bin Laden a significant threat to the United States. What the nature of that threat was, I had no clue. But I knew I was in for a steep learning curve in the months ahead.

We established Alec Station—named after Mike's son—in November 1995. There were eight original plank owners, all handpicked by Mike. The team that took shape included an eclectic mix of analysts, targeting officers, an FBI liaison, and an irreverent, but most efficient, desk officer/program manager we affectionately called "JJ." She was the spark at the center of our operation—brilliant, multitalented, and hardworking. She was blessed with great organizational skills, which any new organization needs. She also possessed a hilarious sense of humor, was energetic, and could cuss like a sailor. To this day, she remains one of my favorite people I worked with during my time in the Agency.

Our experience and training led to a diverse range of viewpoints and talents that Mike made sure meshed well. The core of our team included several female analysts who served as our targeters long before that became an official career track within the Agency. They were dedicated, relentless subject-matter experts on all things Osama bin Laden.

Historically, CIA analysts were segregated from operational folk at our area divisions. They would collaborate but were never colocated. With the advent of the "centers," first the CNC for narcotics and subsequently the CTC, analysts and ops officers not only became colocated but gained full visibility into one another's craft. Blessed with massive brain cells and now infected with our OO's operational acumen and enthusiasm, these select analysts morphed into present day targeting officers—the deadliest animal I know!

Jennifer Matthews was one of our best targeting officers, a consummate professional who mirrored the work ethic and spirit Mike brought to the team. To outsiders, she seemed to be an average married soccer mom of two, with a third child on the way. A 1982 graduate of Central Dauphin East High School in Harrisburg, Pennsylvania, she'd been an accomplished student, a member of the National Honor Society, and active in her local chapter of Youth for Christ. Her classmates voted her "Most Likely to Be the Next Barbara Walters." Even back then, her confidence was magnetic, and she rarely lost her poise.

A decade later, she seemingly lived in a quiet suburb not far from the Fredericksburg Civil War battlefield. Married and settled in her leafy neighborhood, she drove a minivan and shopped at her local grocery store like everyone else. To her neighbors and non-Agency friends, she appeared to be one of them—just another average American living to care for her family.

Once inside our building, she was a relentless hunter of terrorists. She had an intuitive ability to conceive plans to accomplish our mission that few others could even dream up. Mike loved her devilishly clever mind—we all did. There were times she'd come up with an idea that blew my own hair back and made me grateful she was on our side. I later learned that her nickname became "Ruth." For *ruthless*.

In our new virtual station, she was not alone. We had other analysts who grew into targeting officers, including Mary Anne, Joanne, Cindy, and Kami, among others. I cannot forget our most capable, and Arab-speaking ops officer, GG. All were bright, dedicated, and vicious when it came to our mission—in a good way, of course!

In those first weeks, Mike opened up the fire hose of knowledge and pointed it my way. I'd had a brush or two with Islamic terrorists in the past, but I'd never worked that account before, so in some ways I started from scratch that November.

The first thing I needed to understand was why Mike considered Bin Laden such an existential threat. There were plenty of terrorists out there in the world calling for attacks on the Great Satan of the United States. Why did this guy deserve his own task force?

The answer lay in how Mike interpreted the man. He'd studied Bin Laden's life and saw him not as a murderous psychopathic ideologue, as Osama was later portrayed in the world media, but as a leader of a growing movement inside Islam who possessed the resources, connections, organizational skills, and capability to inflict significant harm on the West.

Mike and other analysts had seen a pattern develop around the world. Since about 1990, Islamic radicals kept turning up in places like Algeria, Egypt, Sudan, the Philippines, Somalia, and within the Palestinian community to foment terror attacks against moderate or secular regimes. They were diverse groups causing the chaos, but they shared one common nexus: Afghanistan. Every time Mike drilled down into the details of who was behind these operations, he discovered Arab veterans of the Soviet-Afghan War in the mix. In many cases, they carried out these attacks or financed them. As the attacks, especially in Algeria, grew increasingly bloody, the radicals grew emboldened.

More moderate elements in the Middle East considered this development a mortal threat to their own positions. Tips began flowing into the Agency as to who these actors were from sources in Tunisia, Algeria, and elsewhere. The nuggets of intel, as usual, were fragmentary and sometimes contradictory. Our analysts were split. Some, led by the Near East Division Chief, Fred Anderson, downplayed the role the Afghan vets were playing in the growing violence. Fred, who had led the Afghan Task Force during the '80s, believed that there were enough homegrown radicals in North Africa and the Middle East already operating against moderate regimes. Any study of Egyptian history since the early 1970s underscored that point. The Afghan vets were playing in a field already dominated by local jihadist factions.

Others, including one of our best analysts, Paul Pillar, saw something new developing with the Afghan vets playing a key role in al-Qaeda. The fragments of intel we gathered did not look like the typical state-sponsored terror model of the '70s and '80s.

████████████████████████████████████████████████████

████████████████████████

████████████████████████████████████████████████████

██████████████████████

██████████████████████████████████ the radicals gained enough trac-
tion to pose a legitimate threat to Yasser Arafat's Palestine Liberation
Organization (PLO). Arafat was in the process of negotiating with the
Israelis, something the radicals violently opposed. Hoping to enlist the
CIA's help in containing this threat to his own base of power, Arafat
sent proxies to the CIA ████████████████████████ to connect the dots for
us. The PLO representatives fingered Saudi businessman and Afghan
veteran Osama bin Laden as the man behind the jihadist curtain.

Bin Laden was the seventeenth of fifty-two children in his Saudi-
born family. His dad was one of the wealthiest men in the Middle East,
having made billions in the oil-fueled, booming construction industry.
Osama was educated, well read, and devoted to his faith. A pure, true
believer who not only spoke with conviction but acted with it as well.
In 1986, he traveled to Afghanistan to join the holy war against the
Soviet Union. At first, he functioned as sort of a middleman between
the various mujahideen factions and wealthy Islamic donors wanting
to support their cause. He funneled some of his own money to these
groups as well; at the time his father supported him with a massive
monthly stipend.

At his own cost, he imported and deployed a host of engineering
equipment into Afghanistan—bulldozers, earthmovers, backhoes, and
more. He earned a reputation for bravery among the Afghan fighters
when he personally dug trenches with a bulldozer while under Russian
fire. That willingness to expose himself to danger set him apart from
many of the other foreigners supporting the anti-Soviet jihad.

He built an entire underground network of tunnels, magazines,
and living quarters in a mountain range in eastern Afghanistan near the
Pakistani border. This would serve as his base of operations for years
to come. There, his growing personal force of Afghans, Pakistanis, and

Arab volunteers trained and equipped themselves to fight. Bin Laden earned even more respect among those who served with him, as he lived as they did—a simple and rugged life. How many sons of billionaires were so devoted to their faith that they lived in a cave and fought side by side with others to protect it?

Eventually, Osama's band of Arab volunteers went into battle against the Soviets. He proved to be courageous and calm in a fight. In his last notable engagement in 1989, just as the Russians were completing their withdrawal from Afghanistan, he and his men attempted to seize the airport at Jalalabad. He was wounded in the failed assault.

His time in Afghanistan convinced Osama that Islam stood at a crossroads. He grew convinced that Western influence had triggered a moral degradation of his religion, but that jihad—holy war—was the one path to revitalize it.

A turning point came in 1990 when Iraq invaded Kuwait. Osama was living in Saudi Arabia, surrounded by his loyal followers from his Afghan war days. When it looked likely Saddam Hussein wouldn't stop with Kuwait and intended to invade Saudi Arabia as well, Bin Laden offered to deploy his veteran fighters to stop the Iraqi army. The Saudi government ignored his proposal and turned to the United States for help.

The move deeply shocked Osama. He became an ardent opponent of American intervention in the war, believing that once the infidels were invited into the region, they would never leave. On that, events showed he was not wrong.

In early November 1990, an Egyptian-born American named El Sayyid Nosair assassinated an outspoken Jewish rabbi named Meir Kahane in a New York City hotel. Kahane was one of the founders of the Jewish Defense League in the late 1960s and had just given a speech to an audience of Orthodox Jews, urging them to immigrate to Israel.

When the FBI raided Nosair's apartment, they found reams of material suggesting he was part of a plot to blow up skyscrapers in New York City. Nosair's associates included an al-Qaeda operative and double agent named Ali Mohamed. This was probably the first nascent al-Qaeda effort in the United States. Bin Laden later paid for Nosair's legal bills. The FBI didn't inform the CIA of any of this, and in fact, the Agency didn't find out about it until after 9/11. Had we known in 1995, those puzzle pieces might have provided more clarity for us.

Meanwhile, the Gulf War crystallized Osama's thinking and shaped his entire strategy for the rest of his life. Supporting jihad as a mechanism to revitalize Islam morphed into a view that the United States, Russia, and China were Islam's greatest enemies. The holy wars flaring in the developing world would never succeed as long as the United States in particular reigned unchecked.

He began to plot against American targets. In 1992, his operatives launched al-Qaeda's first known attack against the United States when they detonated two bombs in a hotel used by marines in Yemen as they transited to Somalia, where the U.S. led a peacekeeping force trying to bring stability to that lawless, famine-racked nation. Osama saw the American presence in Somalia as nothing but naked imperialism, and he used al-Qaeda to support the forces fighting the peacekeepers.

After publicly criticizing the Saudi regime, he was kicked out of his own country and exiled, first to Afghanistan, then in 1992 to Sudan. He set up operations in Khartoum, establishing connections to the radical Islamic Sudanese regime that had recently seized power. He greased those ties with generous gifts to its leadership that totaled millions of dollars. He also established a variety of businesses in the city as part of an effort to not only create his own empire separate from his family's but to modernize Khartoum. In a trade with the Sudanese government, he built a much-needed road from the country's primary port to the capital. In return, he was given a large tract of land outside the city, which he transformed into a farm that sought to genetically enhance different crops, including sunflowers.

Behind his legitimate construction business and his agricultural operations, Osama continued to develop his global network. Yet he lived aboveground, worshipping at the local mosque five times a day and interacting with the local Sudanese, who considered him a kind and generous neighbor. How much of a threat did he really pose to the United States? The answer was murky at best. We simply didn't know enough about him at the time.

As he had in Saudi Arabia, he surrounded himself with loyalists who fought in Afghanistan with them. His modest home in a Khartoum suburb was heavily defended with bodyguards armed with everything from AK-47s to reportedly SA-7 antiaircraft missiles.

By 1992, the core of Osama bin Laden's supporters included mainly his old Afghan war comrades or members of the terror group Egyptian Islamic Jihad (EIJ). One of Bin Laden's closest associates, Ayman al-Zawahiri, had taken over EIJ in 1991. The two had met in Afghanistan in the mid-1980s after Zawahiri had been released from an Egyptian prison, where he'd been tortured into revealing the location of one of the conspirators in the 1981 assassination of Anwar Sadat.

The following year, al-Zawahiri's EIJ tried to assassinate two Egyptian leaders. Both attempts failed, and the second one resulted in a bomb blast that killed twenty-one people at a girls' school. The death of a young student named Shayma Abdel-Halim turned much of Egypt against EIJ. During her funeral in Cairo, thousands of people flooded into the streets and chanted, "Terrorism is the enemy of God!"

In June 1995, while Egyptian president Hosni Mubarak arrived in Ethiopia for an official visit, EIJ terrorists attacked his motorcade with machine guns. Two security officers died, along with seven of the would-be assassins. Mubarak survived and returned immediately to Cairo, where he pointed the finger directly at the terror groups operating in Sudan.

Because of these attacks, the Egyptian government loathed EIJ and its al-Qaeda associates. When we first stood up Alec Station, we found the Egyptians to be very sympathetic to our efforts and willing allies in the fight against Bin Laden. Yet even they didn't know much about the man or his organization, which seemed more like a loose coalition of like-minded groups and individuals than anything else.

In the summer of 1995, an Agency brief concluded that Bin Laden was the "Ford Foundation" that linked these jihadist groups together. Associates would approach him in Khartoum, sketch a plan of attack, and ask for the resources to finance it. Bin Laden provided the money and sometimes the weaponry.

Self-funded terrorism was not a new dynamic; Latin American Marxist terrorist groups gave birth to the term *narco-terrorism* because of practice. Early European terrorist groups carried out bank robberies and kidnappings to finance their activities. But with Usama bin Ladin (as the CIA originally spelled his name, and abbreviated it to UBL) it was different. The level of funding rivaled that of state-sponsored terrorism, with seven-figure donations (some say extortion) from wealthy Arabs. Some donors obviously just sought to appease him, but others we found to be sympathetic to his cause.

For us to counter this new threat, the CIA and the United States government as a whole would need to evolve new capabilities and operations. At Alec Station, that would be our greatest challenge: pioneering those evolutions as we struggled to make sense of what Bin Laden and his Afghan War cadre represented.

That challenge was made more difficult by the relationship between the CIA, the FBI, and the Clinton White House. President Clinton focused on his domestic agenda and paid little attention to overseas developments during his first term. His first CIA director, James Woolsey, once went over a year without a personal meeting with the President. Usually, a CIA director met daily with the President to brief him on the current global situation. Clinton preferred distance between himself and the Agency, reading the briefs himself. There had been a debate within the administration as to how to handle the growing terror threat. Should terrorists be considered enemy combatants and treated as such, or should they be prosecuted through the existing legal system? Clinton settled on the legal approach, which ultimately limited what we could do to counter or stop these holy warriors.

The earliest photo we have of our family in Cuba. My Abuelo Emilin is seated in white. My mom and dad are directly above him (second and third from left), I'm standing in the front row center.

My mom and dad and I. The suit I wore in this portrait was the same one I wore when I took the plane to the United States.

The last photo taken of my family in Cuba during our final dinner at the Tropicana in Havana.

My handsome Pops at twenty-one. This was his first driver's license.

Our second home in America, the little duplex still stands and is seen here decades after we lived in it.

Me and my beautiful mom, seen a few years before she was afflicted with Alzheimer's Syndrome.

Me in early high school in front of our Hialeah house, which my dad remodeled.

High school graduation day, with my then sweet girlfriend, Nancy V.

December 26, 1971, the day I left for the Air Force to start my Pararescue Jumper career.

Sensei Jim Alfano.

The night I graduated and officially became a Pararescue Jumper, earned our maroon berets in November 1972.

Geared up with the same 130-pound kit I wore on the night we made our night jump in thirty-eight-degree weather into that Utah Lake.

My first day back home after earning our coveted maroon beret!

My Barracudas, the Miskito divers who successfully destroyed the Puerto Cabeza's Pier. Fierce, fearless, and very capable, they were an outstanding, dedicated group of patriots fighting to liberate their homeland.

Teaching a group of Contras on how to use the Soviet-made RPG-7 rocket launcher. I spend years traveling to each Contra camp helping to develop their tactical and weapons skills in the first half of the 1980s.

Dinner in one of the Miskito camps. I'm at right. The living conditions were primitive at best. This was one of my first trips to meet the Contras.

The 82mm and 60mm mortar systems provided the Contras with artillery firepower they initially lacked. Here I am teaching a crew how to fire a 60mm mortar in one of the camps.

When the Miskito launched their offensive across the Coco River just before I left Honduras, they used canoes like this one to get men and equipment across to establish a foothold in their stolen homeland. The offensive was a complete success and drove the Sandinistas out of much of Miskito territory in Nicaragua.

On patrol with the FDN in the high country. That's me on the donkey. This photo and many like it found their way to CIA Director Bill Casey's desk, and he used them to show members of Congress the conditions on the ground for the Contras.

With Stedman Fagoth at the Coco River crossing where the Miskito offensive began. Stedman was the brave and daring leader of the MISURA.

Mike Lima proudly wearing a medal presented to him by Dewey Clarridge in 2004.

An early photo I took of one of the MISURA camps. Conditions were appalling when I first arrived, and the Contras lacked everything from medical supplies to food, bullets, weapons, and training. The only thing they possessed was courage and a willingness to fight to liberate their homeland.

The weapons I carried on my person to every Contra camp while I was in Honduras. I always had a rifle with me as well.

Colonel Ray's parting gift to me as I left Honduras to return to the United States and get a college degree before starting my training at the "Farm."

In the Philippines, we assisted the Filipinos in their fight against one of the world's longest Marxist insurgencies. Here I am training with an MP5K with Mount Pinatubo in the background.

The remains of the Clark AFB car lot at the BX after Mount Pinatubo erupted. We drove up to Clark from Manila to retrieve some of our sensitive communication gear just as the volcano erupted again, forcing us to clear out and drive through a deluge of falling ash.

A photo of me circa 1998 when I was an SIS-2 and Chief of the Koreas. I never lost my love for operating in the field, and while I was in this senior position, I was still able to take part in several black ops in different areas of the globe. A good leader leads from the front.

Carmen and I on New Year's Eve 1990-91 in Manila.

Before deploying to Shangri-La to stand up our station, working to develop the additional skills we would need to survive in such a hostile environment.

Carmen and my son beside me at Langley on the day I received the Intelligence Medal of Merit for actions in the Gulf of Fonseca during our only Barracuda operation on Nicaragua's western coast.

Our team in Shangri-La, on the rooftop of our compound. In one of the hardest and most intense overseas duties of my career, I served alongside some of the finest men I've ever known.

On one of our few missions outside of Shangri-La, our vehicle got stuck in soft sand. As I was working the jack, the handle flipped up suddenly and nearly took my jaw off. After surviving operations all over the planet, getting KO'd by a jack handle would have been something I'd never have lived down!

After my time at the Agency, I worked for my friend, Erik Prince, at Blackwater. Here we both are, gunning a Little Bird helicopter shortly before leaving BIOP on a security run.

Old friends in retirement. DDO Jose Rodriguez, myself, Billy Waugh, and PJ veteran and USAF legend Wayne Fisk. A life surrounded by such fine men seemed all but out of reach when I first came to America, reading James Bond novels and daring to dream of adventures of my own like 007's.

At home in the Southeast with my pup RED (Retired Extremely Dangerous).

My awards from a life of service within the Central Intelligence Agency, 1980–2004.

The seal of the Counterterrorist Center, started by Dewey Clarridge in the 1980s. It became central to our fight against al-Qaeda in the 1990s and beyond.

When I retired from the Agency, I spent my first night drinking wine under a Virginia night sky, reliving every memory I had since first joining in 1980. For every good experience or person I remembered, I imagined keeping a crystal marble. I later purchased a beer glass and filled it with the symbols of the best moments and people of my time with the Central Intelligence Agency. It sits on my mantle today with precious reminders of the adventures I shared and the people I met and befriended along the way.

Between the FBI and CIA, communications were hampered even with our liaison efforts. At times, there were personal animosities involved, but most often our own legal system prevented the free flow of information between the two agencies. As a result, we each held pieces of the Bin Laden puzzle that we both needed to develop a more complete picture of what he was doing.

We pushed forward furiously in the waning weeks of 1995, gathering more intel, developing ideas and operations. In a perfect world, we would have been able to take him out. It would have saved a lot of lives and massive amounts of resources in the years ahead. That old question: If you could go back in time to 1919 and kill Hitler before he seized power, would you do it? Yeah! I think it haunts all of us in light of what Bin Laden did to America and the world in the years that followed.

Not that there were no attempts on his life. Osama had plenty of friends in the shadows, but he also made plenty of enemies. In 1994, an assassination team tried to kill him while he attended his local mosque in Khartoum. He was late, they were early. A number of innocents died in a hail of gunfire, but Bin Laden escaped harm. The assassins were either killed or captured and then executed.

Given what we knew about him, we settled on a two-front strategy. First, we would hit him where it hurt: his finances. Using every resource at our disposal, Alec Station intended to identify his financial networks and nodes and destroy them. Remove his millions, and what would Bin Laden be? A terrorist Ford Foundation without an endowment.

Second, we needed more information on him. We needed eyes on the ground watching him, seeing who came and went to his upscale compound in the run-down, free-for-all city he now called home. That mission would fall to Cofer Black, our then Chief of Station in Sudan. He had an exceptional team of officers in place, including revered Special Forces veteran and CIA contractor Billy Waugh, already playing a guts game against the Arabs protecting Bin Laden. They'd step up their surveillance of the target in the months ahead.

Of course, if some foreign actor or nation wanted Bin Laden dead, who were we to get in their way? ████████████████ ████████████

As we finalized our initial effort against Bin Laden, our "front office" asked me to transmit our intent to our allies. ████████ ████████████

████████████████████████████████████ ████████ ████████████████████████████████████ ████████ ████████████████████████████████████ ████████ ████████████████████████████████████ ████████ ████████████████████████████████████ ████████ ████████████████████████████████████ ████████ ████████████████████████████████████ ████████ ████████████████████████████████████ ████████

Ultimately, I briefed almost every one of our allies on Osama bin Laden.

████████████████████████████████████ ████████

████████████████ They hated Bin Laden with abiding passion for all the chaos and death he and al-Zawahiri had inflicted with their attacks. They were willing to help. This was not the case with other erstwhile "allies." I soon found that out as I traveled from country to country.

A week later, I flew to ████████████████████████

They met our briefing team with wide grins and open arms.

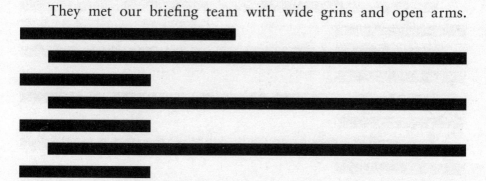

I outlined our intention to go after Bin Laden's financial network, sketched what we knew about him, and signaled our desire to enlist them in our effort. They smiled and nodded and said they'd of course provide whatever support they could.

It all seemed transparently *bullshit*.

That night, we were invited to a banquet ▄▄▄▄▄▄▄▄▄ ▄▄▄▄▄▄▄▄▄

▄▄▄▄▄▄▄▄▄▄▄▄▄▄▄▄▄▄▄▄▄▄▄▄▄▄▄▄▄▄ Everyone enjoyed the finest beef, lobster, fruits, sinful desserts ▄▄▄▄▄▄▄▄. It was over the top and made me supremely uncomfortable.

At the dinner, an anonymous member of our host's party made his personal sentiments clear with a symbolic token strategically placed on the table. I picked it up at the end of the meal and tucked it in a pocket.

██████████████████████████████████████████████

██████████████████████

████████████████████████████████████████████████

██████████████████████████████

████████████████████████████████████████████████

██████████████████████████

█████████████████████████████████████████████

████████████████████████

██████████████████████████████████████████████████

██████████████████████████

Back in Virginia, I returned to our virtual station and went to see Winston and Jeff. I walked into their office and dropped the item on Winston's desk. He stared down at it for a long moment, saying nothing. Message received.

██████████████████████████████████████████████████

██████████████████████

████████████████████████████████████████████

██████████████████████

# 22

## THE GODFATHER OF TERROR

*Alec Station*
*1995–1996*

In any good spy thriller, once the bad guy has been identified, the logical next step is to take them out. A bad guy like Dr. No or Goldfinger always gets whacked in the end, and James Bond emerges unscathed with the woman and his shaken, not stirred, martini.

Osama bin Laden lived openly in the terrorist haven that Khartoum was in the 1990s. He worshipped at the same mosque every day, he stuck to a surprisingly rigid schedule that saw him taking the same routes around the city. He even drove his white Mercedes sedan alone quite frequently. With tradecraft this bad, he was a bad guy looking for a bullet. Except there was no Agency officer to pull the trigger.

You can thank President Gerald Ford for that. On February 18, 1976, he signed Executive Order 11905, which prohibited the Central Intelligence Agency from carrying out political assassinations. Two years later, Jimmy Carter signed Executive Order 12036, which went further and banned indirect United States involvement in assassinations.

Billy Waugh wanted to kill Bin Laden. He had many opportunities to do so while he shadowed the terror leader from 1992 to 1994. Once, he even jogged past Bin Laden as he got out of his Mercedes in front of his residence. Billy figured a two-car operation with only a few officers could trap him on a Khartoum street and assassinate him in his car. No security. No bodyguards. Lawless city. Easy day.

No matter how easy it would have been, there was no legal mechanism to do it. And in the post–Cold War, post-Iran-Contra atmosphere at the CIA, nobody was willing to run an operation that directly contravened two executive orders.

Aside from Billy's personal initiative, there was no formal Agency capability to even carry out such attacks. Unlike the Jason Bourne pulp fiction version of the CIA, we had no assassins on the payroll, so killing Bin Laden was not a realistic option for the CIA of 1996.

With that off the table, our best move against him remained going after his financial empire. At our virtual station, we knew terrorists would come to him for financing and support for their operations. He would dispense the funds and equipment needed for the mission. Yet he was not one to get his hands personally dirty or get directly involved in an operation—not after 1989 Afghanistan anyway.

It took us months to unravel how his own organization, which later we identified as al-Qaeda, fit into this overall picture. It seemed so decentralized, yet global, diverse, yet all roads pointed back to the man in Khartoum. Eventually, we figured it out. He was the Lucky Luciano of terrorism.

Luciano was the first Mafia godfather who pulled non-Italians and non-Catholics into his organization. He was the color-blind Don who cared only about loyalty to purpose and the organization. Bin Laden was the same way. We discovered his connections with Filipinos, Somalis, Saudis, Algerians, Egyptians, Afghans, Pakistanis, and organizations from all over the world. They had one thing that bound them together: holy war. To Bin Laden, jihad was the great revitalizing engine for Islam in the modern age. Who the jihad was against—be it the United States, the Algerian, Egyptian or Philippine government—didn't matter. Ideology and sense of mission did. For those who drank the radical jihadist Kool-Aid, Bin Laden was the great financial provider, the master behind the scenes, manipulating and shaping with strategic use of his massive wealth.

Cut him off from his financial resources, and his whole network would shrivel. But how could we do that? The CIA possessed no capability to search, discover, and interdict Bin Laden's global financial web. Such things were left to other governmental agencies like the Treasury Department. This new mission became the greatest challenge Alec Station faced in its first months after inception. We needed to build our own counter–financial operation that could pinpoint Bin Laden's resources and follow the money trails.

This would not be accomplished overnight—it took years, in fact—but Alec Station's requirement planted the seed that would give birth to a quantum leap in the science of identifying, tracking, and interdicting illicit funding worldwide.

Fast forward to 2000. By then, I was Chief of the International Terrorism Group in the CTC. One of our officers, ███████████████ ███████████████, had been an investment banker prior to joining the Agency. "Phil" was an eccentric chap in a lot of ways; a Wall Street type thrown into a mix of meat eaters and wicked-smart analysts. He was a genius, but a loner who never quite fit in. Always meticulously dressed in a black suit and driving a pristine, freshly waxed Mercedes, he was the quintessential anal-retentive perfectionist. That made him the perfect man for this mission. He played a key role in what we developed in the months ahead.

He took the lead on constructing the CTC's new capabilities from scratch. He asked questions, threw out ideas, and, most importantly, shared his knowledge of the financial world with us—something most of us knew little about. He pioneered the system we used to follow the terrorist money trail. It was Phil's ideas and input that helped us get past Bin Laden's—and other terrorists'—myriad of holding companies, fake accounts, cover businesses, and so on to find where his money was and how he was moving it around. He personally stimulated the development of state-of-the-art technologies for tracking financial activities that became the intel community's envy.

In 1996, we laid the foundations for what Phil eventually created by detecting and documenting the first of Bin Laden's financial tentacles. Our goal was to mesh operational work with the computer skills at our virtual station. Though Billy Waugh had moved on to other assignments, our Chief of Station in Khartoum made sure to keep Bin Laden under frequent surveillance. ██████████████████████████ ██████████████████████████████████████████ ██████████████████████ ██████████████████████████████ Those tidbits from the field gave us ideas and avenues back in Virginia to explore.

It was difficult, byzantine work that never yielded anything close to a complete picture, but we did find pieces of his network. Based on what we developed, Mike conceived further ops against Bin Laden. Many times, the seventh floor—where the senior CIA leadership worked—killed those ideas for being too aggressive or reckless. Other times, the White House did the same. It was the nature of the 1990s. The Agency's senior leadership and our presidential administration defaulted to risk-averse policies overseas. We were hindered by that at times. Yet the CTC's leadership never wavered in supporting Alec Station's efforts.

Part of my role in the team was to serve as a foil to Mike's operational ideas. Being a field officer, I brought a different perspective from Mike's, and it allowed me to suggest a different way of going about something. I'd put the operational realities spin on things, then we'd run it up the flagpole. Unfortunately, too often, we'd be denied.

These were tough months for me and for my family. Mike worked sixty-hour weeks minimum and attacked our mission with all the zeal of a religious adherent. More than anyone else, he saw in Bin Laden a clear and present danger to the United States. Inside the Agency, he was an evangelical force, fighting the bureaucracy as he tried to get the seventh floor to pay attention and recognize the extent of the danger.

When your boss plows through his day with that level of intensity, everyone steps in line—or gets out. We worked harder at Alec Station than just about any other time in my professional life. Even after twelve- or fourteen-hour days at the office, we'd return home only to have work follow us there.

Normally, back in the States, if a department or individual wanted to send a cable out to another station, it had to go through a layered chain of command. It could be a long and cumbersome bureaucratic process to send and receive those crucial communications with our people in overseas hotspots. Alec Station broke that bureaucratic system down. As a virtual station, we could send and receive cables on our own without having to go through the internal chain of command inside the building at Langley. This may seem like a trivial bureaucratic thing. In truth, having the ability to communicate freely with stations all over the world was like a wand of power for us. We could ask questions, get answers, request actions, get results faster than any other Agency organization stateside. It gave us speed, it gave us flexibility, and it sometimes gave us real-time actionable information with very little lag time.

Because of that capability, often we would get Need Immediate Action Cables (NIACs) in the middle of the night. Early on, this meant I'd be sound asleep in bed and the phone would ring. The voice on the other end of the line would tell Mike or me a NIAC had just arrived. One of us would throw on some clothes and drive into our office complex to handle it.

████████████████████████████████████ Mike's pace pushed most of us to the edge of exhaustion. We relished the work. We believed in the mission and its urgency. But the commitment was not for everyone.

As we got up and running, events overseas moved swiftly. For months, U.S., Egyptian, and Saudi pressure on the government of Sudan had been ramped up as a result of Bin Laden's operations. Seeking an easing of that pressure—and an opening to ask for aid money—the

Sudanese approached U.S. officials and asked what they could do to thaw relations between the two countries.

Expelling Bin Laden stood at the top of our list, as well as the Saudis'. The government of Sudan at first offered to send him back to Saudi Arabia, but the Saudis refused. They'd already stripped him of citizenship and sent him into exile for his anti-monarchist activities. Though he had plenty of friends or supporters in high places in the Saudi regime, bringing him home was not an option.

In May 1996, the Sudanese government pushed Bin Laden out the door. He had only one place to go: back to Afghanistan. His departure was forced and swift, mainly so the Sudanese government could sweep up his assets. The fact is, the Sudanese regime, which Bin Laden greased so generously with millions of dollars' worth of bribes, made out like bandits by kicking him out of their country. He left behind all his local businesses, his farm, his construction equipment, and all his property. He had very little time to sell anything. What wasn't just abandoned, he liquidated for a fraction of their worth. We never knew exactly how much the Sudanese clipped Osama for, but it reportedly could have been upward of $300 million.

With his financial empire struck a major blow, Bin Laden faced other challenges as well after leaving Sudan. He had since been opposed by another radical Islamic group known as the Takfiris. They tried to kill him on several occasions in Khartoum. They tried again and failed shortly after he returned to Afghanistan. Subsequently, other would-be assassins made clumsy efforts to kill him. All unsuccessful.

That summer, Bin Laden issued his fatwa and declaration of war against the United States, citing our presence in the Middle East. He quickly orchestrated a terrorist fundraising drive from Afghanistan, tapping into donors and networks he'd developed during the war against the Soviets in the 1980s. He was assisted by elements inside Pakistan ████████████████████ and by the Taliban, who proved to be ideological fellow travelers with Bin Laden. With the Taliban's support, he virtually took over Ariana Afghan Airlines, the country's only air carrier. He quickly turned it into what Mike called "a terrorist taxi service." Its aging fleet of Russian-made aircraft routinely started transporting jihadists, weapons, ammunition, cash, and Afghan opium through Pakistan and the United Arab Emirates. While he took a significant financial hit leaving Sudan, having his own air transport capability supercharged his effort to spread holy war throughout the world. In Afghanistan, he was also much safer from us.

In Khartoum, at least we could keep eyes on Bin Laden, but once he returned to Afghanistan, our ability to conduct surveillance degraded considerably. Ultimately, that led the CIA to reach out to Ahmad Shah Massoud, an old ally from the Soviet-Afghan War who by then led the opposition to the Taliban known as the Northern Alliance.

He was safe in Afghanistan, protected by his Taliban friends, and our opportunity to take him out had passed.

Mike grew increasingly frustrated after Bin Laden's declaration of war. We had adequate funding and resources, but the bureaucracy at Langley stood like a stone wall against the things he wanted to do to counter the Saudi terrorist. The best officers and leaders that I knew at the Agency were black belts in bureaucracy. They were well versed in the subtle art of maneuvering to achieve their objectives—who to cultivate, who to talk to, how to do it, where to go for support and resources—it is a crucial skill to have for anyone working in a large organization. Mike didn't have that skill. He attacked bureaucracy head-on, bull-rushing it with the belief that sheer force of will and determination would get the results he wanted. Too often, it did not. Instead, it burned some bridges for him, and he gradually turned bitter.

At the same time, the threat Bin Laden posed increased dramatically. In November, a bomb planted under a bridge in the Philippines narrowly missed killing President Bill Clinton, who was there for a series of economic meetings. The bomb conspiracy led back to Bin Laden, though that wasn't revealed publicly until a decade later.

Early the next year, as Bin Laden's war against the United States began to heat up, my family suffered a serious medical crisis that demanded my attention. The frantic pace at Alec Station was something I couldn't maintain and deal with my family's situation simultaneously. It forced me to make a choice. I love my country, I loved my job and career, but my family always came first in such situations. With great reluctance, I went to Mike, explained my situation, and told him I needed to be reassigned to something with a more regular schedule. He understood and was very sorry to see me go. As a parting gift, he gave me a book that he inscribed:

*Ric, for the rest of my career, your departure will serve as irrefutable proof that nothing changes for the better. Please accept my sincere thanks and know that my respect, affection, and admiration go with you. God Bless you and yours always.*

*Scheuer.*

I moved over to serve as the Deputy Chief of the CTC's Management Group, which oversaw all personnel, budget and fiscal, security, and logistics for the CTC. For the next seven months, I worked an average 0700–1700 desk job with no midnight calls. Initially, I missed the action, but I soon came to love the job. It gave me newfound respect for the support elements that make all ops possible. I also got to see the quality of people in the group, many of whom I'm still friends with to this day. Honorable mention to my then boss, Roy P., and our Chief of Personnel, Stephany—they were great leaders beloved by their crew.

Not long after our family medical crisis stabilized, King Ralph asked me to come back and work East Asia Division, initially as his XO (executive officer) and subsequently, against the North Koreans again. I gladly headed back into the fray.

Meanwhile, Alec Station remained the central clearinghouse for all things Bin Laden for years to come. I was proud to have been a plank owner with Mike and the other members of the team. We laid the foundation for the pursuit and destruction of al-Qaeda, a fight that some of us saw through to the end in 2011 when, based on CIA/CTC, UBL Task Force, intelligence, Bin Laden was finally killed by a Naval Special Warfare team in Pakistan.

It was a pursuit that came at a heavy cost to our old team, however. Mike's frustrations with the Agency and the Bush administration's policies erupted after 9/11. He penned, anonymously, a furious book entitled *Imperial Hubris* after the invasion of Iraq. Embittered by his bureaucratic battles, he turned on some of the very people who'd supported him for years. He left the Agency in 2004 and became an outspoken critic of it. He published several more books, but became increasingly shrill in his public comments, and that alienated most of his old colleagues. I tried to reach out to him for years to no avail. I finally stopped after watching a documentary where during an interview he harshly criticized the ops officers of our original team and the Directorate of Operations in general. Seeing him say those things wounded me deeply and forced me to shelve my admiration of Scheuer.

Our targeting officers pursued Bin Laden for years, long after the USS *Cole* had been bombed, our two embassies in Africa blown up, and of course, 9/11. Jennifer Matthews, among a few select others, became the institutional encyclopedia of all things Bin Laden after Mike left the Agency. They worked to track him and al-Qaeda from late 1995 until the Obama years.

In 2009, Jennifer was sent to be Chief of Base at Khost, Afghanistan's Camp Chapman, the Agency's hub in theater for pursuing Bin Laden and al-Qaeda. Keep in mind, Jenn was an analyst, not a field officer. She'd been deployed on temporary duty overseas a few times in the past, ███████████████████████████████████, but she hadn't been trained operationally for the field. But Khost was where the Bin Laden action was, and her senior-most superior gave her the base.

On December 30, 2009, a Jordanian asset who appeared to have high-level information on al-Qaeda and Bin Laden was brought to Khost. ███████████████████████

██████████████████████████████████████

███████████████████████

█████████████████████ Jenn was eager to meet and debrief him. She gave
orders to the base security that he was to be treated with trust and respect. There would be no searching his vehicle when he arrived, and no
pat-down of his person.

Dr. Humam Khalil Abu-Mulal al-Balawi, the asset, was picked
up at the Pakistan border by Camp Chapman's Chief of External Security and driven to the base. The vehicle passed three layers of security checkpoints, where they were waved through as per Jenn's orders.
When the car arrived at the heart of the base, sixteen people, including
the Deputy Station Chief for Kabul, were waiting together for the doctor's arrival.

When the car stopped beside the waiting crowd, al-Balawi got out
and detonated a suicide vest. Nine people in the crowd died in the blast.

Medics helicoptered all the victims, including Jennifer, to nearby
FOB Salerno, where an air force surgeon named Dr. Joshua Alley fought
desperately to save her life. She arrived with massive shrapnel wounds
to her abdomen and neck, one leg broken and shredded by the explosion. She had no pulse. They tried to open an airway, but her wounds
were too severe. She died on the operating table.

It was one of the worst days in CIA history. Seven of our brothers
and sisters perished in the attack. A subsequent investigation discovered
we'd been played all along. Al-Balawi was a triple agent, to whom the
Taliban and al-Qaeda fed real and actionable intelligence in order to
build his credibility in the eyes of his handlers. They sacrificed some of
their own people to establish al-Balawi's value and get him passed up to
their real target: the CIA base at Camp Chapman. It was an extraordi-
narily ruthless and cunning operation. Both al-Qaeda and the Taliban
publicly took credit for the attack in its aftermath.

The loss of our friends and colleagues was already enough of a
gut punch to last a lifetime. Jenn's death still wears on me, and I know
it lingers in others, too. She was an extraordinary officer and patriot

whose death proved a major setback to our effort to find and kill Bin Laden. She was also a dear friend to us all.

I was long gone from the Agency when all this happened, so I am in no position to pass judgment. However, according to very senior colleagues active at the time, this incident could have been avoided. If the standard security procedures had been used, there was no way al-Balawi would have gotten close to Jenn and the others waiting for him. Instead, basic procedures were waived for fear they would be seen by a VIP asset as a sign of disrespect.

The Agency studied the debacle and conducted a thorough investigation. A litany of lessons learned came out of it, but I am told that nobody suffered any career consequences. Perhaps there were none to be had, just hard lessons to be learned and never forgotten.

# 23

## THE MEAT EATERS' SHANGRI-LA

*Langley, Virginia*

*Summer and Fall 2000*

In one of Langley's many long corridors, a casual friend approached. Suit and tie, polished shoes, hair clipped short. Tall, handsome, fit. He was a guy with a plaque in his office that read *Death Before Dishonor* with a skull and grenade on it.

He greeted me warmly and said, "Heard you're going out to Shangri-La. Is that true?"

"Yes, it is," I answered.

He smiled and shook his head. "Well, I'd love to be out there with you. But you know . . . I have kids."

So did I. And he knew it.

I wanted to say, *What makes you think you'd make the cut for my team, pencil dick?* We were going into the worst terrorist shithole on the planet. The only guys I wanted with me were the ones who wanted—needed—to be out there scrapping with those murderous sons of bitches.

Instead of de-balling him, I held my tongue. Long ago, I learned to pick my battles. A posturing ride-along was not worth the words. I smiled and wished him well. He did the same.

Even within the ranks of the CIA, some people are born for the fray, and some people aren't. It isn't a bad thing; we each have our strengths and weaknesses. But when you pretend to be a meat eater, yet have never served in the military, never been a case officer, and never spent much time overseas, the poseur factor gets you little respect in our world.

The CIA was always made up of a wide range of personalities: action-oriented operators, cerebral analysts at home in a world of intel puzzle pieces, leaders, managers, and support types. There was space in the Agency for nearly every temperament and personality because the range of what we did required that level of broad diversity.

At times, we clashed more than we meshed, and the tension between the headquarters types and the field operators created bruising bureaucratic battles. Through the dynamics and evolutions of our leadership, the level of risk we took as an Agency waxed and waned. The same happened on an individual level. The longer into our careers, the more risk-averse some of us became.

In 2000, we'd survived eight years of declining national willingness to take risks overseas. The Cold War was over. We were supposed to be enjoying the peace dividend. To some, it seemed our deadliest adversaries were long gone, toppled by the weight of their systems' own ineptitudes. The KGB was once ruthless and cunning and sometimes outmaneuvered us. They played by rules that repelled most Americans. They won their share of battles in the shadow world. We still won the war.

For those of us who loved the field and found meaning in the streets of far-off cities, an ocean away from the safe routine that we Americans considered the norm, there would always be a place for us in the Agency. Those of us who need the juice found ways to get to the pointy end of the spear no matter our rank or place in the bureaucracy.

In 1998, we aimed those spears in three main directions: at North Korea, Iran, and Islamic terrorism. North Korea's nuclear weapons program, massive conventional army, and bizarre cult of leadership presented an existential threat of war that could potentially result in hundreds of thousands of casualties. To this day, North Korea remains one of the most destabilizing threats to peace in the world. In 2000, they were a more regional threat than they are today now that they have had two more decades to develop their long-range, nuclear-tipped missile program, not to mention their capable, and profitable, cyber capabilities.

The CIA's other spear pointed directly at the other emerging threat at the time. Radical Islamic terrorism at the turn of the century morphed into a deadly new enemy, one capable of inflicting death and destruction on thousands of people in a single attack. Osama bin Laden demonstrated that in 1998 when his minions orchestrated the simultaneous truck bombings of our embassies in Tanzania and Kenya that murdered more than two hundred people and wounded at least another four thousand.

There were those in the Agency like Scheuer who saw this new iteration of radical Islamic terrorism as the biggest and most dangerous enemy facing America. After the embassy bombings, he reportedly got into a shouting match with George Tenet, the director of the CIA at the time. That row was the culmination of a series that ultimately derailed Mike's promising career. Richard B. took over the Bin Laden unit and brought it back into the building, where it shared space with the CTC.

Tenet also brought in a new leader to run the CTC. Cofer Black, who'd been Chief of Station in Khartoum in the mid-'90s just before the founding of Alec Station, received the job. He was a hardened, aggressive officer whose firsthand knowledge of Bin Laden and al-Qaeda made him a perfect fit for the position. He was the last COS to have successfully surveilled the Saudi terrorist and even avoided an attempted al-Qaeda hit on him in late 1995 shortly before he left Sudan.

Rounding out the team, besides Cofer Black and Hank Crumpton, was Ben Bonk and Ed W. One Chief (Cofer), three Deputies: primary (Ben), one for law enforcement (Ed), and one for ops (Hank).

Ben was Cofer's deputy and arguably the smartest man I ever met. He was also the nicest man and one of the few in our building about whom I never heard anyone speak anything but praise for his character, intellect, and leadership. He was also an atypical analyst. He drove a vintage 1963 Corvette convertible, carried and could shoot his Colt 1911 A-1. His sports passion, like mine, was Formula 1 racing, a hobby we shared by attending the U.S. Grand Prix in Indianapolis. Unfortunately, we lost Ben to cancer a few years later.

From almost the beginning, the CTC always included a senior FBI agent as part of our front office. They were all top-notch: George A., Chuck F. (who also spent lots of time at the UBL), and, of course, Ed. Ed was a handsome, charismatic, cigar-smoking gent. He was also one of the most aggressive defenders of the CTC and often took sides against his Bureau when turf battles were fought.

The change in leadership was part of Tenet's plan to take a more aggressive posture against radical Islamic terrorism. His plan included returning to Afghanistan to recruit new allies and reconnect with old ones from the Soviet-Afghan war era to develop intelligence, surveillance, and operations against Bin Laden's organization there.

I had missed all of these changes. After our family's medical situation stabilized, I'd returned to the Korea account to work again with King Ralph. We scored some of our best successes during the second tour, and it was one of my most rewarding times in the Agency.

Yet the pull of counterterror never left me. So when Hank, then Cofer Black's Chief of Operations, called me one day in mid-2000 and asked me if I'd be interested in taking over the CTC's International Terrorism Group, I jumped at the chance. The ITG covered every terror organization on the planet outside of al-Qaeda and Bin Laden. It focused on everything from Islamic jihad to the remnants of the Palestinian Black September movement to the Greek Marxist/terror guerrilla group known as 17 November.

The offer was even sweeter. Hank wanted to bring me back to the CTC for a year, then have me take his job when he moved out. If I did well, I'd go from running the ITG to being the CTC's Chief of Operations. It was an incredible offer, made even better because I'd be working for two of our most aggressive leaders in Cofer and Hank. Both men were direct, aggressive, and had little tolerance for red tape. They also were bureaucratic black belts, so when the red tape fouled the way, they knew the best ways to cut through it.

Hank was a Southern gentleman who came up through the ranks in the waning years of the Cold War. He was the youngest officer to ever graduate from the Farm, and he spent much of his career in the field, including a particularly difficult assignment investigating al-Qaeda's 1998 African embassy bombings. Fit and health conscious, I never saw him drink alcohol. To this day, he often grabs his sat phone, a rifle, and a fishing rod and vanishes into the wilderness for weeks at a time, hunting, tracking, and fishing his way through areas few humans ventured. He was my kind of guy, a man devoted to his country and walking his own path of destiny.

Cofer was a man who never lost an argument. He could verbally spar with anyone and outmaneuver them with his cerebral intellect and lightning-quick wit. That made him one of the most formidable bureaucratic black belts in the building. His nickname was "the Hulkster," and his frame matched the moniker. He had the heart and soul of a lion, and his profound intelligence made him a double threat. While I'd only met him once years back when I was working the South American accounts, everyone in the Agency knew his sterling reputation.

I would be part of an exceptional, once-in-a-lifetime team. I wanted this job badly. But first, I had to break the news to King Ralph.

When I talked to him about it, he was totally supportive, even though I'd be leaving the Koreas a year earlier than planned. He knew Hank's offer not only was a career opportunity but that it played to my strengths.

It was all I hoped for and more. Cofer, Hank, and I worked well together from the outset. Their loyalty and trust formed the bedrock of the relationship we built, and Cofer proved to be one of the finest leaders I'd ever met. After a few weeks on the job, I'd have gone to hell and back for Cofer.

As things shook out, I got that chance.

I rejoined the CTC in the summer of 2000, right as it started to take the front-row seat in our national defense. Tenet's focus on terrorism following the embassy bombings freed up resources and gave opportunities to develop new capabilities. This included getting back to where the terrorists hung out—Afghanistan, for one. "Shangri-La" for another.

For security reasons, I still can't share Shangri-La's real name, but it was a city in Africa in a nation ruled by Islamic radicals who had long since allowed terrorists to live openly in their country—provided they pay a bit of protection money to the government.

At a crucial time in this new war, the CIA went blind. No surveillance, no operations. No intel ████████████████████████ on the jihad network. This was a major weakness that Tenet, Cofer Black, and Hank wanted fixed.

Just before I joined the team, Cofer sent a small contingent into Shangri-La to reopen the station and get it operational again. Right after I arrived and took over the ITG, Shangri-La's new Chief of Station returned to Langley to brief Cofer on what he'd done over the past few months in country. Hank and I attended the brief. The COS's report did not sit well with Cofer at all. In fact, the COS's situational briefing on Shangri-La contradicted everything else we were getting from SIGINT and sources outside of Shangri-La. ███████████████

████████████████████████████████████████████

███████████████████

That brief was one of the few times I saw Cofer lose his temper.

After the COS left the meeting, Cofer took me aside and said, "We need to replace him. Find somebody for the job."

Cofer outlined what he had in mind. Usually, this would have been a position for a GS-15, but he wanted somebody with more horsepower in the role. He tasked me with finding a senior officer willing to assemble a team that could go in and establish our presence, develop assets, and get eyes on what these religious fanatics were doing.

I set about doing that. For several weeks, I worked to find an SIS-level operations officer who wanted this difficult assignment. I'd like to say a swarm of hard chargers applied for the position, but nobody did. To be fair, most senior officers already had commensurate positions to their rank. And it was a hardship post—no wives and families, with few recreational opportunities and even fewer cultural experiences to be had beyond lots of ugly, enduring poverty. The only thing it offered was danger and the chance to go toe-to-toe with the miscreant assholes who would do our country harm.

That said, after my tenure in Shangri-La, we had no problem getting several type-A ops officers to follow suit. For years after us, they continued to build on each other's successes.

That September, Carmen and I went running together. We had made this part of our routine since the family's medical crisis. It gave us a chance to talk, spend some time together without the kids, and get some good exercise.

I explained the situation. Important slot overseas. Nobody volunteered for it. I detailed the reasons, then told Carmen why I wanted it for myself. I may have been a senior officer by then, but my heart always lay in the field. I knew I still had enough in the tank to do this job, and do it well. But leaving the family for six to eight months would put a heavy burden on Carmen, and I didn't want to do that to her so soon after what we'd been through together.

After I finished, she stopped and turned to me. "Ric, I know you. This is who you are. You need it. Go do it."

There is nothing like having this kind of support at home, and I knew how blessed I was to have it. Life in the CIA is difficult for families. Divorces are common. Somehow, Carmen and I weathered every storm together. She was one of the rarest women I've ever known—a person who knew that my sense of service to our country formed the bedrock of my identity. Instead of resenting it and the time it took away from the family, she embraced it. It was who she'd married, the man who ran to danger. She once even told a friend that, through me, she lived the life she wished she could. Notice she did not tell *me* that!

Without any hesitation, she let me go do this one last crazy tour. Looking back now, while Shangri-La proved all I'd hoped and more, I regret leaving the family for as long as I did. My absence created hardships back home we hadn't anticipated, and Carmen paid the price. Still, Shangri-La was central to the fight against the jihadists, and that's where I needed to be in the moment—especially when nobody else wanted the job.

The next day, I went to see Cofer. "Hey, boss," I said, "I've found somebody for the Shangri-La job."

"Oh yeah? Who?" he asked.

"Me."

He looked at me in silence for a long moment. Finally, he said, "Ric, are you really sure you want to do that?"

"Hell yes."

"Then let's pull a team together and get your training."

"Hooyah, sir."

In about a week, we assembled an eight-person team: five operations officers, my deputy, a logistics specialist, and our analyst. Two of our ops officers arrived freshly minted from the Farm. They may have been rookies, but they were moon-baying hard chargers of the finest order. Ranger was a young officer who could have been Daniel Craig's doppelgänger. Same haircut, same facial shape and structure. He walked with a jaunty, almost cocky hitch to his stride that telegraphed he took zero shit from anyone.

No wonder, before he joined the Agency, he served in the U.S. Army, became a Ranger, and fought in Somalia. He was a captain during the Bloody Sunday Black Hawk Down battle in Mogadishu in 1993. He came to us as a combat-hardened veteran. Wiry but whip-strong, he could run like a Tomahawk missile—I swear he had jets on his feet.

Ranger served as our team's paramilitary officer.

We paired him with Hunter, an experienced and brilliant officer in whom King Ralph saw tremendous potential. Yet he was troubled and came with some baggage. He'd yet to be promoted to GS-13, and he was the last in his class at the Farm to reach that grade. Personal demons probably hindered his advancement. Quick to anger, he was a glass-half-empty kind of guy. Somebody once said Hunter could be alone in a closet and get in an argument with himself. Nevertheless, I saw the same potential King Ralph saw, so we pulled him into the team, and I made him a project. Meanwhile, Hunter would serve as Ranger's mentor and coach—a role he filled quite well.

John, our other rookie, never served in the military. He joined the Agency as a civilian, went through the Farm, and emerged eager and willing to do whatever was asked, including going to a shithole for his first tour. I assigned our DCOS to mentor John, and he did not disappoint. He scored some major operational successes (recruitments) in the months ahead.

I had told my officers that if I ever saw any of them in a Yellow state of mind, I would send their asses home in an "atrial flutter" (less than half a heartbeat in paramedic terms). John was a young lion, and he was hungry! There was no way he was going to be benched.

I remember once I was working out on the heavy bag we'd installed on a balcony that overlooked the compound. Undetected, I watched as John prowled the expanse between our residence compound and ███████████ building. His head on a swivel, forward-leaning stance and with a growl tattooed on his face. He made Doc Holliday look like a sissy. I could not have been prouder of John if he was my son.

Our analyst, Jeff, came to us with little to no operational experience. Given the level of threat we faced in Shangri-La, I made it a point to train Jeff as if he were one of our operations officers. In the weeks ahead, he went through ██████████ every range day and every tactical scenario thrown our way. Years later, I found out that during his retirement ceremony, he thanked me for allowing him to do some of the most exciting things he experienced during his CIA career. Hearing that meant a great deal to me. Jeff may have been an analyst, but he sure as hell fit in well with the ops team. In tough situations, we found him to be solid.

Before we headed to Shangri-La, the team deployed to ██████████ for thirty days of intensive training. This would be one of the hardest assignments in the Agency at the time, and we needed our skills honed to a razor's edge. We were sequestered in what amounted to a ██████████████████████████ compound ███████████ here we stayed in barracks, had our own chow hall and dayroom where we could hang out after our day's work. It was a perfect place to focus on the intensive level of training I knew we needed; plus, it gave us an opportunity to gel and bond as a team.

Going into this monthlong mini deployment, we crafted a general plan for what we wanted to focus on and develop. Then we handed our plan off to our two training instructors—Jimmy, who was another Black Hawk Down veteran of Delta Force, and my best friend, Frog, a steely-eyed veteran of Naval Special Warfare's SEAL teams. Steve B., a retired SEALs' Force Master Chief, was the senior-most NCOIC in the teams. These two exceptional characters designed one of the toughest training programs I'd ever seen during my time in the Agency.

Our days started with PT—usually a long run. From there, we spent hours on the range getting intensive trigger time. We all developed calluses on our index fingers, and collectively we must have fired tens of thousands of rounds by the end of our month.

In our final shooting competition, we were comparing our targets and scores. Ranger grew upset. I asked him what was wrong.

"I'm supposed to be your PM guy, and you outshot me!"

I did, but barely.

I loved that kind of butthurt. It signaled a hard-charging competitor all the way. I laughed and said, "Yeah, but you forget I came out of PM."

That mollified him, but from then on, our friendly rivalry on the range pushed us hard to become better and better with our weapons.

When not on the range, we went through total immersion in real-world tactical scenarios complete with role players, ████████████ ████████████████████

████████████████████ We learned the latest vehicular evasion techniques. We practiced shoving cars out of our way, learning that the best way to bash through that sort of roadblock was to aim for the rear axles.

I made a point of going through every scenario and iteration first. Leaders lead, they set the example. The mentors I'd had over the years drilled that into me. Now, I shared it with my own team. Going first also allowed me to understand the scenario and watch how my own guys handled it. I got to know their reactions, their thought processes, and how cool they were in tense situations.

Jimmy and Frog threw a lot of things at us. To simulate surprise, they put us in vehicles with welders' masks over our faces. The little glass viewing port would be taped over. We'd head over to the driving range like this, then at the right moment, they'd pull the masks off us and see how quickly we responded to the situation we found ourselves in.

In one of those scenarios, Jimmy and Frog set Hunter up for a particularly dangerous real-world situation. When they pulled the welder's mask off Hunter, he discovered a car sideways blocking the road ahead, while a second team blocked his rear in a huge truck. This is the best way to neutralize a target in a car—by setting up a mousetrap for the target vehicle between two other vehicles.

The move here would have been to barrel straight for the car's rear axle, T-bone it, and push it around to clear a path. Instead, Hunter suddenly reversed and went straight at the huge truck, bouncing into it, with no effect, time and time again. I was sitting in the back seat and stopped the exercise. Hunter was going to be buying us a lot of beers that night.

Hunter's outside-the-box thinking could sometimes be a double-edged sword. I noticed this during a couple of these scenarios, and I began to worry that we'd have to watch him closely when we got to Shangri-La. Still, his brainpower was sufficient to justify his participation, and his shooting was well above average.

One afternoon, I went through a vehicular scenario where I had a driver and I rode shotgun in a sedan. We rolled up on a checkpoint manned by some simulated militia types. This is a common feature in the developing world, and talking your way past these things required a little diplomacy. Delta Jimmy role-played one of the militia guys, Frog the other. And it was Jimmy who strode up to the driver's-side door. Now, you never have your window rolled down in these sorts of real-world situations, but for the training reasons, we were supposed to have it cracked in order to facilitate better communication.

My driver didn't do that. He was a cheeky bastard who always looked for an angle and advantage in these training scenarios, so he kept the window firmly rolled up.

Jimmy tapped on the window, gun in hand but not pointed at us, and said something I couldn't hear. The next thing I knew, my driver shouted, "Contact left!"

In a flash, I threw open the passenger door, bailed out of the car, rolled, and came up over the roof of the vehicle, weapon drawn. I put two Sim rounds right onto Jimmy's face mask at nose level, spun, and put another one into his backup man. Both down, the scenario EN-DEXED (ended). We gathered with the role players for the after-action critique.

"How'd we do?" I asked, smiling at the splotch of paint my Simms rounds had left on Jimmy's face mask.

"Um. Well, your solution worked," Jimmy said hesitantly. "And after all, you are the boss; it was your decision to engage, and engage you did," he added, holding up his face mask.

"Was that not what you wanted from us?" I asked.

"Well, sir, we just wanted some money. We weren't looking for a fight."

My jaw dropped. It was not uncommon to be forcibly panhandled at gunpoint in the developing world. Long experience with these sorts of things had proven the best response was to avoid a fight and hand over a wad of cash. A firefight is always a risky proposition, especially if the checkpoint is in the middle of some lawless, Wild West kind of third-world city. That could quickly get out of hand.

We should have just given them the money.

"Well, you won anyway," Jimmy said.

"Yeah," I replied, anger growing, "but I just got us into a gun battle in the middle of town."

Jimmy nodded. "Yep. That's the lesson learned here."

I chewed my driver a new asshole for that one. Those were the kind of mistakes that, if made in the real world, get people killed and cause international incidents. There would be none of that on my watch.

We worked for thirty days straight, seven days a week, twelve- to fifteen-hour days. We loved every minute of it. When we'd get back to our team area, we'd grab some chow and sit around marveling at the fact that we got paid to do this stuff. Anyone with a pulse and a need for action would have been in heaven. I saw every day on the faces of our guys that we had the right team in place. They loved this stuff. Especially Jeff.

In our few hours of downtime, we simulated the atmospherics we'd face in Shangri-La. No TV. No satellite. If we wanted to relax, we'd have to do it with VHS movies. We brought a few goofy comedies with us ████████████, but the one flick we returned to time and again, first in our thirty-day workup cycle, then later in Shangri-La, was the 1993 epic *Tombstone*.

We watched that film so many times we memorized the lines. The screenplay is simply brilliant, salted with Old West slang we absolutely loved. "I'm your Huckleberry" and "Well, Johnny Ringo, you look like somebody just walked over your grave" became part of our team's internal lexicon. There were plenty of times in the weeks ahead we just needed to unwind with something stupid and funny like *Van Wilder*, which starred Ryan Reynolds and was definitely *not* PC! Yet it wouldn't be more than a few days, a week tops, before we busted out *Tombstone* again. Part of it I suppose was that we knew we'd be going into a modern-day version of that Wild West town—a lawless area filled with bad guys bent on our destruction. The rules in Shangri-La mirrored those in Tombstone. There was no rule of law, only men exerting their will with the barrel of a rifle.

We emerged ████████████ a cohesive, disciplined team. We were our own kind of Band of Brothers, bonded over our many shared experiences and hardships Jimmy and Frog threw our way. It was the best training I'd ever been through in the Agency.

In November 2000, a few weeks after al-Qaeda nearly sank the U.S. Navy destroyer USS *Cole* in Yemen with a suicide bombing attack, we boarded our flight for Shangri-La. The war in the shadow world was heating up, and we were flying into the middle of it to rebuild our Agency's capabilities in hostile territory. I knew we were ready.

# 24

## TOMBSTONE RULES

*Shangri-La*
*November 2000–May 2001*
The ride through Shangri-La in the armored sedans that picked us up at the airport and took us to our new homes in a gated, guarded compound was like nothing I'd ever experienced. I'd seen poverty in the developing world throughout my career—South America, the Philippines, Cambodia, Vietnam—but nothing prepared me for Shangri-La.

Trash rotted in the streets. It was everywhere, including in the trees. As we left the airport, I saw the fence surrounding it was peppered with plastic bags, blown there by the hot African winds. "Know what the national flower is here?" one of our escorts asked us when he saw me staring at the fence.

"What?"

"The plastic bag."

No joke. Every tree seemed to blossom with plastic bags speared on their bare limbs.

The city itself sat in a bowl of brownish haze, a mix of desert dust and pollution that made the atmosphere even more oppressive than the 110-degree heat. There were few traffic lights, few paved roads, many without sidewalks. There was a semblance of a central downtown, but the rest was just a long, sprawling jumble of low-built, drab houses and shacks interspersed with open-air markets rife with swarms of thick, black flies.

Most everyone on the street or in the markets appeared malnourished. Some, shirtless and shoeless, others dressed in traditional African or Muslim clothing. Others, reduced to filthy rags, wore the scars of unending warfare and violence—burns, missing limbs, and other disfiguring injuries. Starvation stalked the side streets and refugee camps that ringed the city. Families here sometimes became so desperate they would leave their children at orphanages as a last hope that they may find steady meals.

Salted into the crowds were soldiers and security types, hefting rusty, poorly maintained weapons. Other armed men stood in front of buildings or guarded compounds from their high concrete walls. Guns and flies were the only things Shangri-La had in abundance. In roughly forty years of independence, this country had only known a few years of peace. The rest of the time, a civil war racked the nation, creating famine and displacing millions while killing at least two million more.

The sense of hopelessness was palpable here, and we hadn't even gotten out of the cars yet. It was a mixed bag of poverty, third-world despair, and evidence of a state so dysfunctional that it officially discouraged taking photographs of its own capital.

We rolled to our compound, the guards opened the front gate, and we settled into the well-appointed town houses. This place would be our only respite from the realities of this hellhole. We had a basic gym, a swimming pool, and clean homes to live in.

As we drove in, I noticed a small kiosk just outside the gate and across the street. Inside sat a couple of men watching us intently.

Just because you're paranoid doesn't mean there aren't people after you.

━━━━━━━━━━━━━━━━━━━━━━━━━━━━━━━━━━━━━━━━━━━

the few American diplomats here operated out of an old consulate compound whose location was not as publicly known. The embassy ███████████████████████████████████ still dealt with the occasional walk-in traffic. The very few State Department functionaries would move back and forth between the consulate and the embassy as needed.

. You could taste the stale air and moldy dust. It gave us an eerie feeling to be inside the place.

How do you pick up pieces like this and start an entire intelligence network? It was an immense challenge for our small team. We set to work figuring it out.

Moving around the city would not be easy. The street maps published on Shangri-La were out of date and inaccurate. There were hardly any street signs or even street names. We would have to rely on rudimentary GPS systems and build our own maps of waypoints and landmarks. For the meantime, we'd have to simply factor in that we would get lost whenever we hit the streets.

Another complication was our light skin. We stood out here in Africa to a degree that made us a curiosity to the locals. Dodging surveillance teams and avoiding terrorist attacks and random street violence would be a lot more complicated as a result of the racial differences between our team members and the people of the city. Fortunately, we brought a solution with us. Some truly clever special-effects types had crafted for us a whole kit of disguises. A couple of minutes in a bathroom could transform me from a graying white guy into a sub-Saharan Black African. The disguises would not hold up at speaking range, but for vehicular operations around the city, they were perfect. We even had long-sleeved gloves that matched the color of our face masks. We could evade easy identification even if a hostile car pulled right alongside us.

While there was plenty of crime and violence in Shangri-La, that would not be the biggest threat we faced. Every major Islamic terror group from Hezbollah to Bin Laden's al-Qaeda maintained a presence here. The city was almost a throwback to the pirate bays in the Caribbean during the era of the Spanish Armada. They networked and cooperated, shared intel and resources. Some of the most notorious assassins and terror leaders went to ground here to avoid capture.

Overlapping all these groups was the host nation's security and intelligence services, plus its army. As we studied the situation, it grew obvious to us that there was little difference between these national institutions and the terror groups. They mingled and worked together, shared information, and carried out operations together. Early on, I met an army colonel who exemplified this. To our faces, he was friendly enough, but behind the scenes, he'd orchestrated several operations that had killed Americans. Part of our responsibilities included meeting with liaison types from the government, and he was one of them. I will never forget sitting across from him, wanting only to put a bullet between his eyes as justice for what he'd done to our fellow Americans.

Unfortunately, that doesn't fly in the real world, only spy novels.

We didn't have many friends in Shangri-La, either. ████████ had a presence, but they were supremely arrogant (no surprise there, it is a national trait) and played their cards close to the vest. They essentially refused to work with us, though their home nation was ostensibly one of our closest post–World War II allies.

In contrast, we received significant assistance from a surprising source. They turned out to be our closest allies in the city. They provided us with leads, information, and support whenever they could.

While they were not of any intelligence value, there was a small presence in country, and they welcomed us warmly. In a desolate place like Shangri-La, they gave us access to some much-needed socializing.

Most of the time, when not on the job, we were stuck behind the walls of our compound, limited to whatever entertainment we could find. Usually, that meant recycling our VHS movie collection.

On the advice of the ▮▮▮▮▮▮▮, we hired a local chef they recommended—▮▮▮▮▮▮▮ Normally, part of an overseas tour includes cultural immersion. We eat the local food, we visit bars and go see shows in our off-hours time. That wasn't possible in Shangri-La. There were few restaurants and fewer hotels. Eating the local food could be dangerous to us, and patronizing those restaurants served as choke points, just like it had been back in my Contra days when the Sandinistas orchestrated that hit I was lucky to avoid.

▮▮▮▮▮▮▮▮▮▮▮▮▮▮▮▮▮▮▮▮▮▮▮▮▮▮▮▮▮▮▮▮
▮▮▮▮▮▮▮▮▮▮
▮▮▮▮▮▮▮▮▮▮▮▮▮▮▮▮▮▮▮▮▮▮▮▮▮▮▮▮▮▮

▮▮▮▮▮ For the next six months, we ate almost all our meals within the compound.

Meanwhile, the men in the kiosk kept a careful eye on us. We watched them back, sometimes sending a surveillance team to the roof to see what they were doing. Watching the watchers watching us became a routine part of life in Shangri-La.

To discover others observing us, we used ▮▮▮▮▮▮▮▮ ▮▮▮▮▮ teams who deployed to Shangri-La for a few weeks at a time. They'd come and go so the locals wouldn't see familiar faces on the streets. These guys were exceptional at their job.

Beyond the government-directed static watchers at the city's un-
avoidable choke points (areas in any given city that we have to routinely
cross), we also soon established the surveillance patterns of several local
government types following us. This was actually fairly easy, as they
had limited resources, with very clumsy and blatant surveillance tactics. In short order, we had identified and memorized the vehicles they
frequented, along with their preferred staging areas. We'd leave our
compound, drive through the city, and sure enough, the usual suspects'
car would tag along, a couple of goons inside.

We pretended we didn't notice them, then played a little game.
They ran their operations on a shoestring and didn't have much money
for gas. So we'd lead them on wild-goose chases until their tanks ran
low and they aborted the tail.

Those were the government guys. The terror groups had eyes everywhere, too. We could sometimes deduce the official surveillance from the
jihadists, but not always. Everyone watched everyone else in Shangri-La.

Of course, the watchers could turn violent at any moment. I told
my guys over and over to stay at Yellow and be ready to move to Orange in a heartbeat. The fact was, to avoid being prey, you gotta look
like a carnivore. We made sure we postured aggressively to discourage
any surprise attacks.

One day, as we returned to our compound in two armored vehicles, we picked up a tail. We watched the two cars behind us as we
approached our gate. One suddenly broke off and looped around ahead

of us through some side streets. As we stopped at our compound gates and radioed our guards the security password, one of the surveillance cars suddenly reappeared and came speeding toward us from the right. Simultaneously, the second car sped toward us from the left. Both were driving well beyond the reasonable speed for that terrain in an aggressive, focused manner that suggested we were about to be attacked. Or probed.

They were in for a surprise. All bite, no bark. That was my team.

"Guns up, everyone out!" I ordered. All six passenger doors of our two vehicles suddenly flung open as we bailed out, fanned out, dropped to a knee, and leveled our long guns at the approaching cars. The "attackers" inside had no stomach for that. Both surveillance vehicles pulled tire-squealing one-eighties and bolted out of sight.

Message delivered: We are not the victim type. The watchers never tried that again. At the next meeting with our "local counterparts," we reported the incident in great detail. They of course acted indignant and promised to look into the incident, and even offered us protection. My deputy (one of our few Arabic speakers), smiled and said, "It's okay, we can take care of ourselves."

Often, our missions entailed confirming some piece of SIGINT we'd received. A fragment of a conversation heard over a cell phone or radio might indicate a particular place was being used by a terrorist cell as a safe house. We'd go and case the target location, noting license plates and taking photos. We would add the geolocation to our files

Very slowly, we began to build files on the local bad guys, their homes, vehicles, and so on. Still, it was fragmentary intel at best.

Of course, simultaneously, our officers were developing local sources. Not an easy task in this environment, but we indeed succeeded in resuscitating some former contacts and even recruiting some new sources. Some were volunteers, others were classical, full-cycle recruitments. For obvious reasons, I can't discuss this any further.

We needed people inside these organizations, local government and terrorist organizations alike, to gain a real understanding of them. Jihadist groups are the hardest to penetrate because they are true believers. They know each other intimately. They're insulated and insular. Outsiders aren't trusted, and insiders are almost always loyal to the death, so penetrating them is exceptionally difficult.

In Shangri-La, though, money talked. The true believers in each jihad group were sustained by a network of locals, who sometimes came to us with tidbits of information they were willing to share in return for some cash. These are called *walk-ins*—people who would come to the embassy gate and wanted to talk and bargain.

Walk-ins are like panning for gold. You can sift and sift day after day to find nothing but sand. But every once in a while, a nugget turns up in your pan.

All the operational members of the team spent many hours over at the embassy talking to these walk-ins. It was never a fun process. Most were grifters with nothing to offer, looking to spin a good story for a quick bit of cash. We'd bring them inside, search them very thoroughly, then sit them down and listen to their tale.

We cross-checked their stories with questions we already knew the answers to. Sometimes, we showed them photos of alleged members of the group they were reporting on to see if they could identify some real targets or guess and pick fictitious characters we included in the photo piles. Most failed these tests, and we knew they were full of shit.

We did have a couple of nuggets come through the embassy gate. Most had one or two pieces of the puzzle they traded for quick cash. Transaction complete, they'd be on their way and we never saw them again. However, a select and valued few looked like they could be promising longer-term assets. In their case, being seen around our embassy could get them killed.

For these, we had to implement "high-threat meeting" protocols. These sensitive operations were based on complex tradecraft disciplines and not easy to carry out under the usual surveillance to which we were subjected.

In a place like Shangri-La, a twenty-first-century outlaw kingdom like our Tombstone once was, you trusted others at your own peril. We made a point of never trusting anyone. Our assets could have been compromised and turned, their families threatened if they did not work against us. They could have become embittered because we weren't paying them what they thought they were worth. They could have been playing us all along, waiting for a moment to detonate a suicide vest or lead us into an ambush. We took no chances. Every asset was searched down to the spot under his ball sack before he ever got into a vehicle with one of our team.

██████████████████████████████████████████

████████████████████

████████████████████████████████████████████

███████████████████

███████████████████████████████████████████████

███████████████████

██████████████████████████████████████████████

███████████████

It was a thorough, time-consuming, and exhausting process just to get a nugget or two of information, but it had to be done. Meeting assets in a high-threat environment is an exceptionally dangerous thing. Keeping them alive required detailed planning and thorough execution. Our team became quite adept at it. There were times we had to abort one of these operations after we detected surveillance. In such moments, caution was the order of the day because our asset's life was at stake. Our own, too, potentially.

At times, we had walk-ins who came in and seemed to be probing us to see what we were interested in and what we might know. Terrorists know all about the walk-in process and use it to their advantage at times. It didn't usually work with us. We were careful about what we did and did not reveal, but the mere fact these groups were probing us demonstrated a level of sophistication that surprised us.

Gradually, thanks to the nuggets from a few of the walk-ins and the SIGINT tips that led us to safe houses, we developed a few threads we could pull. We started detecting individuals and vehicles connected with different organizations. ████████████████

████████████████████████████████████████

██████████████████████

████████████████████████████████████████

██████ Occasionally, a sympathetic local would dime them out. We put eyes on them whenever we could to see what they were up to, passing whatever we discovered up the chain of command.

These operations underscored the importance of having people on the ground able to get close to these terrorists. Satellite imagery, SIGINT, and drone coverage can only go so far. But once you mesh all the electronics and techno-wizardry with actual eyeballs in the street, then you have something. In Shangri-La, we meshed all those aspects of intelligence gathering together to find more threads to pull.

Of course, with Shangri-La being so wild and underdeveloped, it was never easy to do this. We'd sometimes get word that a known terrorist's car had been spotted at a particular house. The overhead surveillance couldn't give us an address, of course, just a roof color and a GPS coordinate. We'd have to drive into the neighborhood at night in full disguise, looking for the house with the right roof color. Once we finally found it, we'd take photos, note cars and license plates in the immediate area, and leave undetected. Setting up surveillance in these areas was out of the question; we would not survive the almost immediate compromise. Inevitably, a strange car in the neighborhood attracted unwanted attention.

"The average person in Shangri-La is sitting around waiting to die," somebody had told us. There is little work. Little entertainment. At night, it is so hot, everyone sleeps on their rooftops out in the open. So a car cruising down the street below made enough noise to be heard. Heads would pop up over the parapets to see who we were and what we were doing. Sometimes, they'd even approach our cars.

Another threat came from the complexities of driving in the city.

No matter how familiar we became with it, we always got lost on these ops. That alone could be a dangerous thing.

Shangri-La had a curfew at night. The government would set up snap checkpoints all over the city to enforce it. More than once, we stumbled into one of them. Sometimes, we'd be far enough away down the street from them that we could just turn around and get out of Dodge, but other times, we'd just have to go through. This meant quickly shucking off our disguises, hiding our weapons, and busting out our papers.

Once, I rolled up to one of these checkpoints, and an emaciated teenage soldier appeared at my window. When I showed him my ███████████ identification, he stared at it uncomprehendingly. He couldn't read. It took several minutes of me using the few words of the local language I knew to convey to him who I was and why I was allowed to be out after curfew. After several tense moments, he waved us through. This happened to almost everyone on the team several times during our tenure there. Those were some of our hairiest moments in country.

There were other checkpoints established by armed men around the city at night as well. Most consisted of a vehicle parked to partially block the road, a couple of guys with AKs out in front. As a car rolled up, they'd shake the occupants down for some cash or goods. After running into several of these on ops at night, we started carrying cartons of cigarettes with us. Smokes were currency in Shangri-La.

Leaving the city was forbidden by the government, unless we had express permission. Several times, we received missions that required us to go out into the countryside. We gained permission to go sightsee some historic location, then used our time outside the city to carry out the operational act. ██████████████████████████████████

████████████████████████████████████████████

████████████████████████

████████████████████████████████████████████

██████████ We went out deep into the desert to scout locations—dry lake beds being the best—and took lots of photos and measurements to satisfy the headquarters' taskings.

Those were interesting trips, like traveling back in time. We slept in our cars near some historic site and rose at dawn to see caravans of camels traveling across the desert in the distance. It felt a little like being in the movie *Lawrence of Arabia*. Again, I had to pinch myself as to my luck: the Cuban-born kid from Hialeah, looking for clandestine landing zones in a hostile desert for my beloved CIA. Hooyah!

There were few opportunities to see the country's history like that, or even get out and see any other part of it, for that matter. We used to joke, "How bad is Shangri-La? It's so bad you have to go to Chad for R&R."

A few of us were fortunate to get a chance to go SCUBA diving in the Red Sea, ███████████████████████████. The area was far off the tourist beaten path, so the reefs and sea life were absolutely stunning and pristine. Between dives, though, it was all business. We took note of all the ships coming and going from the port, the type of facilities, security postures, military readiness, and any other little detail Langley might have found useful.

In the six plus months I was there, I returned home to the family only once for a very short visit. I could see my absence was affecting Carmen badly, and I grew to regret taking the assignment because of the burden it placed on her. Still, this was the sort of place we all felt we were born to be in, a full-contact, free-for-all city filled with shadowy figures and menacing terror groups. Unraveling their secrets to keep other families safe was the path we had chosen and were meant to travel.

Those six months were some of the toughest of my career, both on my family and on me in the field. Yet we did good work. We achieved what Cofer Black wanted: a presence on the ground to keep eyes on the terrorist menagerie operating out of Shangri-La. We'd developed a couple of good assets, we'd scored some good nuggets of intelligence, and we successfully stood up the station on an aggressive footing. We'd shown the local security types that we could play the game a lot better than they could. We also delivered the message that we were *not* prey! If they messed with us, there would be consequences. Additionally, we'd developed new tactics and nuances to carrying out asset meetings in a high-threat environment that were later incorporated throughout the Agency.

Still, at the end of those months, I left Shangri-La with no remorse. The city and country were a case study of failed government, failed institutions riddled with corruption, and the desperate poverty that results from both. I've never seen a more hopeless place. I never want to see one like that again.

I remember there was a family living in a shipping container near the street entrance to our compound. Three kids, a husband, and a wife existed inside that metal box in 110-degree heat, day after day while we were there. After our team watched the kids playing with a plastic bag and a rusted spring in the street by our compound, I wrote to Carmen and asked her to make a trip to Toys "R" Us and send us some goodies. Ranger, John, and the others did the same. We ended up with a stockpile of treats, toys, and goodies for this family, and each time we passed their shipping container home, we stopped and gave them some token gifts. Sometimes, we included a little bit of cash and often dropped off a bag of fruit and vegetables.

It seemed like throwing bricks in the Grand Canyon. There were so many hopeless, lost souls in that city with no means to survive the war, famine, and disease racking the nation. But here was tangible help to five people we saw every day. The goodwill that grew between us touched all of us and left an indelible impression in my heart. Practically, it also made sense to do this because if we were in danger, they'd be more likely to tell us since they benefited from our presence. But that isn't why we started helping them. Americans have always done this. From giving candy to French kids during World War II to adopting orphans during the Vietnam War, we are a people who care, and we give to those less fortunate.

In Shangri-La, I think it was just a way to hold on to our humanity in the face of such overwhelming human misery.

I'll never forget the last time I saw them and bid them farewell. The kids were playing with toys my own kids would have played with at their age. One sat in the street, coloring in a coloring book with markers my thoughtful wife had purchased back in Virginia. Not so different, yet from circumstance chasms apart.

I came home more grateful than ever to be an American.

# 25

## HEADQUARTERS STATION

*Langley, Virginia*
*July–September 2001*

I returned home from Shangri-La to find Carmen and the boys in good shape. My oldest was already doing two-a-day workouts in the Virginia heat, preparing for his last season of high school football. My youngest boy was just about to start his freshman year at Fairfax High and was trying out with the freshman squad's defense. I knew with the job I would soon be taking that I wouldn't be traveling as much as in the past. After all the moves, the foreign stations, the long nights away from the family, I'd have the opportunity to attend my sons' games and spend more time with them.

I was fifty years old now, and that night I'd crossed the bridge with my grandfather in Cuba seemed like a distant memory. We'd moved on from the Cold War to an even more uncertain world still taking shape around us. For me personally, lots of change seemed in the works, too. I was starting the last third of my career, heading toward a new role in the CIA that would take me out of the field. Mandatory retirement age in the CIA is sixty years old. That gave me ten years left. I intended to make them as exciting and meaningful as the first twenty. One thing was clear: it was time for me to grow up and do some senior headquarters (HQS) time. That meant I'd be riding a desk, but I figured I could sneak away and get in the field once in a while.

I have never allowed myself much time to be sentimental or nostalgic. I'd learned a long time ago that you can't cling to the phases of life as they come and go. They are to be experienced as you keep moving forward, setting goals and staying on the path God intended for you. Still, it was hard not to get a little choked up when I thought of these past decades. The orphan from Cuba, the street kid from Miami. The Pararescueman whom the Agency rolled the bones with and gave me a life like none other. I was grateful for every phase, every experience. The way ahead? I'd never planned my career. I'd never looked down the road. I just kept focused on doing the best I could in the job I had, throwing my heart and mind into every assignment. That paid off throughout my career, and I was blessed with promotions and opportunities I will always cherish. But it was never planned.

The path I walked had always been made clear to me. Even in moments where I was at my most lost, there were signs that pointed me in the direction I needed to travel. And yes, some of the paths—like leaving Cuba or my divorce—were painful parts on the way to my chosen path. Now, as I entered the last decade of my Agency career, I was not about to coast to the finish line. I wanted to be in the fight in whatever way I could contribute. Beyond that, I knew the path would reveal itself, so I didn't dwell on the uncertainties that lay over the horizon.

Fortunately, the next couple of years were already in focus for me, thanks to Hank Crumpton and Cofer Black. When I returned to Langley, the coolest management job for any action-loving ops officer awaited me: Chief of Operations for the CTC. Hank had just moved out of that slot to become a Chief of Station overseas. The job was mine now. This made me the third-ranking officer in CTC under Cofer and Ben. We were the leadership cadre, spearheading America's effort against global terrorism.

If I had to take a desk job, this was the one to take. It was an incredible opportunity that gave me a chance to help evolve our response to terrorism's growing threat. It would also give me the opportunity to help groom future CT officers and maybe even get me in the field from time to time.

After all, age is not as big a factor in our profession as it is in the more kinetic careers. In the "special" side of the military, few officers will be leading action after making major (0–4).

First days on the job found me thrust into a new realm of political and administration battles. The House Permanent Select Committee on Intelligence wanted to know why we were funding the Northern Alliance in Afghanistan and giving them helicopter parts. Apparently, some of the committee members thought the Northern Alliance was composed of a bunch of drug smugglers. I had to explain to them the drug runners and poppy growers in Afghanistan operated in the south, protected by the Taliban. They also didn't seem to realize that the Northern Alliance was our only real ally in that country.

Meanwhile, we faced friction with the U.S Air Force on a critical program. The USAF kept wanting to charge us ridiculous amounts of money for the Predator drone modifications the Agency wanted to develop. Cofer believed in those mods and knew the Predator could become a deadly effective weapon against terrorists. Yet at times, Cofer grew so upset with the way the military behaved that he threatened to abandon the program altogether. Fortunately, he was never serious, and Ben always talked him off the ledge. But those meetings led to a lot of fireworks. In the end, the Predator ███████ turned out to be one of the most important assets ████████████.

The Predator was born after the Gulf War as a joint project between the CIA and the USAF. The CIA wanted a light surveillance platform that could loiter for hours undetected above bad guys, observing them with a sensor suite that included high-resolution video camera technology. The Predator fit the bill perfectly. It was light, quiet, small, and hard to see. With its fuel-efficient propeller-driven engine, it was capable of spending hours over a target. After al-Qaeda's attacks in the late 1990s, the CIA wanted to enhance the platform into something more than just a surveillance asset.

Starting in 2000, the USAF and the CIA worked together to develop an armed version of the Predator that could carry two AGM-114 Hellfire antitank missiles. While I was in Shangri-La, the first live-fire test was conducted in February 2001 outside of Las Vegas. Three missiles launched, three hits. It was a great success, ███████████████████ ██████████████████ advocating using the new weapon system to hunt Bin Laden in Afghanistan.

Just before I returned to Langley, the CIA and USAF created a replica of Bin Laden's Afghan compound at Tarnak out in the Nevada desert. There they ran simulated, then live-fire attacks on it with armed Predators, scoring a hit on a targeted room in the compound with a well-placed missile shot.

For all the potential, working with the air force was a constant strain for Cofer and Ben. At one point, coming out of a briefing after the air force demanded the CIA inject more money into the program, Cofer exclaimed, "Fuck them! I can't justify taking any more money from other operations. We're bailing on the Predator!" I looked at Ben, whose eyes told me: *Don't say a word, I'll take care of it.*

Despite the frustrations, everyone in the building knew the Predator's potential could not be abandoned. In 1998, after al-Qaeda's attacks on our embassies in Kenya and Tanzania, President Clinton struck back at Bin Laden with Tomahawk barrages aimed at supposed al-Qaeda targets in Sudan and Afghanistan. These subsonic cruise missiles were launched from ships and did little significant damage to al-Qaeda, though an aspirin factory in Sudan was destroyed. The TLAM (Tomahawk Land Attack Missile) was not accurate enough to conduct the kind of surgical strike conceived as our response in 1998. Worse, one of them failed to detonate when it struck near one of Bin Laden's training bases in Afghanistan. The terrorists recovered it and sold it to the Chinese, giving a global rival valuable insight into our weapon technology. The incident led directly to the Chinese military developing a copy of it called the CJ-10.

The Hellfire-armed Predator gave us a much more accurate means of striking back at these terror groups. Instead of launched from ships thousands of miles away, the Predator would be in the sky directly over the target area, watching it with its sensor suite and cameras. We would know if the people we needed to take out were on-site or not, unlike with the 1998 TLAM attacks when we just fired the barrage and hoped Bin Laden might get caught in it. (He wasn't; he'd gone to Kabul.)

The Hellfire was originally designed as an antitank missile for the AH-64 Apache attack helicopter. It was smaller, more maneuverable, and more accurate than the TLAMs. The test program so far was generally quite promising. The Predator looked to be able to fill a niche in ███████ antiterrorism toolbox. It was just a headache to develop.

While I experienced a bit of these internal wranglings and politics, my new role as C/OPS consisted mainly of overseeing every operation that the CTC ran. It was an incredible opportunity to get the thirty-thousand-foot perspective of the things we'd been doing in the field for decades. I went from being in the streets, eyeball to eyeball with America's enemies, to the operations center at Langley where we coordinated the entire counterterror war. Talk about going from a telescopic view to a wide-angle one! The learning curve was often like drinking out of a fire hydrant.

That summer of 2001, the CTC kept eyes on dozens of dangerous groups, everyone from Iran's Hezbollah Party to the Filipino jihadists of Abu Sayyaf in the Southern Islands who had just unleashed a campaign of kidnappings in June 2001 that included two American missionaries as their victims.

At this level, the CIA operates with delegated authority. The Agency is so large and there are so many people keeping watch on so many different threats that there is literally no other way to run the organization. For me, this meant our Group Chiefs had the authority to conceive, plan, and conduct operations. They kept me in the loop, asked permission when necessary, and carried on with an autonomy not found in many places today. We entrusted our group leaders with great responsibility and flexibility so that they could respond quickly to fast-developing situations.

Each day, I would be briefed by each of the Group Chiefs. They'd give me updates for ongoing operations, latest developments, and resources they might need to carry out missions.

The threats America faced that summer came from many quarters, but two in particular were seen as significant threats. Hezbollah was considered among the most dangerous. They had carried out operations all over the world that killed thousands of people. They also were responsible for the barracks bombing in Beirut in the 1980s that killed 241 U.S. marines. They were well trained in the dark arts of clandestine operations, highly motivated, and thoroughly supported, controlled, and directed by Iran. They represented the worst of the state-sponsored terror groups, and our Hezbollah section included some of our most dedicated and intelligent ops officers and analysts.

Along with Hezbollah, al-Qaeda remained the most immediate threat to the United States. Alec Station was now under "Rich." His Bin Laden unit reported alarming chatter from the terrorists. Rich and his dedicated team were convinced something big was in the works, but nobody could figure out exactly what it was.

It is hard for average Americans to understand just how difficult intelligence work can be. It is nothing like in the movies, where a set-piece puzzle is assembled throughout the film's running time. There's almost never an aha moment where suddenly everything fits into place and the heroes know where the bad guys are and what they're doing. It just does not work that way.

The intel on al-Qaeda came in penny packets and pieces. ███████
████████
███████████████████
███████

We didn't even know what the puzzle was, just that there were an awful lot of pieces that indicated an attack was coming. The CTC was so alarmed that Rich briefed Cofer, Ben, and me three times a week or more on al-Qaeda's activities. Everyone concurred an attack seemed imminent; that was never in dispute. The problem we faced was how we could penetrate al-Qaeda's operational security and figuring out what they planned to do.

After the embassy bombings in 1998, al-Qaeda attacked the USS *Cole* in 2000, nearly sinking a U.S. Navy destroyer with a suicide bombing attack. We knew Bin Laden's organization possessed a global reach. We knew they had the capability to carry out a diverse range of attacks. We knew they counted in their ranks jihadists willing to die in suicide attacks. This made planning an operation against us much easier since the trickiest part of any mission is always the postattack extraction of the team that carried it out. Bin Laden's attacks so far had been largely one-way missions. That gives them an additional advantage and streamlined their own planning.

Our black ops are designed not to lead back to us. With the proliferation of video cameras, facial recognition systems, traceable travel documents, and so on, post-incident forensics investigations make it extremely difficult to remain anonymous. Terrorists do not have to worry about that. They don't plan to survive the mission. Besides, they are always ready to take credit for their misdeeds. It is how they achieve fame, recruit adherents, and obtain further funding.

It was a maddening time, not knowing where they would strike. Some of us in the CTC believed Bin Laden would strike at the homeland. Others saw signs of overseas operations. The problem was, we simply did not have enough pieces of the puzzle in front of us.

We just knew they were up to something. That was keeping our analysts up late, culling through thousands upon thousands of cables from our overseas stations, searching for any clue that might give us a thread to pull on.

On September 9, 2001, three Tunisian al-Qaeda operatives posing as Belgian journalists secured an interview with the Afghan leader of the Northern Alliance, the CIA's old friend Ahmad Shah Massoud (not to be confused with his younger brother, Ahmad Zia, who went on to become vice president of Afghanistan). When the fake reporters arrived, they detonated a bomb concealed in their video camera that mortally wounded Massoud. He later died in a helicopter en route to a hospital outside of Afghanistan. One of the assassins also died in the blast. One was shot and killed trying to escape. The other was captured.

The news electrified the CTC. That al-Qaeda could conceive and execute such an incredibly complex operation as the assassination of the leader of the Afghan resistance left some of us astonished. That was next-level shadow-world ops. I think some in the intel community, even in 2001, viewed these terror groups as second-rate actors in the dark world—the bottom-of-the-barrel types who got lucky once in a while. Lucky? The synchronized bombing of two of our embassies and the *Cole* was not the work of "camel jockeys"! Still, many believed they were nothing like our oldest and most capable adversary, the KGB.

But this? Killing Massoud like that took vision. What was the objective? Bin Laden was looking at the big picture in Afghanistan. Taking him out redrew the balance between the Northern Alliance and the Taliban. It would set the Northern Alliance into disarray until a new leader could unite them again. Plus, it solidified Bin Laden's relationship with Mullah Omar, the head of the Taliban, the militant Islamic faction that seized power in Kabul and brought the Afghan Civil War to an end in 1996.

Conceptualizing the attack took considerable understanding of the hardships any assassin would face. Getting close to Massoud would have been difficult. His bodyguards were capable, hardened veterans, totally loyal to their leader. Beyond them, his Northern Alliance headquarters was always filled with scores, if not hundreds, of other loyal fighters. Massoud had survived twenty-six other assassination attempts. He was no easy target.

Bin Laden conceived a means to penetrate that security by preying on Massoud's one weakness: publicity. The Northern Alliance faced long odds against the Taliban. Massoud needed the world's help. A news team from Europe eager to interview him seemed like the opening he needed to bring his cause to the attention of the world. It was a devilishly clever scheme. The journalists were not searched, and penetrated Massoud's headquarters with guile, not guns.

Most impressive of all, somehow al-Qaeda managed to keep this entire operation secret. Bin Laden compartmentalized the mission, and his men adhered to strict operational security protocols. Though we were searching harder than ever for signs of impending al-Qaeda attacks, Massoud's assassination came as a complete surprise.

If they could do that, what else were they planning? For those of us in the CTC, that question kept us up long into the night of September 10.

# 26

## THE LAST NORMAL MORNING

*Langley, Virginia*
*September 11, 2001*

Tuesday-morning rush. Typical traffic getting into the office. I drove my vintage 1986 red BMW 635i into work at my usual 0630 that day, listening to my favorite country music radio station as the late summer sun rose. I'd slept like crap the night before. I suspected everyone had. I think Massoud's assassination left us all rattled.

*If they could do that, what else could they do?*

I reached HQS, parked, and went through the layers of security into the building. Twenty before eight, I posted up in front of Ben's office, waiting for him to come out of a meeting. Ben and Cofer shared an office area. Their secretaries had desks across from each other. Beyond them lay our bullpen of desks and cubicles. It was bustling as usual, everyone heads-down in their morning assignments. The bullpen was so large that they had actually posted "street signs" on the cubicle lanes to help visitors navigate the maze, with street names like Hezbollah Highway.

I knew both Ben's and Cofer's secretaries well by now. So while

I waited, I chatted with them, making small talk that concealed how unsettled I felt.

On the wall just outside of Ben's offices was a wide-screen television tuned to one of the cable news channels. At some point during our conversation, I glanced up and saw the World Trade Center on the screen. It looked like a telephoto shot from miles away, hazy despite the transcendent, cloudless blue sky over New York City that morning.

Smoke billowed out of the north tower.

I stared at the scene. The secretaries looked up and were riveted with me. Passersby stopped and saw the smoke on the television and moved closer to find out what was going on. Somebody turned up the volume, and we heard the announcer talking about an aircraft hitting the World Trade Center.

*Small plane. Accident. Happened in 1945 to the Empire State Building. Could happen now, for sure.*

"Mr. Prado?"

I turned to see our Federal Aviation Administration liaison officer standing behind me. By 2001, the CTC had become a true joint operation, filled with reps from every federal agency from the FAA to DEA, NSA, DS, ATP, the USSS, and so on.

Our FAA guy looked sheet white.

"Yes?"

"We have a problem," he said quietly.

I leaned into him. "What's going on?"

"Four airliners are not responding to us. They all sent distress calls. Since then, we've been unable to contact them."

*This cannot be happening.*

As if in slow motion, I nodded, then turned back to the screen, considering what do to. Just then, a blur moving right to left appeared on the news feed. An airplane, going fast, in a sharp bank. It disappeared behind the north tower. A split second later, a flaming explosion shot out from one side of the south tower. Confusion, gasps. Shocked cries filled the bullpen. All eyes locked on the scene unfolding.

One airplane could be an accident. Not two. And there were two more unaccounted for.

Cofer's Chief of Staff stood nearby. I grabbed him and said, "Send a cable to every station. Tell them we're under attack. Tell them to watch their six. And find out who is doing this. Hit all sources, leave no rock unturned. Cash every chip we have with our liaison services."

He nodded once and disappeared to get it done.

Flames boiled from both towers now. They rolled out of the shattered sides of both buildings. Transfixed, I almost felt the heat of fire on my face. Again.

In an instant, I was taken back to Miami, riding through the streets in a ladder truck, geared up and holding on to the bouncing rig as we sped toward a warehouse fire. When we got there, flames roiled out of the sides of the warehouse, wreathed in black, acrid smoke.

I climbed into the bucket with a brother firefighter, and the ladder team lifted us above the flames and over the roof. We needed to cut a hole so we could vent the heat and direct a hose right into the heart of the conflagration. I grabbed an ax and leaned out over the bucket, holding on with one hand as I prepared to swing.

The roof was made of zinc, and the heat below had made it as easy as paper to cut through. My ax came down again and again, ripping a hole until an entire chunk of the roof just fell away, leaving me dangling over a hellscape of furious red embers and burning bales of hay. It was like looking down over Dante's *Inferno,* the heat blasting me even through all my protective gear. My body shook, and I held on. The scene below seared into my memory.

I remember saying to myself, "What the hell am I doing here?"

A moment later, the bucket swung away.

The heat was terrifying. While with Miami-Dade, I probably responded to a couple of dozen fires in those early days of adulthood. Inside each one, I remember the furnace blasts of heat that hit in waves so powerful the visceral feel of them transcends time. You never lose that memory, that fear that must be conquered to go inside those burning hellscapes in search of anyone still alive.

There is nothing worse than burning alive. Nothing. It is every firefighter's worst nightmare, because we all have seen the horror flames visit upon human flesh.

"Oh my God . . . Is that a person?"

I jerked out of the memory. More shocked sounds from my brothers and sisters. On the screen, bodies fell from the upper stories of the towers. Falling. Inexorable, arms flailing, they plummeted past windows, story after story until they vanished from the camera's vantage point. An impossibly awful scene juxtaposed against the stark blue sky.

I knew at once. Our brother and sister Americans faced an impossible choice: burn alive in the furnaces their offices became as flaming aviation fuel drenched the buildings, or jump clear of the fires and heat to face the agonizing plunge to the plaza below.

The blasts of heat drove them over the shattered side of the building. And I understood.

I understood. Nobody could withstand that heat. Their last act was to choose the lesser of two ways to die.

And all because they showed up to work a little bit early that fateful and awful day.

People were in tears around me. Tears of horror. Tears of anguish. Rage. Fury. Impotent, we stared at the sight of the people we were sworn to protect dying in ways unimaginable before this late-summer Tuesday morning.

Something happened inside me that moment, like tumblers of a lock falling into place. What opened was every fiber of hate, fury, and vengeance I had ever felt. It poured out of my heart like blood from an open wound, pain-racked and agonizing. I stood there, feeling it course through me, watching the deaths unfold in front of us. I trembled from its power.

*I don't care what happens in the months ahead,* ████████
████████████ *of the motherfuckers responsible for this* ████████
*My career, my future, my path—it boils only down to this.* ████████
████████████████████████████ *They will have justice.*

It seemed so trite, so pathetically weak of a response in the moment
as we stood in the bullpen, safe in our headquarters building. But none
of us in there that morning had any doubt: we would respond, and this
wasn't like 1998. We were going to war with whoever did this to our
people.

Our FAA guy appeared beside me again. "Mr. Prado. The Pentagon's been hit by another aircraft."

It was a little after 0940.

They were hitting strategic and economic targets as well as our
command and control centers—all in high-concentration, high-casualty
areas. In minutes, word spread to evacuate the building. The headquarters of the CIA was a logical next target, and one plane remained as
yet unaccounted. An order came from the seventh floor ordering all to
evacuate the building.

People filed for the exits, heading to clear the building and get
home to their loved ones. In the CTC, almost nobody moved. Already,
workstations were being set up in conference rooms, maps of Afghanistan appeared on walls. We knew the CTC would be the epicenter of
this fight, especially at the beginning. Our first mission was to find out
who did this to our people and our country.

Twenty minutes later, we watched the towers collapse, engulfing the
fleeing people in the streets with falling debris, body parts, glass, and
billowing clouds of slate-gray dust that would cause lingering health
issues for tens of thousands present that day for years to come.

In that moment, I got a chilling vision that our friend John O'Neil
could be dead.

I'd first met John in the mid-1990s while doing my UBL gig. I actually
taught a class called "A Day in the Life of a Case Officer" to his agents
and analysts. More recently, I met up with him in NYC in 2000 just be-

fore I departed Shangri-La. I had to fly to New York City to meet with some FBI counterparts, and John was the Chief of the FBI's counter-terrorism section at the time. We got along well in spite of the reputed friction between our two agencies. John was an intense, laser-focused guy, and I think he saw that aspect of himself in me. He also had seen that I understood the threat we faced from Bin Laden. John had spent most of the late '90s trying to convince the bureau that al-Qaeda could inflict significant harm on the United States. He'd led the investigation into the 1998 embassy bombings. Later, after we met in New York, he investigated the attack on the *Cole*.

He was spirited, passionate, outgoing. A larger-than-life type of guy I couldn't help but to like and admire. While a colleague and I met with several FBI agents that day in New York, John greeted us warmly and invited us to lunch. There was no way we were going to say no to that.

He took us to his favorite submarine sandwich shop in the shadow of the World Trade Center. When we walked in, it was as if a godfather had entered. People approached John with near reverence, shaking his hand, laughing and talking to him. The owners at first wouldn't let John pay for our meals, but he insisted. Even after we sat down, well-wishers came over to say hello.

We ate great food and talked not like colleagues but friends.

I'd heard through the grapevine he'd left the FBI earlier in the summer. And he became the Chief of Security at the World Trade Center.

I knew that whatever happened, John O'Neil would never have abandoned his post. Somewhere in that monstrous growing cloud of ugly gray dust that was consuming lower Manhattan, John O'Neil lay dead or dying. Ten days later, we found out he'd helped survivors down to the street, then turned back and rushed back into the shattered buildings to save as many as he could. His body was found under the rubble that deluged Liberty and Greenwich Streets, his wallet still tucked into his perfectly tailored suit coat.

As Flight 93 spun into a field in Western Pennsylvania, the CTC burst into *find out who is doing this* mode. We culled the cable traffic, reached out to all our stations, searching for information and answers. Long into the day, even as the fires raged at the World Trade Center and President Bush addressed the nation, we worked to find out who did this.

Only a few of our people went home that day, even though the entire building was evacuated. Those who did leave went home to hug their families and secure childcare and came rushing back. Toward evening, with everyone at their desks feverishly culling for clues, our Chief of the Management Group, "Cash," broke the windows to our abandoned cafeteria and raided it for food. Snacks and drinks were passed out among the cubicles and offices. Better food would be forthcoming.

We worked long into the night. I know in the back of our heads, we wondered if Langley would be hit. By then, all planes were grounded, but if Bin Laden was behind this, who knew what follow-up attacks he'd planned. Suicide bombings? Light planes? We were absolutely a target.

Yet the vast majority of our people in the CTC stayed behind, ignoring their own safety.

Sometime after eight that night, I decided to walk the CTC and check on everyone. As I walked through the Hezbollah group, I spotted one of our senior and most talented officers still at her desk. Christie was eight months pregnant with her first child, and there she was still here, on the first day of a new war in a building with a big X on it.

My disbelief at her presence must have been all over my face. She looked up from her computer and greeted me. She was sure Hezbollah must have had a role in the day's attacks. She was furiously searching for a link that could tie them into this. So far, all indications pointed to al-Qaeda and Bin Laden. She remained behind with us because she did not want Hezbollah to escape our wrath if they had been involved.

When I think of the best people I've met in my Agency career, I think of Christie, alone at her desk in the worst moments our nation has ever experienced. She was there, ignoring her own safety and the safety of her unborn child to find out who had attacked our nation and killed thousands of our people. She worked through the morning, even as the building was evacuated and Flight 93 had yet to be accounted for. She stayed at her post until I finally discovered her there that night.

Eight months pregnant, in a chair for hours. She must have been miserable. Enough was enough. I asked her to get home, get some sleep. This would be a marathon, not a sprint. She wanted to stay, to follow up on a few leads. Instead, I tracked down one of our logistics guys and asked him to drive Christie home. She smiled through her exhaustion, picked up her purse, and headed out with him. She would be back in the morning at the crack of dawn.

People in our business frequently equate courage with a calm reaction under gunfire or in a tight undercover moment. Courage comes in many forms. That night, I saw a remarkable aspect to it I'd never encountered before: a woman so dedicated to our mission she was willing to risk her unborn child to carry out her duties.

After I watched Christie depart the CTC, I returned to my own office and worked until I fell asleep at my desk. The next morning, I noticed that many of us had done the same thing. For three days, I stayed in the building, showering in our gym and raiding the cafeteria for food. Around me, others did the same.

Cofer, who'd spent much of this time either briefing the president or meeting with our leadership on the seventh floor, set the pace. He was a machine, working nonstop with fiery energy. The attacks had infused him with a singular sense of purpose. The president ordered him to get whoever did this ███████████████. That became his mission, and nobody would get in his way.

The pieces began to fall into place within hours. All through the eleventh and twelfth, we listened. We asked questions. Around the world, we tapped our assets, called in every chit, exploited every avenue. The pieces we collected all pointed to al-Qaeda. The worst part was reading how these evil terrorist fuckers were celebrating their great victory.

The hours passed like a blur. I barely remember any of it, just the sense of pandemonium, the intensity and emotions of it all. At one point, on day two or three, one of our FBI counterparts, "Mike," came to brief us on what they'd learned. The evidence they'd developed pointed straight at Bin Laden as well.

"We're pretty sure this was al-Qaeda," Mike said. Then he added, "Thank God."

That threw me. "Why 'thank God'?" I asked.

"Because if Hezbollah was behind this, they would bleed us for months." I looked over at Cofer, confused.

"Huh?" I said.

Mike proceeded to explain that the FBI had uncovered networks of Hezbollah cells scattered all over the United States. They were functioning as smugglers, running drugs, black market cigarette cartons without the tax stamps, and other scams. The FBI strongly suspected that on a word from Iran, those fundraising cells could be activated and used to launch attacks throughout the country.

The FBI didn't think al-Qaeda possessed that sort of well-developed network in the United States.

"Mike," I said, "this is the first I've heard of this."

Communication between the FBI and CIA always had issues. We had different cultures, different ways of doing business. The FBI focused on building legal cases against criminals. We were under no such structured approach to our job. In years past, I'd run a program designed to show the FBI how we did business. I liked the FBI a lot and enjoyed working with them. Our own CTC FBI liaison was a great asset to us, and he often went to bat for us against his own people. Yet there were communication lapses, and that was something we clearly needed to fix.

Friday night, I left HQS and found my red BMW in the parking area. I was wrung out, smelly after three days in the same set of clothes—even with the showers. We knew we faced a long war ahead. This wasn't going to be a hundred-hour fight like the Gulf War. We were fighting an insidious new type of enemy—an actor without a state, with tentacles in nations all over the globe. I drove home through light traffic in the shadows of a summer sunset.

At home, I parked and wearily headed for the door. As I opened it, my youngest son flung himself into my arms. He hugged me so tightly he bruised my ribs. I hugged him back in the doorway, fiercely. Protectively. A rush of emotions hit me all at once.

Together, we went to find Carmen. She was cooking in the kitchen, just as she'd always done. It felt odd to see such a routine thing in a week filled with so many life-changing moments. Even in the midst of a crisis, Americans lived on. We went through our daily routines, even as the world changed overnight around us. There was comfort in that. It felt resilient. Like despite the soul-pain the entire country felt, we would get by. We'd be okay.

Then I saw the tears streaming down her face. She came to me, and our embrace was at once a comfort and a caution. These moments could be so easily taken away. In the past hundred years, our homeland was barely scratched by war. Now, our very people here at home, our loved ones, were the targets. As I held my wife, I knew there were families missing fathers, husbands, mothers, and wives in New York. The lampposts around Manhattan were covered with missing person photos, including John O'Neil's.

Civilians. Missing in action. Buried somewhere in the rubble at One World Trade Center, their families clutching to slender reeds of hope that the first responders digging at Ground Zero would discover a miracle and pull their loved ones from the wreckage alive.

I knew miracles would be in terrible, short supply.

My folks came to this country and found not a haven from communist oppression but heaven. All they wanted was a chance to build a life with their own labor and effort. America gave them that opportunity, and they thrived with this second chance. They loved this country like few people I've ever known. Even in the darkest days of the Vietnam War era, when protests and radicals made national self-loathing chic, my parents always stood for the flag and our anthem. Their loyalty never wavered.

For me, 9/11 was personal. It was a direct attack on my friends, my family, and my country. We were not going to be fighting for some abstract concept. This wasn't communism versus capitalism. We weren't about to send our troops overseas to protect an ally. This was about keeping our own families alive.

I would use everything I'd learned—every tactic, every trick, every tradecraft nuance—to crush the enemy that robbed us of our American sanctuary.

I felt Carmen crying, her head on my shoulder, tears on my suit coat. I pulled her closer, comforting her through my own mix of renewed rage and anguish over what we'd just gone through. There in our suburban kitchen, safe in the arms of my beloved, feeling her own pain even as she eased mine with her mere presence, I knew right then we could never take such a moment for granted again.

# 27

## THE PAYBACK BEGINS

*Undisclosed Location Overseas*
*September 2001*

"Mufasta" boarded the airliner, moving through the aisle until he found his window seat. He peered outside at the airport terminal, his first view of freedom in fourteen years. He should have been dead. A cold-blooded killer responsible for both point-blank executions and a mass-casualty event that killed or wounded 141 people, he'd been caught by an erstwhile ally's Special Forces team and taken down with three of his minions.

Condemned to death for his deeds, regime change saved his life. His sentence was commuted to life in prison. ████████████ years later, he was released.

His victims included people from around the world—the UK, India, Italy, Pakistan, the United Arab Emirates, and of course, the United States. ████████████████████

████████████████████████████████████████████████

Thanks to an astute analyst, ████ learned he would soon be released. A special greeting was arranged for this psychopath.

Mufasta thought he was flying home ███████████

████████

████████████████████████████

████████████

████████████████████████████████

████████████

████████████████████████████████

████████████

████████████████████████████████

████████████

████████████████████████████████

████████████

████████████████████████████████

████████████

████████████████████████████████

████████████

Mufasta sat quietly in his seat as other passengers boarded and found their seats around him. The last time he was in an airplane, he'd been dumped facedown and cuffed by an ally's Special Forces team. Since then, all he'd known were bars. His freedom seemed a godsend.

As the hustle and bustle calmed around him, passengers clicked their seat belts and settled down for the long flight. The middle seat next to Mufasta was empty, but an "Asian" male took the aisle. He nodded casually at Mufasta, synched his lap belt in place, and pulled a magazine from his carry-on bag.

██████████████████████████████████████████

████████████████████

This was scant days after 9/11. The remains of the dead in New York were still being recovered. The fires at Ground Zero still burned. The country was in a state of shock, reeling from the attack, grieving for lost loved ones. Wanting to strike back at whoever did this.

██████████████████████████████████████ Too risky. Too many unknowns. Lack of political will to strike back at these maniacs.

But now, the whole country realized we'd indulged these shitheads long enough. It was time to start taking them down. ████████████
████████

The flight took off, climbed to altitude, and began cruising at forty thousand feet. Mufasta glanced over at the man in the aisle seat.

████████████████████████████████████
██████████████████████████████████████████████
████████████████████████
██████████████████████████████████████████████
████████████████████████
█████████████████████████████████████████████████
████████████████████████
█████████████████████████████████████████████████
████████████████████████
█████████████████████████████████████████████████
████████████████████████
█████████████████████████████████████████████████
████████████████████████

The murdering psychopath spent the entire rest of the flight ogling a magazine.

████████████████████. Condition White achieved.

The plane landed at a scheduled stop in a different foreign nation. Mufasta's itinerary included a change of flights to grab a connecting one home. Passengers began to pull their carry-ons from the overhead bins. Others filed toward the front and rear exits. Mufasta's ticket put him in the rear of the plane, so he should have debarked via the back stairs under the tail. Unbeknownst to him, a van was waiting for him down there.

As he got into the aisle, he spotted a woman on a cell phone. Briefly, they made eye contact. It was one of those little moments that go unremarked a dozen times a day for average people carrying on with their lives. But in the dark world, that's a tripwire. Mufasta's situational awareness returned in a rush. He'd made one of the officers, and she knew it, too. Mufasta bolted for the front of the aircraft, rushing past her and pushing passengers out of the way.

A scramble ensued. If Mufasta made it down the stairs into the terminal, he'd be beyond ██████ reach. One officer contacted the van and told the driver to swing around to the front of the airplane.

Mufasta made it to the front exit stairs. He was halfway down, then saw the van, door open, waiting for him. Wide-eyed in terror, the terrorist spun around and ran back up the stairs—and right into ██████ Navy SEAL.

The Senior Chief stopped him in his tracks, spun him into a headlock, and said, "Welcome to America, motherfucker."

Seconds later, the Chief tossed him into the van, where FBI agents cuffed him. He was driven to an aircraft waiting not far away and was soon on his way to the United States to stand trial for his crimes against Americans.

Mission accomplished. ████████████████████████████ ███████████████████████

████████████████████████████████████████████Though he wasn't part of the 9/11 attacks, he was a fellow jihadist traveler. We needed this win ████████████████████████████████.

That success following so quickly on the heels of 9/11, it should have been ██████████████████ celebrated publicly. The country needed the morale boost.

████████████████████████████████████████████████

██████████████████████████ And the terrorists needed to know it, too. It didn't matter when they carried out attacks against Americans, ██████████████████████ Sooner or later, we will track them down and bring them to justice.

While the CTC focused on 9/11 and al-Qaeda—it had become clear within a few days of the attacks that Bin Laden was behind them—I'd made a point of telling our Group Chiefs to stay on their targets. This was the sort of moment in which other terror organizations would smell opportunity and come after us, too.

At the same time, we began ramping up our capabilities and team for the war on al-Qaeda. That meant going into Afghanistan and working with the Northern Alliance. We'd need somebody to spearhead our covert operations there who thoroughly understood al-Qaeda.

Nobody was more qualified for the job than my *tocayo,* Hank Crumpton (*tocayo* is a Spanish endearment for someone who shares your first name: Henry/Enrique, in this case). He'd been part of the team that investigated the 1998 embassy bombings as well as the USS *Cole.* He'd worked right alongside the FBI in their International Terrorism Operations Section for a year, focusing on Bin Laden and al-Qaeda. He had the creds, and he was aggressive, creative, and willing to take risks. He'd also been on the ground in the thick of things in the past. He was an operator who understood the street and how things got done at HQS.

Tenet and Cofer wanted him back. The covert operation in Afghanistan would be under the CTC's auspices, which meant technically he'd be part of the ops groups. This could have been awkward because he was senior to me.

I called Hank a few days after 9/11 at his new home overseas. He'd just taken his dream job as Chief of Station in a great country—heck, he hadn't even fully unpacked yet. My call came through late in the night in his corner of the globe.

He answered it at once.

"This is Ric. Get to the office. Call me on the secure line."

About fifteen minutes later, he called me back.

"Cofer asked me to call," I said to him. "This is not an order. This is a request. We are going into Afghanistan. We want you to organize and lead the war. Tenet has approved it."

He remained silent, waiting for more.

"I don't need an answer right now, but soon. Think about it."

Hank didn't need to think about it. "When do you want me back?" he asked.

I gave him another out. "You can think about it."

"I already have. When do you want me back?"

"Okay," I told him. "Get here as soon as you can. But take care of your family first."

"I'll book a flight now and let you know. Tell Cofer thanks."

"Yeah. And, Hank?"

"What?"

"All of us here, we knew your answer."

Hank later wrote in his memoirs, "At that moment, the only thing that matched my faith was my hatred for al-Qaeda. I wanted to kill them all."

We all did.

Not just those of us in the CTC. In the days that followed, people from different branches flowed into my office, willing to do anything to get into this fight. "John M." was a recent Chief of Station. He'd had an incredibly distinguished career, both in the field and here at HQS. Set to retire in a few weeks, he stormed into my office and announced that he'd tear up his retirement papers for a job in the CTC.

I knew John by reputation only, but it was a stellar one. He was a former college sprinter, a U.S. Naval Academy grad who'd served in the fleet as a nuclear engineer. He held an MBA and worked for a while in the private sector after leaving the navy. John was one of the few officers to infiltrate overseas tribal groups in pursuit of terrorists, including one particularly notorious assassin. He'd carried out covert actions around the world throughout his career. In the process, he became one of the most highly decorated officers in the Agency. His missions were so secret, however, that very few people below the seventh floor knew his deeds that earned those medals.

He would be an incredible addition to the team. I told him I needed a few days, but I'd get back to him. I called Hank. "I think I've found your deputy," I told him. "John M."

"I know John," Hank replied. "He's a great guy. But didn't he retire?"

"He changed his mind. On 9/11, he refused to evacuate and came to the CTC to do whatever he could."

"That guy's a stud. Yeah, I want him."

The new team was coming together.

From the flow of volunteers who came to me looking to help, two others stand out. "Tom" and "Bud" were both former officers who'd left the Agency for six-figure jobs in the private sector. They wanted back in.

That was the spirit that burned in all of us after 9/11. Our nation had been attacked, and we all wanted to fight back. When I see how CIA officers are portrayed in movies, I recoil in anger. We're painted as drug-dealing crazies (like in *American Made*), or amnesiac killers à la Jason Bourne. The truth is, we are patriots to the core. It defines who we are more than any other part of our identity. From that love of country comes our sense of service and duty to our people. It is a calling, not a career. The days after 9/11 drove that home when so many good men and women stepped up and were willing to do whatever it took to defeat al-Qaeda.

When Hank arrived in the building again, our seniority issue proved to be a moot point. I functioned for his group as a source for support and resources. Cofer, Ben, and I let him plan and execute what he thought was best. What they developed and engineered has been detailed in many other books, so here I'll just say that it was a brilliant, outside-the-box black op that combined operators on the ground with technology that seemed to come straight out of science fiction. A handful of CIA officers, and subsequently Special Forces teams, helped the

Northern Alliance regroup and help drive the Taliban out of power. It was a remarkable achievement, and the credit for it goes entirely to Hank and his remarkable team. They are a case study of what can be achieved with the right balance of intellect, aggressiveness, and a willingness to try new things.

The armed Predator drone system was among the new things ███ deployed to Afghanistan that fall. As American special operations teams went into action, they were heavily supported by airpower— USAF heavy bombers often flying from stateside bases along with U.S. Navy aircraft ████████████████ or carriers thousands of miles from the battlefields. The distances involved sometimes meant short loiter time over targets for the navy planes. Until we secured our own air bases in Afghanistan, that would continue to be a problem. Reportedly, some of the pilots flew twelve- to fourteen-hour missions, using amphetamines to stay awake between tanking up from aerial refueling aircraft. It was a grueling experience for them.

Meanwhile, the Predators could be launched ████████████ ███████████ without having to worry about pilot fatigue. Plus, their loiter time in the battle area was nothing short of incredible. It didn't take long for the Predator to become one of our most vital assets in the covert war in Afghanistan. ██████████████████████████ ██████████████████████ it paid massive dividends. History will remember the weapon like the World War II–era jeep and the Vietnam War's Huey helicopters. It was that influential.

Predator operations included looping the CTC into the missions. At our operations center inside HQS, we kept a team in place 24-7. ████████████████████████

████████████████████████████

████████████████

████████████████████ Ben, and I, along with a senior FBI agent working with us.

On a Saturday in October, I filled in for Ben at the "Predator feed center" while he had a high-level meeting in D.C. to attend. It never

failed to astonish me that I could ████████████████████████████
████████████████████ see in real time bad guys on the ground twelve
thousand miles away. The technology was positively futuristic. The
camera resolution, the near-instantaneous communication between the
drone pilots, the stakeholders, and the weapon platform itself relied on
satellite technology that seemed the stuff of pulp spy novels.

It was the next best thing to being there myself.

On that day, with guidance from multiple INTs (in the intelligence community, we refer to the different disciplines as INTs: SIGINT,
HUMINT, etc.), one of ██████ Predators discovered a heavily armed Taliban compound. This place was a veritable Afghan fortress, complete
with guard towers, antiaircraft weapons, one primary, large building,
and tidy rows of military vehicles.

████████████████████████████████████████████████████████
███████████████████

██████████████████████████████████████ A couple of fighter-
bombers raced to the area, but for whatever reason, their crews could
not locate our target.

The senior military officer ███████████████████████████ suggested one of the Hellfire missiles at the largest building to mark the
target for the navy. ████████████████
████████████████████████ The missile impacted into the largest
building, leaving a hole in the roof. The blast didn't do a lot of damage,
but it did cause an almost ant-like frenzy in the compound. Scores of
people bolted from the target building, racing around in all directions
in a panicked frenzy.

A moment later, about twenty guys emerged from the building in
a cohesive group. This was where our military background kicked in;
this group stood out to me and my SEAL companion Hal, who was
standing next to me watching the scene unfold. Armed with assault
rifles, they moved with military precision until they were clear of the
compound. Then they set a 360-degree perimeter with several men we
assumed to be leaders in the middle.

Those guys looked like senior people protected by a cadre of personal security types who really knew their business. From that moment, they became our target.

"Keep the Predator on those guys," I ordered.

The drone pilot adjusted course. The leadership group began to double-time farther away from the compound again in a tactical formation.

In 2001, Predators could only strike stationary targets. ▉▉▉▉ ▉▉▉▉▉▉▉▉▉▉▉▉▉▉▉▉▉▉▉▉

▉▉▉▉▉▉▉▉▉▉▉▉▉▉▉▉▉▉▉▉▉▉▉▉▉▉▉▉▉▉▉▉▉ that October, we had to wait until a group like this one wasn't on the move.

They kept moving. We followed them, watching their every move with the drone's camera beaming the scene to us via satellite on the other side of the planet. This went on for an hour. By then, the navy planes had to come off station to refuel and start the agonizingly long flight home.

Finally, the group reached an L-shaped building where most went inside. A few took up security outside in what looked like a shallow trench.

This was our opportunity. The Predator possessed a powerful laser that could be used to designate a target for another aircraft's laser-guided bombs. We waited until a couple of USAF planes reached the area. We coached them onto the building, then lased the target for them.

They dropped two bombs. The first sailed down to impact right in the space between each bar of the *L*. It smacked into the ground and failed to explode. Dud. Unbelievable. The second landed a hundred yards upwind, blowing up in open ground and causing no damage.

The leadership team boiled out of the building and started running for safety. The air force planes soon ran out of endurance, too. They headed for home, leaving ▉▉▉▉ Predator with one missile left to keep station over these guys.

For hours, ▉▉▉▉ the Predator played cat and mouse with these guys. Finally, they came to a tractor with a flatbed trailer towed behind it. It was sitting on a dirt road, and as our target group approached, the driver jumped out. A second later, a dog jumped out as well.

███████████████████████████████████████████████████

███████████████████████████

███████████████████████ The Taliban crowded around the tractor. A few of the men climbed onto the trailer in back.

███████████████████████████████████████████████████

████████████████████████████

I looked around the room. Everyone was vociferously worried for the dog. After all, we're Americans.

I turned to Hal and said, "We're trying to kill twenty-some people and everyone's worried about the dog." We had to laugh.

He smiled and shook his head. For a nation raised on *Lassie, Homeward Bound, Benji, Air Bud, Marley & Me, All Dogs Go to Heaven,* and others, I suppose it was too much to figure we'd fire without giving thought to the pup down there.

At the time, ███ aircraft could not fly below ten thousand feet. That was to protect them from the Taliban's known antiaircraft gun and missile systems. So we couldn't just order a gun run to strafe these guys as they rode along. Besides, we had another gap in our air support. Until they stopped and looked like they'd be sitting there for a while, all we could do was follow.

Nearly six hours after we first discovered these guys, they rolled up to a big, hangar-style building. The tractor came to a stop. The driver opened his door, and the dog leaped from the cab. Everyone in the ops center cheered.

A second later, ███ last Hellfire struck the trailer.

Our screens went black as smoke boiled up over the impact site. Everyone held their breath. Where was the dog?

The breeze blowing across the Afghan countryside soon dispersed the smoke cloud. Our view of the target area resolved into a horror show of broken bodies lying sprawled all around the charred remains of the tractor and trailer. A few men, still alive, were crawling toward the building. The dog appeared at the edge of the blast seat, unharmed.

The dog lived. The bad guys died. A win-win kind of a day if there ever was one. Later that day, when Ben came back from his meeting downtown and I briefed him on what happened, he was extremely disappointed that he'd missed it.

We all wanted a piece of the enemy that fall, even our most senior officers. In our eyes, the Taliban was just as bad as al-Qaeda. They gave Bin Laden sanctuary. They gave al-Qaeda logistical and material support. They allowed Bin Laden to train an army of clandestine warriors to carry out the fatwa against the United States he had issued in 1997. Bin Laden and Mullah Omar, the head of the Taliban, were personal friends, and al-Qaeda took out Massoud to curry his favor. Now, they were going to die, or be driven into the mountains and countryside by our Northern Alliance / special operations teams.

*That was for you, John O'Neil. And there will be more to come.*

As the fighting unfolded in Afghanistan that fall, the CTC kept tabs on many other terror-related crises around the world. The CTC was growing, flexing to meet the newest challenges wartime brought to us, but at times this left us stretched. Our answer was to work even harder. The people in the CTC continued to put in twenty-hour days, sleeping in their cubicles, on the break room couches. We showered and cleaned up in the gym. Our families saw little of us.

Even when we did make it home for events, we were distracted. I remember my oldest son's football team played Cofer's son's team one Friday night that fall. As our kids dueled on the gridiron, we sat on either side of the field, texting back and forth on our secure government BlackBerrys.

If we weren't at HQS, we were at home thinking about what we faced. We had epiphanies in the shower or while out exercising. Our families found us distracted at best, distant at worst. But this war—at least this phase of it—fell largely on the Agency's shoulders. We owed it to the dead of 9/11 to bring everything we had. Total commitment. The dedication I saw in the CTC that fall was second to none, and I will always be proud to have been a part of it. Blessed, in fact!

Very quickly, it became clear this was not a war that would know national boundaries. Yes, the nexus (for the moment) was Afghanistan. But jihadists allied with al-Qaeda operated on every continent. For us to disrupt their operations and keep Americans safe, those groups had to be dealt with as well. In late 2001, nowhere was that more evident than in the southern Philippines. Abu Sayyaf's campaign of kidnapping and murder continued unabated. Dozens of local Filipinos died horribly at their hands, usually by beheading. The Philippine Army units trying to track these cells down found the local population largely supported the terrorists, by fear if not ideology. Every move the army made would be reported to Abu Sayyaf by the locals. This made it almost impossible to surprise the terrorists. In fact, Abu Sayyaf sprang several ambushes on the army, inflicting heavy losses among its soldiers.

In response, President Bush offered American troops, training, and technology. The Philippine government accepted, with the caveat that our men and women could not conduct active operations. We would be there only as training support.

It had been almost six months since the Burnhams had been kidnapped by Abu Sayyaf. Pressure mounted on the president to do something about the two missionaries who had been celebrating their eighteenth wedding anniversary when they were captured. Finding them in the jungles of the southern Philippines in an area where outsiders were instantly viewed with suspicion—and often attacked—was an exceptionally difficult challenge.

As the hostages languished in the jungle, Senator Dianne Feinstein, the chair of the Senate's Intelligence Committee, reached out to the National Security Council and demanded a brief on the Burnhams' situation.

Briefing the senator fell to General Wayne Downing, then the new deputy national security advisor, who had come out of retirement to coordinate the war on terrorism. Since I frequently briefed the NSC and the general, I was tasked to be the Agency's rep at that meeting.

The two of us showed up at Senator Feinstein's office prepared to give her the rundown of the situation in the Southern Philippines.

She greeted us brusquely. We sat down in chairs, right across from each other, only a few feet apart. No pleasantries, all business.

"I want to know what we can do to get the Burnhams out of the Philippines," the senator said.

The question caught us off guard. We had no authority to initiate a rescue operation.

The general spoke first, attempting to outline the situation. Feinstein interrupted him, then cut him off. Clearly, she didn't want a briefing, at least not one to which she had to listen.

"Senator," I said, "I've been to that area. The terrorists control it. You can't just show up. Outsiders get their throats cut."

"What about sending troops in?" she asked.

"The locals tip off the terrorists to any troop movements. You can't move around in those islands without being seen or heard. A surprise attack is impossible."

Feinstein glowered at us, then in a shrill, cold voice demanded, "You mean to tell me that after all the money we've given to the CIA and the special military that we can't get our people back?"

I blinked. Was a sitting senator ordering us to carry out an unsanctioned rescue mission with Special Forces troops?

General Downing said, "Yes, Senator, we can do that. But we have no authority to do it."

"That's up to our government leaders to authorize. After all, if we go in there without host government approvals, that is considered an act of war," I added. That really set her bottom on fire!

We tried to explain the situation again, but she would have none of it. It seemed she was angry that we hadn't already unilaterally invaded an allied nation, descended with the full force of a SEAL or Green Beret team, and taken down Abu Sayyaf on our own.

For the next ten minutes, she upbraided us and our supposed impotence to rescue the Burnhams. It was an astonishing display of ignorance to the basic functions of how the United States employed its special operations assets. This coming from the chair of the Senate Intelligence Committee, who has been read into our world probably more than any other civilian leader in Congress, was especially disheartening.

When in history has a senator personally ordered a military operation be conducted?

Wayne tried yet again: "What you're asking, Senator, would be an act of war. Any sort of operation to get the Burnhams would require authorization from the National Command Authority along with coordinating with the Philippine civilian government."

She ended the meeting as curtly as it began, standing up and storming off in a huff as if we were beneath her. Worthless.

She didn't want a briefing. She called us there to abuse us. And by extension, the Agency and the military.

It was my first briefing with a United States senator. I remember leaving the room thinking, *Is that the kind of civilian leadership we really have?* Feinstein had a lot of power over the Agency and the military. Her scorn for both oozed out of her with every sentence.

And her scorn was directed straight at General Wayne Downing, a man who'd served his country for nearly forty years. He served in Vietnam, first with the 173rd Airborne, then as a company commander with the Twenty-Fifth Infantry Division, he wore two Silver Stars and the Purple Heart. In Somalia after Bloody Sunday, he went to visit the Rangers who'd been through that terrible battle. While there, a mortar landed practically right beside him, wounding several men nearby and nearly killing him.

In the hall outside her office, General Downing looked at me and said, "What would you give to have that on tape?"

I thought about it for a moment. "General, my left testicle."

As we walked out of the Capitol Building, I couldn't help but wonder how we were going to fight and win a war when some of our own civilian leadership had such little understanding of how to fight it beyond the optics and the political posturing for votes.

# 28

*Langley, Virginia*
*Early 2002*

What if we had killed Bin Laden in 1995? Billy Waugh, my old friend and mentor, legendary Special Forces icon, and CIA paramilitary contractor, had plenty of opportunities. He'd even come face-to-face with Bin Laden as he got out of his car one day in Khartoum. Billy jogged past him close enough to touch him.

The answer is clear, thanks to the history and hindsight. Those four thousand people killed and wounded in the U.S. embassy attacks in Africa would still be alive today, untraumatized, unscarred by their terrible luck to be nearby when those truck bombs went off. The USS *Cole* would never have been attacked.

The Pentagon would never have been hit by that American Airlines flight. The Twin Towers would still be standing. The three thousand people who died in the World Trade Center would still be among us, living ordinary lives of average Americans. Their families would still be intact. Their children would still have mothers and fathers. The rings of pain and anguish that rippled across the social fabric of New York

City, then New York, and finally the entire country would never have been released.

Arguably, there would have been no invasion of Afghanistan. No invasion of Iraq. Arab Spring probably never would have happened. Syria's descent into civil war? Wouldn't have happened. Libya's? Egypt's? Probably not.

There would have been no ISIS burning people alive in cages.

And what of Europe? If Billy Waugh had killed or captured Bin Laden in 1994, would waves of desperate, illegal immigrants from Africa and the Middle East have deluged the EU, increasingly radicalizing the Islamic population there?

The entire world changed the day Billy Waugh was not allowed to kill a single man, a known terror broker. A man whose machinations foresaw a world redrawn under the crescent banner of jihad and sharia law.

William Colby and Bill Casey both banned assassinations internally within the CIA in 1972. Gerald Ford issued his executive order banning them a few years later, which Jimmy Carter strengthened. Meanwhile, our Cold War enemies creatively assassinated dissidents and defectors with poison-tipped umbrellas and other deviously clever means.

While we fought a clean fight, the unscrupulous enemies of Western civilization changed the world right under our noses. Not for the better, either.

I know I was not the only Agency officer to dwell on this reality in the wake of 9/11. The missed opportunities in Khartoum, then later in Afghanistan, plagued us all. It rightfully later came back to haunt former president Clinton, whose reluctance to go after Bin Laden received considerable press after we went into Afghanistan. Many cognoscenti in the CIA place the blame of Bin Laden's actions squarely on Bill Clinton.

In early 2002, we assessed the Agency's performance and role since September 11, 2001, evaluating our strengths and identifying our weaknesses. We were doing great work inside the combat theater in

Afghanistan, where our officers, assets, and technology were busily carrying out Find, Fix, and Finish operations against the Taliban and al-Qaeda. The three *F*'s were military jargon for finding where the enemy is, fixing his daily patterns, and finishing their/its existence. This even as Kabul

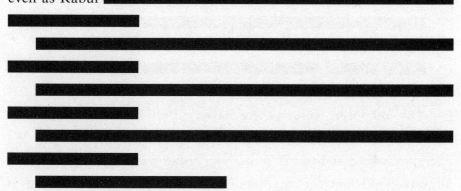

At a meeting with Cofer and Ben one morning, I mentioned this. He agreed that our counterterror efforts outside Afghanistan were almost anemic in light of the threat the homeland faced. We were still postured for the early post–Cold War environment of the 1990s, not a global war against a capable and deadly network of jihadists willing to die if they could murder Americans.

We needed a better way to react to cells plotting against us and our allies in other countries. After all, many of the 9/11 terrorists operated from Hamburg before they came to the United States for flight training.

Cofer listened to my brief on the subject, then gave me curt instructions: "You're my Chief of Ops. Fix it."

I left Cofer's office and went to work. As I crafted a concept, I drew upon every lesson and experience I'd had with the Agency for these past twenty years. I'd spent my adult life swimming in the shadow world, learning its rules and nuances. From my time working CT, I'd gained a thorough understanding of how these terror groups function and how North Korean criminals operate worldwide. They all had commonalities no matter their goals and purposes. Every underground network includes those features, and I set to work figuring out how we could attack them.

Throughout my career, there'd always been rumors of ultrasecret elite teams carrying out vital operations in defense of our country. We operators would sometimes talk about those rumors, and I think we all wanted to be invited into that inner sanctum; that "other Agency in our basement." But as I climbed the ladder, I learned that these rumors were just that. There was no ultrasecret elite operations team to join. It wasn't like James Bond or the agency within the Agency of *True Lies*.

We learned from our 9/11 experience that you cannot develop these capabilities at the last minute. I remember briefing Tenet on this and saying, "Sir, we cannot build the firehouse when our house is already on fire!" Then I simply proposed to Cofer that the CTC start a program that most ordinary Americans assume is in the Agency's toolbox already.

When I outlined the idea to Cofer, he loved it. Then he said, "All I need now is your recommendation for who's going to lead it."

"Chief, I already have someone in mind. Me."

With that, he threw me out of his office. "You have a job. Now go do it. And find me a team leader not named Ric Prado."

He didn't think a fifty-one-year-old member of the Senior Intelligence Service had any business returning to the streets. But that's exactly what I wanted to do; this dog could still hunt! After being strapped to a desk for many seven-day workweeks, my zest for doing ops hadn't slackened. Working as C/OPS was pretty sexy, and as advertised. But there was no escaping the fact that fieldwork called to me.

I left the office, but in my heart, I wanted this assignment more than anything else in my career. It would be a lateral move at best, so from a professional, career-progression point of view, it did not make sense. But developing a counterterrorism initiative capable of filling the gaps in our capabilities would be a tangible, and crucial, way to have a direct impact on the war. Plus, the things I'd learned over the course of my career made me a natural pick for the job.

We needed an initiative that could determine who and where the threats lay, and for that, we needed stealthy professionals with a long history of getting eyes on bad guys.

The truth was, information was a key resource in the war on terror, as important as ammunition or food for the frontline troops fighting in Afghanistan. In past wars, we usually knew who the enemy was and where to find him. Even in Vietnam, when the Viet Cong slipped through villages in civilian clothes to launch attacks on our forces, we at least knew that they would be confined to one geographical area in the world. Not so with international terrorist groups. They operated on every continent except for Antarctica. We had no idea who most of them were and had virtually no inside assets to give us a better picture of who and what we were dealing with in this new war. Contribution from our liaison partners was spotty at best.

Years of CT work convinced me the low-level true believers are the "useful idiots" of jihad. They're human missiles on a one-way mission of destruction and carnage. They're as expendable as a magazine of hollow points. Once it's empty, you drop it out and slap another mag home. They also receive most of the media coverage, as the attacks are designed to maximize shock and publicity.

Those guys are a dime a dozen. We could kill them for generations with drone strikes, special operations teams, JDAM satellite-guided bombs, with armored divisions and marine expeditionary forces, and they'd keep coming. Working against the Marxist revolutionary terror groups in South America showed me where the weaknesses lie in any shadow-world organization. I wanted to exploit those weaknesses and use them to really hurt al-Qaeda's many tentacles.

As the usual Prado luck would have it, my good friend and future boss, Jose Rodriguez, had also joined the CTC front office. JR was yet another of those godsent leaders to join the CTC at the very start of the war. We had a dream team in place. I knew we would win the war with men like that around me. They were aggressive risk-takers willing to do what was necessary to protect American lives. They thought outside the box, listened to new ideas and operational concepts. This would be the exact right time to develop new capabilities we could use to hammer al-Qaeda, as well as other enemies of our country.

I needed to be on the tip of this spear!

Later that day, I corralled Ben Bonk, Cofer's senior deputy, and the two of us went back in and pressed the case with Cofer. This time, we were successful, and Cofer gave me the job.

As we left Cofer's office, Ben waved me into his office and asked me to close the door. He extended his right hand to me, and with his left hand on my shoulder, he said, "Look, Ric, I know where your heart is, and I could not be prouder to call you my friend. Just understand that whether you fail or even if you're successful, this mission will be the end of your thus far spectacular career."

Ben's words haunted me as I drove home. What did he mean? I understood that at best this would be a lateral move, not a step up. But how could success doom my career?

In the years to come, my mind wandered back to Ben's words many times. They were prophetic indeed. But I did not care about that then, nor do I regret any of it now.

# 29

Construct

*Virginia*

*2002*

Once the new initiative was approved, I brought in guys like my dear friend Frog, a crusty twenty-five-year veteran of the SEAL teams and a navy Force Master Chief (more respected than a three-star admiral); the worldly ops guru and former USAF pilot "Caped Crusader"; the battle-proven Ranger and his good friend Chesty; and a five-language femme fatale, Lisa.

I invited a few members of my previous "Muslim Africa group," including surveillance experts "Taz" and "Buddha" and several CTC analysts and targeting officers like Joanne from the UBL task force, Jeff, and our NSA veteran Vogue (she was the best-dressed woman in the federal government, and deadly dedicated, too!).

I inherited my first deputy, Marc, and a young female operations officer, Jen. To this day, both are dear friends. Jen has risen through the ranks, and Crusader, Ranger, and Chesty are all SIS-4s in our directorate of operations. Last but not least was "Genghis," a retired Green Beret colonel who opted for the sure action of an Afghanistan deployment before he joined us operationally. Supported by the talents of a SIS-level admin/security officer of note, Cash, the ███████████████ was born.

Our targets were located worldwide.

There was not a member of the team who had not been touched in some personal way by the 9/11 attacks. I know that fueled my own drive. Anytime the exhaustion started to take hold of me, I would flash back to watching our people jump from the World Trade Center. Instantly, I'd be filled with rage—it was like an adrenaline rush. I'd throw myself back into my duties with all the passion and experience I possessed.

They say a professional never makes business personal. That was supposed to be our way in the clandestine realm as well. But after 9/11 and seeing those people fall to their deaths . . . all of it was personal for me and to every member of our team.

We trained for weeks on high-speed driving scenarios, full kinetic scenarios, and anything else our trainers dreamed up. They were endlessly creative. We spent hour after hour firing live ammunition in scenarios that got as close as possible to real-world situations. In the movie *Glory,* there is a scene where Matthew Broderick's character watches as one of his Union soldiers demonstrates his marksmanship. Standing, with no stresses on him, the soldier nails the target every time. Then Broderick steps up to him and starts firing his pistol into the air next to the soldier's ear. The stress of that quickly made him nonfunctional.

We developed a modern training system that incorporated real-world stressors. We rarely shot on a range the way you'd see at a civilian facility. Instead, we would move and shoot targets arrayed in different locations and from different distances. We'd shoot from behind cars and other cover. The point was anyone with practice and discipline can hit a stationary paper target from the ready position without any stress applied. We needed to be able to shoot accurately in dynamic circumstances. Our training reflected that, and our people rose to the occasion. By the end of our workup cycle, I knew that all our people we'd put into the field were deadly accurate shots in any situation with any of the weapons we'd be using.

We gelled quickly as we rolled through our training syllabus. At the end of our workup, I thought it important that we show Cofer Black the kinds of capabilities we'd developed. I invited him down to our black site to show him what we could do. I knew when we were done, he'd tell the seventh floor that he'd seen us flash our teeth.

In the early spring of 2002, he joined us at our remote black site, which was secluded enough that nobody would hear any gunfire or explosions. I escorted Cofer to the crow's nest, an observation deck that overlooked our shoot house.

A shoot house is an enclosed live-fire range, built to resemble the interior of a building, be it an office, a home, a bar—whatever. Elite SWAT and SOF warriors practice in these sort of facilities, as do special army and navy top-tier units.

Different types of ammunition can be used depending on the scenario. This includes live ammo and Simunitions, also known as sims rounds. While they sting like the dickens, sims rounds are not lethal and do not inflict bodily injury.

A couple of our analysts and support people joined Cofer on the crow's nest, where we passed eye and ear protection around to everyone. The crow's nest provided a great top-down view of the scene below. I made sure Cofer was settled, then went down to join the rest of the crew for the scenario.

For our demonstration, we set the shoot house up to look like an Irish pub, complete with a full-size bar on the right tended by a mannequin, and eight to ten tables in the general sitting area. The target perp, role-played by our communications guru, Coy, sat on a couch in the center of the room, flanked by a female mannequin and four mannequin bodyguards. Stacked outside the entrance waited our entry team, dressed in tactical black and kitted up with body armor, masks, eye protection, and weapons galore.

On my command, Ranger breached the door and pitched a flash-bang grenade inside the pub, which lit up the room. Even with their eye and ear protection, the audience above recoiled. Immediately, Crusader,

Ranger, Chesty, Frog, and I dynamically entered the room and shot the notional bodyguards using live ammo from our M4 carbines. We exited through the rear of the pub, where Jeff rolled up with our getaway car. We piled in and sped off.

Time on target: 110 seconds.

We fired ten to twelve shots.

Cofer came down to greet us and was as excited as I'd ever seen him, beaming with pride like only a "father" could. I told him that as good as this was, that scenario was not going to set us apart. Bystanders could have been killed or wounded, or a local off-duty cop might have been inside the pub. We'd thought through those possibilities, then developed capabilities designed to minimize those risks.

I asked Cofer to take a break, come back in an hour, and he'd see the *real* show.

For the second act, we were dressed in civilian clothes. As Cofer took his place in the crow's nest, I explained that no eye or ear protection would be necessary.

Inside the pub, Coy sat at his couch with the same mannequin tending bar. However, this time he had four live bodyguards. All were former tier-one special operators, independent contractors with the CIA. Their instructions from me were simple: play the damn role for real. If something raises your concern, address it. If all seems normal, then act accordingly. I did not want them to cut us any slack.

They fully understood the game; they were professionals. This time, we trickled into the bar without the forcible entry. Bourbon, one of my surveillance specialists, and I sauntered in, got two beers from the bartender, and started conversing in our native Spanish.

Crusader and Frog followed and sat opposite us, the former speaking in his favorite foreign language and Frog nodding (not understanding a bloody word). Ranger and the others casually walked in to take their assigned places. Then in strolled Jen and Mark, the latter my original deputy. Jen possessed an innate gift of gab so good that she could verbally out-spar a truck driver. She looked around at the place and immediately started bitching at her notional husband, Mark, at how dumpy the place was. The crowd above started to chuckle. Jen and everyone else played on, not missing a beat. The unhappy couple moved to the back wall of the pub, Jenn's complaining escalating. She went full Hollywood, and everyone above was distracted by her tantrum.

Suddenly, she turned and slapped Mark right in the face. He recoiled, knocking over a preplanted pitcher of ice.

The people inside our saloon roared with laughter as all eyes remained locked on the disturbance. A nanosecond later, my concealed handgun, loaded with Sims rounds, appeared right in the face of the nearest bodyguard. Ranger, Chesty, and Crusader did the same. That left all four tier-one operators paralyzed, staring at the barrels of our Glocks and subsequently prone, facedown on the floor. Frog duct-taped the perp, and off we went.

Time on target: ninety seconds. Shots fired? Zero. Collateral damage? Zero. A Predator drone or Tomahawk Land Attack Missile we were not. Surgical, deliberate, avoiding unnecessary casualties—that was our greatest asset to the war on terror.

At the debriefing, I explained to Cofer that this was our intended style. We were surveillants with teeth.

That night, we celebrated our final exam with Cofer at our black site compound. At one point, he told me, "If I brought in a hundred civilians and asked them to guess what your guys did, none would have any idea of what you really do for a living."

"Boss," I replied, "that is our goal."

Now it was I who was as proud as any father could be. We were formed, trained, ready. Cofer went back to Langley and told the "head shed" we were open for business.

It was time to see what we could do in the real world.

# 30

## CRYSTAL MARBLES

*2002*

One morning at HQS while we were still putting together an operational contingency, Jose Rodriguez came to see me. He had recently taken over the CTC from Cofer Black. He was an outstanding officer and leader, a man who made it clear from the outset that he believed in our mission. He was also irreverent as hell with a subversive sense of humor and no fear of unleashing it in even the most hallowed of places. While we missed Cofer tremendously, and I'd personally remained close friends with him ever since our time together at the CTC, we didn't miss a beat with Jose. He was an operator's operator—eager, aggressive, willing to take risks to strike at those threatening our country.

Jose told me that Director Tenet wanted to see us in his seventh-floor office. The summons excited both of us. My mind already started running through the options we had been working through.

Together, Jose and I headed upstairs, where we were in for a total surprise.

Jose and I reached the seventh floor and presented ourselves to Director Tenet's secretary. A moment later, we were standing inside the head of the CIA's office.

"Gentlemen," the director said to us, "mark your calendars. In a week, you're going to brief Vice President Cheney at the White House on the initiative."

Jose and I exchanged glances. This was our chance at last. If we got the White House on board with the new mission, and we'd be in business.

Finally.

I don't think my feet touched the ground once on our way back to the CTC. For the next seven days, my guys circled the wagons and built our executive brief. We went through every possible question they might throw at us. Every point we wanted to make was honed. This would be no PowerPoint presentation, no electronic trail. But I would have some key visuals to show the vice president that would drive home our capabilities.

The morning arrived, and I dressed in my best charcoal-gray suit and black Johnston & Murphy dress shoes. I grabbed my notebook and headed out the door for HQS, as excited as I've ever felt.

At Langley, Jose and I joined Director Tenet and three other senior Agency officers for a final run through of our brief. Director Tenet would introduce us, Jose would outline our concept, and I would explain our training and capabilities.

When finished, we were driven downtown in several black sedans. The drivers had no clearance, so Jose and I sat beside each other in silence as we watched the D.C. scenery go by through the car's tinted windows. It was a short trip, and we soon reached the White House gate, where the guards checked our IDs and waved us through. A moment later, we were escorted inside.

There I was, the dirt-poor kid from Cuba who grew up with almost nothing, walking through the center of American power with the senior leadership from our Agency. I savored the moment. Every step I took, I thanked my adopted country for the opportunities its freedoms afforded me and my family. I was here because the American dream made it possible. But I was also keenly aware of the price of that freedom—a price we were willing to pay if necessary.

This walk through the White House was the culmination of a long journey that started on that bridge with my abuelo back when the Soviet Union presented the greatest threat to the world. My story would never have been possible in any other country.

I said a silent prayer of thanks. I only wished that I could tell my mother and father. Someday, perhaps. Just not today. I never did get to tell them, and now that I am legally cleared to tell them, they are both gone.

Our escort showed us into a situation room deep inside the White House. Nothing elaborate but comfortable and functional. A long, rectangular table dominated the room, and extra chairs lined the walls. A moment later, Vice President Dick Cheney and then National Security Advisor Condoleezza Rice entered the room.

The vice president wore a dark suit and appeared to be all business. He possessed an intensity I immediately liked. Condoleezza Rice wore a suit jacket, light blouse, and dark skirt. She mirrored the VP's intensity. Introductions were made, handshakes around the room. Then everyone sat down and got to work. Cheney sat at the head of the table, Condi Rice to his left. Director Tenet took the opposite end of the table, and everyone else sat down in between. Jose was on the VP's right, and I next to him.

"Mr. Vice President, we are here this morning to brief you on a special capability we have developed," Director Tenet began. A moment later, he turned the floor over to Jose, who outlined our overall concept.

My turn came next. I started with our composition and the incredibly talented people who joined us. I gave a little background on them, making a point to highlight how much experience we possessed. I moved on to the training we'd undergone to develop and hone our capabilities. I added, perhaps unnecessarily, that this was a capability we needed to have in our toolbox now, before any future 9/11 events hit the country.

Both the Vice President and Condoleezza Rice asked questions as I spoke. It did not take long to realize that Condoleezza was an intellectual force. So was our vice president. After my run-in with Senator Dianne Feinstein, I was not sure what to expect that morning, but the difference between these two and the senator was dramatic. Feinstein could never hope to match the intellectual horsepower I saw in the room that day.

The meeting ended a short time later. As the vice president and I shook hands, he said to me, "It has been a pleasure to meet you, Ric, and thank you for the risks you are all willing to take. Please convey my sincere appreciation to your people. They're doing great work."

The meeting left a deep impression on me. Condi Rice in particular was poised and polished with genuine grace. At the same time, she possessed an authoritative air that commanded respect. One minute in a room with Condoleezza Rice and anyone could see she was a truly remarkable person.

Dick Cheney was the same way, but more physically intense as he entered and commanded the room. Not even President Bush, whom I had earlier met and admired tremendously, commanded similar presence. He made eye contact with me whenever he asked me a question.

I was confident that when the time was right, we would have the support of the White House.

While we waited for approval, we studied al-Qaeda's many tentacles across the globe. The reality was that we Americans often fight
our enemies under tremendous restrictions that limit our ability to save
lives. Our enemies operate with no such constraints.

That was a source of deep frustration for us. We knew these guys
were despicable, murderous human beings bent on supporting attacks
against innocents around the world. Al-Qaeda, though thrown into disarray in Afghanistan, still had active networks carrying out attacks. In
April, al-Qaeda operatives carried out a suicide bombing against the
El Ghriba synagogue, the oldest one in Tunisia. The attack killed fourteen German tourists, three French nationals, and two local Tunisians.
Thirty others were wounded.

On October 6, 2002, a two-year-old, thousand-foot-long oil tanker
called the MV *Limburg* was hit by a suicide boat, much like the USS
*Cole* had been in 2000. The blast ripped a hole in the side of the ship,
spilling ninety thousand barrels of Iranian crude oil into the Gulf of
Aden. The burning ship was towed to Dubai. One crew member died
in the blast, and thirteen others were wounded. This proved to be an
al-Qaeda operation as well.

Two days later, two jihadists attacked a marine unit conducting a training exercise on an island off Kuwait. The terrorists were veterans of the fall fighting in Afghanistan and had returned to their country of origin to conduct other operations against Americans there. The marines were using blanks in their rifles for this exercise, but some carried loaded pistols, and they were able to kill both attackers, but not before one marine was killed and another wounded.

So the threats were there. Al-Qaeda's senior leadership cadre may have been disrupted and dislocated from Afghanistan, but the tentacles still carried out operations.

We needed to be going after those tentacles, as well as those of other terrorist organizations.

Finally, several months after the White House briefing, I was summoned to Director Tenet's office for a briefing on our latest developments.

When I sat down in Director Tenet's conference room on the day we were scheduled to brief ███████████████████ I don't think I'd ever been more thoroughly prepared. ███████████

[REDACTED]

The DCI's conference room was well apportioned with beautiful luxury furniture, while the walls were adorned with photos of the director with presidents and other key officials. Signed books, oil portraits, and paintings completed the décor.

I found a place at the long, dark wood table with Director Tenet at one end, a few feet from its edge, leaning back while chewing on a Cuban cigar. Deputy Director for Operations James Pavitt sat down to my right, ACDCI "John"—who had come up through the analyst ranks—sat down at the table as well. The only other operator in the room was "Robert," the Division Chief [REDACTED]

Jose did not attend the meeting. He trusted me to give the brief and didn't want to appear to be looking over my shoulder. When we'd talked about it earlier, he said to me, "You've got this, Ric."

I had never felt more confident.

[REDACTED]

Robert made the introductory statement. When he finished, he turned the floor over to me. I began. As I did, I glanced over at Tenet. He was still leaning back in his chair, cigar in his right hand now. His eyes were fixed like lasers on mine.

They began to ask questions. Thanks to good preparation by my innovative and diligent crew, we had anticipated and prepared for everything we figured they would throw at us.

Before this briefing, I faced a panel led by a senior officer from our seventh floor, "Buzzy."

I was able to answer every question based on our rehearsals. My crew had anticipated every question posed to me around that table. As I fielded them, I could see Buzzy's wicked smile come to life as we engaged and destroyed question after question. We were well prepared and had anticipated all of them. Given the sensitivity of our program, there were no PowerPoint slides, just a black notebook with sketches and briefing notes.

Just then, DDO Pavitt spoke up. He looked like an Ivy League professor, with his frost-colored hair, white dress shirt and striped tie, and a huge signet ring.

"Mr. Director, as you can see, there is no doubt in our minds that Prado's team cannot only accomplish this mission but that they can actually get away with it."

But then he dropped the bomb: "However, Mr. Director, we will seriously need to look at the political considerations of this mission, even if it succeeds without a trace."

Tenet plucked the cigar from his mouth, leaned forward, and nodded at once. "Agreed." He responded a little too fast. I realized he and Pavitt had planned this response all along.

I looked across the table at Robert. The Division Chief was a meat eater, aggressive, willing to take risks, an excellent leader ████████ ██████████████████████ ████████████████████████████ We made eye contact. In that instant, I knew he realized it, too.

Robert abruptly stood up, closed his notebook, adjusted his Brioni suit, and walked out without a word.

I stared at the men remaining around the table, but this time, they refused to make eye contact with me. The shock of it left me numb.

What could I do? There were no options. I couldn't argue this. They'd clearly made the decision long before I'd ever entered the room. I could go full Scheuer on them, screaming and yelling ███████████ ████████████████████████████ But what good would that do? The decision would not be altered. There would be no credit to take, no success for the seventh floor to trumpet if we succeeded. And if we failed or were compromised, their careers would be on the line. In the mind of a politician, that was a lose-lose scenario. It offered them nothing.

████████████████████████████████████████████████
████████████████████

I stood up and left, the deep sense of shock making everything seem surreal and in slow motion. As I left Tenet's office, I knew this would be the last time I'd be invited to the seventh floor. Robert lingered near the elevator. He looked at his notebook, then to me. With barely controlled fury, he said, "Well. We'll just shitcan this."

████████████████████████████████████████████████
██████████████████████
████████████████████████████████████████████████
██████████████████████
████████████████████████████████████████████████
██████████████████████
████████████████████████████████████████████████
██████████████████████
████████████████████████████████████████████████
██████████████████████
████████████████████████████████████████████████
██████████████████████
████████████████████████████████████████████████
██████████████████████

When I went to tell Jose what had just happened, he seemed resigned. "I'm not totally surprised."

What did this all mean? It meant our team was out of business.

I had to consider their careers as well. I wasn't sure where my career would go from here, but my people were all extremely talented, driven risk-takers who believed in the necessity of countering terrorists.

They had bright futures ahead. I couldn't force them to stay in a team that would not be utilized.

"Jose," I said, "we need to review the validity of this. We can't keep some of the Agency's finest officers just doing nothing."

They deserved an opportunity to excel in their careers. Excel they would in the years ahead. Despite what had just happened, I could not be prouder of them.

Ben's words three years before came back to me over and over in the days ahead. *"Look, Ric, I know where your heart is, and I could not be prouder to call you my friend. Just understand that whether you fail or even if you're successful, this mission will be the end of your thus far spectacular career."*

I applied internally for a number of positions. The one I wanted the most was a spot-on position in Lieutenant General John Campbell's staff, where I would function as his Deputy Director for Military Affairs. He was the Associate Director of Central Intelligence for Military Support, an incredible officer, gentleman, and leader. It would have been a tremendous honor to work with him.

I didn't get the position. Years later, we ran into each other and talked about that position. He was astonished that I'd applied for it. "Ric, your name was never even brought in front of me. I would have loved to have had you."

That there had been some behind-the-scenes manipulation of candidates for the slot infuriated him, and it twisted the knife already stuck in my liver.

For six weeks, I applied for positions and heard nothing back. It became very clear that I was not welcome in the Agency anymore. At first, I had a hard time accepting that. Why? We'd been successful. I'd been a good soldier. I'd taken orders, I'd created capabilities. I'd led successful missions and operations all over the world.

Heartbroken, I put in my retirement papers.

In the weeks that followed, I was awarded the Distinguished Intelligence Medal (the highest medal presented to a retiring officer), the George Bush Excellence in CT Medal, and even a medal from the Directorate of Intelligence, presented by my dear friend Ben Bonk. Old friends came to see me, job offers from contractors flowed in. I sleepwalked through this final lap at headquarters as if in a dream. It didn't seem possible after all the fun I'd had. All the incredible adventures, the places I'd seen and the impact we'd had; these were things that I would cherish.

I never thought I'd go out this way. They say that the CIA is an ungrateful mistress. The careers of those with hearts like Bill Casey's too often came to crushing halts. Meat eaters do not politick well. Even though the Agency's origins in World War II grew out of the OSS's legacy action, risk-taking and aggressive operations in defense of our country, that spirit all too often does not burn bright at the top anymore.

Somebody once said that Tenet was an excellent peacetime DCI. But he wasn't a wartime one like Cofer Black would have been. Cofer was driven out as well shortly before I was. But he would have been an incredible leader as director in the war on terror, a man wholly consumed with a sense of purpose. And that sense of purpose was the destruction of al-Qaeda through any and all possible means. Men like Cofer bring victory. Fortunately, we eventually had Jose as DDO. But he, too, paid an excruciating price for his forward-leaning efforts to protect our country and his subordinates.

Cofer or Jose never weighed the risk to their own careers against those sacred tenets of our job: to protect our homeland and our people.

In two months, it was all over. The final farewells, the retirement parties and medal ceremonies. I turned in my security badge—the same color, same style as the one I'd started with back when I was a GS-nothing. There is no pretention of rank or status in the Agency, and those security badges reflected that.

My office cleared out. My personal things gone. I walked through the building a final time. As I left the lobby, I looked over at the wall of stars. When I first arrived here in 1980, I was young, in awe of my surroundings. A hard charger ready to make my own mark. Those stars seemed larger than life to me. The message was clear: we were a clandestine force willing to give all for our nation. Not a job. Not a career. A calling. The best of us embodied that.

But now the wall was personal, for some of those stars represented people I'd come to love as brothers and sisters.

I headed home, for the first time in decades my path ahead uncertain. I knew I was burned out. I turned down job offers because of that. I just wanted to process and be with the people I loved.

In truth, I needed to heal.

That first night home, no longer an officer in the Central Intelligence Agency, no longer of a rank equivalent to a major general in the U.S. military protocol, I selected a bottle of Italian Barolo from our cabinet, found the best Arturo Fuentes cigars I owned. Maduros. Dark and rich, very hard to acquire. Although Dominican, they were the product of Cuba via the tobacco growers who sought refuge there and brought with them their Cuban seeds. The smell of these gems always brought me back home to those days of my childhood and my grandfather's tobacco-rolling business across the street in Manicaragua. I've had a lifelong love of Maduros because of that connection to my roots.

My roots. I thought of the silver spurs my father wore in his wild youth. Gone. All the artifacts of my heritage wiped clear thanks to the thievery of Castro's revolutionaries. *For the people,* my ass. I spent half my adult life beating back Marxism and its cultish adherents. The zealots who drank the ideological Kool-Aid all acted the same, from what I saw in my family's hometown to the jungles of Central America, the Philippines, and elsewhere. They were just predators, everywhere they existed. And when they took over regions or nations, the people always suffered. And like my family, their own heritage was stolen.

These cigars remained like tokens of a lost way of life.

I took a Maduro from the humidor, the bottle of wine, and a glass, and I went out to the little gazebo we built in our backyard. Carmen and my sons knew that I needed some space. They watched from the house, periodically checking on me while I sat alone under a darkening Virginia sky and sipped my Italian wine.

I hurt. I couldn't lie to myself about it. I'd put up a good façade in the final months. I'd never shown my pain to the family, but I know they sensed it. How I dealt with it would determine a lot about my future and how I looked back at the past.

Scheuer had imploded, left the Agency, and had grown increasingly embittered and vitriolic after his experiences. I couldn't be that way. It would mean flushing all the good from twenty-five years of my CIA life.

Half of it. The best half spent in service of my country doing things I could only dream of doing as a kid huddled in that simple bed in a Colorado orphanage. I jumped out of airplanes. I led raids into hostile territory. I helped crush the ideology that took everything from my family.

I inhaled the cigar's rich smoke, letting it linger for a moment as the memories flashed through my mind. The river bridge crossed. My father's patient guidance, always setting the example with his own behavior. I learned to be who I was because of him. The action side, the steady side. The gentleman. With his meticulously arranged tools, he taught me everything had a place. With organization came order.

I smiled at that. Because of him, whenever I traveled, I arrayed my kit with the same exact care. Razor beside shaving cream. Toothbrush. Hairbrush, all arrayed with precision. Every time I went through that ritual in a new hotel, I thought of his van full of tools, not a screwdriver out of place.

It all began with my father and his love for me. I knew I had made him and my mother proud with what I'd done with my life.

Another sip of wine, memories spilling out in a jumble. For a moment, I saw myself as a young man, lying on the floor of a Huey helicopter and peering down at the wreckage of Eastern Airlines Flight 401, an L-1011 wide-body jet that had crashed into the Everglades twenty miles off the runway at Miami International Airport. Our PJ and air rescue detachment at Homestead Air Reserve Base was the first to respond to the crash. I was young, shocked by the sight of this aircraft torn apart on impact. The fuselage lay broken and scattered across the saw grass, the plane's wings mostly ribbons of aluminum debris.

I didn't realize my mic was open, and as I lay on my stomach looking down at the scene of destruction, I said aloud, "What can we do here? There can't be any survivors."

But I was wrong. When we landed, we encountered stunned and traumatized passengers limping from the wreckage, their clothes in tatters. Among them were the remains of the dead. Heads without bodies. Bodies without heads. A beautiful woman, not much older than my twentysomething self, had no visual signs of injury to her body, yet her eyes were unseeing and glassy in death. The rescue work began, and my air force brothers saved many people that night. I helped some of the walking wounded to waiting transports, the magnitude of the disaster imprinted forever on my young mind. Seventy-five of 163 people survived.

I turned away from that memory.

The bottle in my hand again, the thick red fluid flowing into my glass. I took a long drink and gazed up at the night sky.

*With how this all ended, what can I do here?*

████████████████████████████████████████████ They were all still out there, plotting, conniving, slipping through the cracks in our defenses and security to find ways to deliver another body blow to America or her allies.

████████████████████████████ The people these terrorists killed from here on out? That would be on us, the very Agency sworn to protect the country from such catastrophes. The result of decisions made that valued career more than the lives of our fellow Americans. In that moment, I felt like I was hovering above it all, looking down at the wreckage of what I thought my life would always be, looking for any sign of hope.

*I cannot let bitterness destroy all that I gave. All that I love. There is no path forward from that destruction of my past.*

I knew right then that I needed to always shield my family from this pain. I couldn't let their view of the Agency be poisoned by their protectiveness toward me. If that happened, we'd all sulk in bitterness in the years ahead. It would redefine us from an Agency family to something much darker and rootless.

My father did not raise me to become a malcontent.

The stars shone brightly now against the crystal black backdrop of a perfect Virginia spring night. Crickets sang. Carmen peered out the window from time to time, giving me space but checking on me quietly.

I closed my eyes. The memories came like a flood again without order or context. The opposite of my father's van. The mad-dash rush to a scene of an accident with Miami-Dade Fire & Rescue. The night I plunged into that Utah lake in the dead of winter to finally become a PJ. Lying in a doctor's care, as sick and febrile as I've ever been after the Agency evacuated me from my beloved Contra camps.

I thought of Dewey Clarridge and Bill Casey. The moment I was recruited into the first CT group from Ground Branch. We developed an attack technique for going after terrorists' camps with something more effective than distant TLAM shots. Two helicopters. A low bird with the assault element aboard. High bird tasked with providing support, using the door guns to hammer watch towers and gun positions as our team of former Green Berets wrought havoc on the ground. That VHS tape still exists somewhere in Ground Branch's archives.

Those were incredible experiences, riding through training exercises as we developed this technique.

Then I remembered the 1991 investigation ███████████████████ ████████████████████████████████████

███████████████████████████████████████████

████████████ There in the gazebo in my own backyard, I winced at that memory.

I had to make some sense of all this. Find order to defeat the chaos.

I closed my eyes and took a long, deep breath. My head cleared. I needed to purge the pain and protect the good parts of all that had happened. Order from chaos would start with dumping the baggage.

I imagined a jar made of simple glass, sitting in my mind's eye, empty. I set it down to my left. Then, very methodically, I laid out my entire career, one memory at a time. It stretched across my memory with soldierly precision, each waypoint on this journey neatly aligned to the next awaiting inspection.

Here in front of me were the tools of my own healing. I started at the beginning, picking each memory up to examine it for the lessons, the people, the operations, the successes and failures, the good I tried to do. And achieved.

For each I wanted to remember, I placed an imaginary crystal marble in my jar. For those moments and people who brought the pain, I visualized a dark, misshapen marble and tossed it away into the void of my imagination. One at a time, I picked through the memories of my career, saving the best and jettisoning the worst.

*Oh yeah, that guy was a shitbag. No sense wasting any memory space on him.*

A dark marble flew into the void.

*Dewey Clarridge, peering around a bookshelf in his immaculate suit, a colorful handkerchief tucked into his breast pocket. "Heard you were back."*

He always was there for me, a mentor in the shadows, looking out for his young acolyte with steadfast loyalty. It was hard not to love a guy like that. I placed his crystal marble reverently into my jar.

The more I thought through my career, the more that jar filled up. I had to reimagine it, enlarge it as I moved on through the '80s and into my time in the Philippines. Far fewer marbles ended up in the void than in my jar.

As I went through this process, I realized I'd been blessed. The Agency gave me a life surrounded by people whose loyalty and devotion were exemplary models for me. They were of my dad's character, cut from similar cloth. The path our Maker opened for me afforded me the honor to walk parts of it with them. That was an enormous life gift. How many people can say they've gone into harm's way with some of the finest humans our country produces?

Not many. I was among the lucky few.

Long into that warm night, I stayed at this process. When I finished, I'd purged the pain and the people not worth remembering. My jar was filled to the brim, each marble a testament to the value and good fortune I found in my journey through the CIA, and pararescue, which got me a shot at the Agency.

Carefully, I packed up every waypoint in my journey worth remembering. I tucked them away with the same order and precision

I'd laid them out for inspection. Order from chaos. Organization. The keystones of discipline. My father's gifts to me.

In the morning, I would order a jar, or perhaps a beer stein. I would fill it with real crystal marbles as tangible reminders of the life the Agency gave to me. I would find a place of honor somewhere in my house so I never would forget this night and the meaning I'd found in the memories.

Bottle empty, cigar now a stub, I stood up, turned, and walked into the house to face my new life filled with gratitude for my old one.

# 31

## NOT NINE-TO-FIVE MATERIAL

*Virginia*

*Spring 2005*

I tried the suburban white-collar worker thing, commuting into an office and clocking my nine-to-five before coming home to Carmen. It was a great opportunity with excellent compensation at a company that was growing and vibrant. After decades of dangerous missions, sleuthing under the noses of rival intelligence teams, and finding myself in tropical hellholes fighting Marxists, terrorists, drug, runners, and associated scum, I needed to experience a bit of domestic American middle-class normal. It was safe. It was routine, and I could knock it out in my sleep.

To be honest, my new normal quickly drove me crazy. Worse, I was driving Carmen bonkers, too.

As I was leaving the Agency, Erik Prince, the founder of Blackwater Inc., had offered me a job. I'd turned him down, despite his generous offer. I wasn't ready to jump from the Agency's spy world to the world of military contracting. I needed to explore a tamer version of life while I recharged. He took my refusal personally, which saddened me. I liked Erik a lot. We'd met while I was working in the CTC, and I always found him to be a devoted patriot and a genuinely compassionate guy.

We became friends. When his wife died of cancer in 2003, I attended her funeral.

In May of 2004, at Erik's invitation, we attended the Virginia Gold Cup, a classic horse country event that culminates with a steeple chase. Carmen and I were eating lunch at the Blackwater tent when Erik dropped by our table. Carmen is normally a very shy, reserved person in social settings, but Erik had a way of setting her at ease. After pleasantries, Carmen spoke up and completely startled me.

"Erik, would you please give Ric a job? He's bored and driving me crazy at home."

Erik lit up. "Are you serious?" he asked, then looked at me.

I thought about it for maybe a tenth of a second. Calm, quiet, steady days. Commuting in a sensible car. Cubicle dwelling. Suburban barbecues and tranquil Sundays spent reading the paper in my gazebo.

I wanted to barf.

"Yeah, we should talk again," I said, trying to play it cool.

*Get me the fuck back into the fight, brother!*

I started work at Blackwater a few weeks later.

While Erik and I came from very different worlds, we had one very strong common denominator: our love for God and country. Our friendship quickly grew from mutual respect. He was a former Navy SEAL who longed to be in the thick of the action. The founder and CEO of the most important contract security company of the war on terror would often stand right alongside his employees in harm's way. During multiple deployments to Iraq from 2005 to 2006, we flew together as door gunners in Little Bird helicopters. We also helped pull security in South African Mamba armored personnel carriers (APCs) while escorting convoys through "IED Alley" in Iraq. He was definitely a man of great personal courage who wanted to strike devastating blows against the enemies of his beloved United States. I could identify with that.

He brought me on board to build new capabilities for Blackwater. The company excelled at personal security missions, kinetic operations in combat zones, and supporting the deployments in Iraq and Afghanistan. Blackwater contractors also helped provide security along the Gulf Coast and in New Orleans after the devastation wrought to the region by Hurricane Katrina in 2005.

Blackwater's frontline operators scored some notable successes—and lost good people. In 2007, Iraqi insurgents targeted the Polish ambassador and his entourage in an upscale, normally quiet Shia neighborhood. They hit his convoy with three roadside bombs, crippling his vehicle and wounding ten people. The survivors pulled the badly burned ambassador out of the wreckage but were soon pinned down as the insurgents hit them with small arms fire.

Outnumbered and surrounded, the Poles called for help. The nearest friendly force was a Blackwater team that had no security contract with the Polish government. Nevertheless, on their own initiative, the Blackwater guys sped to their rescue. They drove the insurgents off and extracted the Poles, saving the ambassador's life.

Shortly after that incident, the Iraqi government made headlines complaining about Blackwater's heavy-handedness in Baghdad. No good deed goes unpunished.

Another time, a friendly compound came under heavy attack by hundreds of Shia militia. Every time army and air force medevac choppers tried to get to the compound to pull the wounded out, heavy small arms fire drove them off. A Blackwater Little Bird crew decided to risk all to get ammunition to the beleaguered men while extracting a wounded marine. Under heavy fire, the Little Bird crew reached the compound, touched down on a rooftop even as bullets cracked around them, and offloaded crates of ammunition for the men. A moment later, they pulled the wounded marine aboard and got him safely to the Baghdad combat support hospital.

While I did some time in Iraq with Erik, gunning Little Birds and rolling in those South African APCs, my main role at the company was to build its black operations capabilities to support the intel community (but not for the CIA). In that role, I recruited operators, foreign and domestic, from my worldwide contacts stretching back decades.

As part of my duties in support of Blackwater's business development, I recruited my dear friend Cofer Black and subsequently Rob Richer, a former Chief NE and ADDO. Both proved to be worth their weight in gold and brought the company plenty of high-end business. Erik never forgot that contribution (nor did Cofer let him forget: "We are here because of Prado"). For the first time in my life, I was making corporate money, doing what I loved best: "intel ninja team leader" work.

It is important to note that the support to the intel community that Blackwater provided was never a for-profit part of the company; our work in this realm was for the most part "at cost." Among other things, our job included tracking terrorists and other hard targets. In return, the federal government paid our expenses. This was not a business venture for Erik, it was a vocation.

To showcase our capabilities to potential U.S. government "clients," Erik personally funded several initiatives overseas designed to act as "proof of concept" for our new division in the company. I am comfortable speaking to this because it was a corporate venture and *not* a USG-connected effort. Basically, we wanted to showcase the remarkable capabilities we developed, thanks to our network of daring and inventive operators. In one notable instance, we created a completely fictitious persona for one of my foreign contacts so he could pose as a businessman from another country in his region. We carefully built an entire cover for him that included cover companies, bank accounts, addresses, telephone numbers—everything he would need to pass scrutiny should somebody want to see if he was legit.

Again, we did this totally on our own without any governmental involvement or knowledge, using Erik's personal financial resources. It was an exceptional moment for us, because what followed succeeded far beyond our expectations.

Thus equipped, the "new persona" flew into a hostile nation known for being exceptionally difficult to penetrate. Our asset intended to exploit that nation's interest in developing business ties with nations in his region. Sure enough, he was able to gain access to key governmental officials eager to foster financial connections with him. He collected business cards and later drew diagrams of every office and governmental building he was allowed into. If we could do this from a corporate platform, imagine the potential service we could provide the U.S. government!

After that unilateral operation, I'll never forget briefing a group of officials from a U.S. government agency on what we'd accomplished. When I handed them some of the material our man on the ground brought back, they were thunderstruck. In thirty years, nobody had pulled off anything like that.

In truth, we were able to be more flexible, develop more capabilities, and do more damage to the enemy than we were *allowed* to do at the Agency. Why? We were lean, committed to the mission for the right reasons, and we didn't have the competing tensions between safe career-protecting decisions and doing what it took to defend the American people. That was our greatest asset, and it opened the doors to operations we'd only dreamed of being able to conduct. We would put together an all-star group of experts, ██████████████████████████ ████████████████████████

Unfortunately, we have to leave the story there. Unlike the many stories that have subsequently leaked from our Agency days (*none* from me or mine), our post-Agency work remains secret, and we would have to obtain even more special dispensations to speak of these. Who knows, maybe in the future, they, too, will see some light of day. Much to be proud of, nothing to be ashamed of.

Nothing.

Through it all, I learned a key truth about America. Our nation does not lack warriors. Time and again, I saw the youngest of our brethren stepping onto the training ranges, eager to learn the skills that would make them a deadly threat to Bin Laden's legions. They wanted to strike back, defend the nation they loved as we did. They were wartime volunteers.

It was our nation's leadership that often failed to measure up. When you have pit bulls ready and willing to go after America's enemies, only to be chained in the yard by career-obsessed managers, you cannot win a war. It only gets prolonged.

███████████

A year later, ████████████████████████████████ my phone rang. I glanced down and saw the 619 area code and knew at once who it was.

"Hello?" I said as I connected the call.

"Ric," said Dewey Clarridge's polished voice on the other end of the line, "I need you to come see me."

I got on the next thing smoking to San Diego. Dewey and I had kept in touch long after he retired from the Agency in 1991. For years, he'd run his own company, contracting with the community as I was doing now. Back when I attended ██████████████████████████████ Navy SEAL training—BUD/S—to recertify on the specialized Draeger rebreathing system ███████████████████████████ ████████████████████████ While at Coronado among all the young eager guys, ██████████████ I stood out like a sore thumb.

At night, we'd go have dinner with Dewey. Always meticulously dressed, a perfect gentleman with a wicked sense of humor and a flair for drama, Dewey was the consummate host. He used to take us to a place in San Diego that we were convinced was run by the Russian mob. After all his Cold War battles, he loved the idea of sitting in a restaurant in the United States run by our former adversaries. The food was terrible, the waitresses hot. We'd sit outside in a usually empty patio, smoking cigars and drinking excellent hooch as Dewey regaled us with stories of his life overseas.

Later, I introduced Dewey to Erik Prince after he'd asked me what I was doing in my retirement. "Fucking with the bad guys," I told him.

He loved that, mainly because that's exactly how he'd spent his retirement, too. So I invited him to come see our fledgling operation. He arrived at the Blackwater office dressed in a Buffalo Bill–style buckskin jacket, huge grin on his face, eyes filled with life. I swear, the guy was ageless.

This time, I rented a car at the airport and drove into the hills north of San Diego. Dewey lived atop a hill in a beautiful home, a C5 Corvette in his garage. To dissuade any would-be car thief from poaching his gray sports car, he'd emplaced a World War II–era howitzer next to his beloved ride, its muzzle pointed directly at the driver's seat.

I parked the car in the driveway and walked over to the front door. A knock, and a moment later, Dewey was standing in front of me, wide grin, shaking my hand. He was casually dressed—for him, anyway—in a button-down dress shirt, khaki slacks, and expensive moccasins. Behind him, I saw one of his wife's cats cleaning itself in the entryway.

He ushered me inside, and I glanced down the side hallway off the entryway. Yep. The machine gun was there. He'd mounted an M1917 liquid-cooled .30-caliber Browning at the end of the hallway, pointed right at the front door. Anyone raiding the house would get a burst of World War II firepower from their nine o'clock blind spot.

We walked through his living room, which was covered with awards and framed photographs that served as signposts of Dewey's illustrious career. There he was with President Reagan. In another, he smiled alongside Ollie North. There were dozens of these moments immortalized on his wall with leaders from all over the globe.

We sat down on his back patio. The day was warm, but a gentle Southern California breeze took the edge off. The view was spectacular. Rolling hills, blue skies, California dreamin' at its finest.

He poured me a drink as we made small talk, catching up on news of our kids and families. As we talked, I saw the agelessness in his face was gone. Every man faces it sooner or later—at least the ones lucky enough to get to that point in life. Dewey was never one to go gentle into that good night; he was a fighter all the way. But in the end, Time always wins.

He produced a bottle of red wine, poured me a glass.

"Cheers," he said simply.

"Always a limey at heart," I replied and clinked his glass with mine.

He smiled at that—he had a sly, *the things you don't know* sort of smile that he often used when photographed.

This man was cut from the same cloth as Wild Bill Donovan. He was Bill Casey's go-to guy. Aggressive, daring. Willing to hammer our adversaries and enemies throughout the shadow world, he would have made an excellent wartime DCI. He hated the pencil dicks, the politicians who equivocated and dithered. He was action-oriented and knew the underlying nature of the CIA better than anyone else. Our job was to break the laws of other nations without getting caught to defend ours. It is dark and murky work. The press is never on our side. But those of us who understand the measure of the menace lurking in those shadows know the dangers our people face every day, even as they go about their peaceful routines.

How many schemes have we foiled? How many terrorists captured before they could carry out their plans?

I feared the country would never know, because the Agency tells few tales.

We finished catching up, rounding out the small talk with where mutual friends were these days and how they, too, were still fucking with the bad guys.

"Listen, Ric, we need to talk," Dewey said, all business now. "I have . . . certain very successful initiatives underway in Afghanistan and other parts of the world."

He paused a beat, then added directly, "I'm getting older now. It's time for me to get out of the game."

I suppose I saw that coming, but hearing him accept it made my throat choke up.

His eyes bored into mine. "These are superb initiatives, Ric. I want you to take them over. Are you interested?"

"Hell yes."

"Excellent. I knew you'd say that."

In that moment, I realized Dewey had passed me his torch.

# POSTSCRIPT

## THE FORTY-YEAR BRIEF

Mission: To preempt threats and further US national security objectives by collecting intelligence that matters, producing objective all-source analysis, conducting effective covert action as directed by the President, and safeguarding the secrets that help keep our Nation safe.

—*Central Intelligence Agency's Mission Statement*

It has been forty years since I first saw the wall of stars in the lobby at HQS. Since that first time in the building, I lived a life of adventure and meaning without regret in the service of our country. There is nothing more important to me than the sanctity of our union and the security of our people. As I grew up in the Agency, I took part in operations around the globe in dark alleys and deepest jungles. Along the way, I kept my eyes and ears open, learning all I could while applying those lessons to every aspect of my life on the path ahead.

I had no intention of ever writing about my experiences. The memories are more than enough for me. Fame is not something I've ever sought. A platform to espouse my views also held no appeal. I'd prefer to save those things for those more articulate than I. Since my days at the Agency and at Blackwater, I've kept my hand in the game, training the next generation's warriors with our company, Camp X Training. I continue to give back to my community by working at Fort Bragg, where our special operations forces train. I am also co-owner of Camp X Training with my legendary partner, Henk Iverson of Lone Operator fame. For the past seven years, I have been an instructor at the John F. Kennedy Special Warfare Center and School at Fort Bragg, North Carolina. I do several exercises during the year supporting our special operations forces: Green Berets, SEALs, Marine Raiders, and AFSOC operators. All studs.

If I won the lottery, I'd drive a faster car and wear a better suit, but I'd still do what I do with Henk Iverson and my coaching of U.S. Special Operations Forces. On the latter, I come in three weeks into the three-and-a-half-month program to show the young guys how to beat the other instructors in the war games they play. I am their mentor, the good cop.

I make no fewer than 170 new "special" friends every year. It's so rewarding. They approach me and say, "Sir, how do we get into Ground Branch? That's got to be sexy!"

I tell them, "Oh, it's not that special, not compared to what you do. I come here because I am in awe of *you*." One guy I had this conversation with had done eight tours in Afghanistan. I could tell he had bullet holes in him by the way he walked.

Even at sixty-nine, I relish the range time. Moving and shooting, defensive driving, the scenarios we create born from a lifetime of operations in the field—this is the way I contribute—and stay in touch with who I am and always will be, no matter how hard time pushes back. There on those training sites, I can impart the lessons of a career that spanned almost half a century and prepare young men and women in ways I never was.

A book was the last thing on my mind in my postretirement, non-retirement years. Carmen and I settled in a beautiful town. We had our painful moments, saying last goodbyes to my father and hers, then my mother a few years later. My boys grew up and became proud members of the U.S. military, one serving in combat overseas as the global war on terror dragged on in Iraq, Syria, and Afghanistan. My daughter was a school principal for more than five years and today runs a company providing oversight, best practices, and guidance to magnet and specialty charter schools.

At night, we'd settle down on the couch, Carmen and I together, like countless other American families, searching for a bit of entertainment on the television. The Jason Bourne movies, Robert Redford in *Spy Game* decades after he headlined *Three Days of the Condor,* Tom Cruise's *American Made*—the list is endless. As I watched these films about my beloved CIA and its people, I realized a truth about American culture: no other aspect of our government receives the amount of attention from Hollywood, the publishing business, and the media than the Agency does. Not the FBI, not the White House or Congress or even the U.S. military. The CIA is uniquely portrayed and almost always negatively.

And they never get it right. Not a single movie I've watched in the forty years I've been in the game has even come close to a proper portrayal of what I'd seen in the Agency. Robert Ludlum, Vince Flynn—they wrote brilliant novels, but the worlds they created bore little resemblance to one I lived through from the Cold War to the global war on terror.

The point was driven home to me on a personal level when a book was written in 2012 that purported to be about me and my life and career. It was part fantasy, contained many factual errors, including that some of the photos the author said were of me were not even me. I have no idea who they were.

The CIA's vow of silence mirrored my own belief in the persona of the quiet professional. Through the years, I avoided the spotlight. I avoided reporters. So did the vast majority of my peers.

But in the years since I left the CIA, I've come to realize that our institutionalized silence left a void. Into that vacuum came the movies, the novels, the salacious newspaper articles and melodramatic cable documentaries. We surrendered the helm, and others seized it. For decades now, we have let others drive the narrative of our own Agency. The result has been anything but an accurate depiction.

The FBI never faced this issue. J. Edgar Hoover realized very early on that to control the narrative of his agency, he needed to forge contacts within the American pop culture scene. For decades, the FBI carefully polished and crafted its image with the American people through radio shows, television series, movies, and books. The CIA has never done anything like that, and it has had real-world consequences.

The threat of bad press since the Church Committee hearings of the 1970s has created generations of senior leaders who are often more fearful of the media than they are devoted to the protection of our people. All too often, we are cautious when our adversaries are daring. We are risk-averse when we should be proactive.

How do you attract the next generation to our calling if the next generation only sees us as burned-out, amnesiac killers and drug-smuggling mercenaries? Mothers do not let their sons or daughters grow up to be CIA officers. Young men and women who would thrive in our ranks don't give the CIA a second thought. We've been tainted by our own country's pop culture image of who we are and what we do.

I wish that were not the case. Our people need to know we're out there in a world few understand and fewer have ever experienced. We're in the shadows there, listening, watching, whispering—for one purpose only: to protect our people and our nation from those bent on doing us harm.

I sat down to write this book as a modest attempt to help change the narrative. The CIA I knew included some of the finest, most dedicated, and most value-driven human beings I've ever met. They were principled, loyal to each other and to our flag. They recognized the threats we face on a daily basis and worked tirelessly to expose them before our fellow Americans were hurt.

The truth is, we foil far more plans than the Agency will ever admit. The vow of silence that has characterized the CIA since its inception ensures those successes go unmentioned for years, sometimes decades.

It would also be good for our adversaries and enemies to know that we are out there. They need to be looking over their shoulder—or, even better, discouraged to even attempt anything against us.

In the years ahead, as the world becomes increasingly dangerous, destabilized by non-state actors and rising superpowers, the United States will need the Agency's capabilities more than ever. The CIA falls between diplomacy and total war on the spectrum of action available to our presidents. We are the third option, and as we approach quarter-century, many of the threats we face exist in the realm of the shadow world, beyond the reach of diplomats and soldiers alike.

In the aftermath of World War II, the CIA was established to keep the pulse on foreign governments and nations who posed a threat to us. That Cold War paradigm defined the Agency for its first forty years. We battled Soviet-backed Marxist revolutions around the world bent on toppling regimes and spreading the toxic authoritarianism that embodied such ideology. But in the 1980s, a new threat began to emerge. Non-state actors—terrorists, drug cartels, and weapons dealers—found safe havens in corners of the world to operate against American power. We could not be directly confronted by such types, but with the support of the Soviets, Iran, and other states, they could strike from the shadows against us.

And they did. We learned on 9/11 that such organizations, even when not backed by a foreign government, could deliver body blows to our homeland and change the tide of history forever.

The attacks caught the Agency struggling to make the transition from the Cold War paradigm. We'd begun to flex to meet the challenges of these non-state actors, but we had yet to develop the kind of black ops capabilities needed to proactively interdict and disrupt their attacks against us. In some cases, our own rules were used against us. We discovered that the enemy practices excellent fieldcraft. They are capable of complex missions all over the world. Their operational security is nearly airtight. Their rank and file are true believers, willing to die for their cause. This makes planning and execution of major attacks considerably easier, as they do not need an exit strategy, just an adherent eager for the martyrdom of a suicide mission.

We learned quickly that our traditional methods of recruitment don't work at all with these people. We can't go to a diplomatic function and find a terrorist willing to work for us, as we'd been doing against the Soviets and other nations since the CIA's inception. That is the wrong paradigm for the new threats we face.

The answer to stopping these non-state actors lies in the shadow world. The only way to gain visibility into these organizations is to penetrate them by any means necessary. I learned long ago in the streets of Latin America that this is no gentleman's game, but it is a vital one that must be played. It is almost impossible to turn a terrorist. They are loyal ideologues or religious fanatics who cannot be bribed, bought off, or otherwise enticed into selling out their networks. More often than not, they must be compromised, and that requires resolute, strong-arm tactics that are not for the faint of heart.

Satellite imagery and SIGINT are useful tools but will never replace eyes on the street or assets inside an organization. Because of all these factors, the shadow world went from an ancillary battleground of the Cold War to the primary theater against terrorism.

That shift underscores the need for the Agency to have robust covert operation capabilities. Now more than ever, we need those skill sets to penetrate their world and expose their capabilities, plans, and networks. There is no other way to keep the pulse on our terrorist enemies.

Yet that is not enough. In the aftermath of 9/11, it became clear we needed the ability to interdict and disrupt enemies like al-Qaeda wherever their operatives lurked. That was the only way we could preempt their attacks and save American lives. In the combat theaters, this was not an issue, but terrorist cells flourish all over the world, including in our own country. It was up to us to figure out how we could discover them in these parts of the globe, then find ways to thwart them in places where we could not strike with military special operations teams or drones.

We lacked that capability. The enemy knew it and ruthlessly exploited it. They continue to do so today. The result? Our nation still has a major weakness in its war effort on terrorists, and it is one they continue to exploit.

The drone program, which the Obama administration expanded, is an effective tool in the war on terror. Yet it has its limitations and many pitfalls. All too often, there are innocents killed in these attacks, and that collateral damage always serves to create more terrorists. The drone campaign has become a recruiting tool for ISIS and other terror groups, ultimately breeding more terrorists than we can kill. While we have been able to take out key leaders with the Predators operating in Afghanistan, ██████████, and the Horn of Africa, those leaders are swiftly replaced by others from the ranks. And drone strikes do not exploit available intelligence from computers and cell phones, nor do they capture terrorists to be interrogated.

The limitations of the program reveal weaknesses ████████████████████████████ Drones cannot be used in cities. They cannot be used in certain nations for political reasons. For example, we cannot send Hellfire missiles into a car on a Norwegian highway—even if the person in the backseat is a senior ISIS official living clandestinely inside that nation's refugee community.

████████████████████████████████████
████████████████████
████████████████████████████████████
████████████████████████████████████████
██████████████████

Think of what the history of the last twenty-five years would have looked like if we'd wrapped up Bin Laden in the 1990s when Billy Waugh used to jog right by him in the streets of Khartoum. Think of the lives saved had we been able to operate against the al-Qaeda network that bombed the London subway system or blew up the trains in Spain in 2004.

In the years ahead, the shadow world will continue to be the front line for this new type of warfare thrust upon us by terrorist enemies. Terrorism is not going away anytime soon, and the chance of another catastrophic attack on our homeland remains real. In fact, it is probably only a matter of time. The only way to stop such a plan before it reaches fruition is to play in the terrorists' own murky world. It is a dangerous and amoral place. Historically, we've tried to uphold the Hollywood image of the white-hatted cowboy, rolling into Wild West towns to establish law and order. Call it the Lone Ranger syndrome. We want so badly to be the good guys that we often have crippled our ability to protect our people by our own strict rules of engagement. Think of a noble boxer adhering to Queensberry rules. That's the Agency. But our enemies ignore such niceties. They're the street-brawling MMA fighters to our boxer, willing to eye-gouge, nut-kick, and head-butt. They have no rules. Yet we insist on confronting them on our terms.

Time and again, we are outmaneuvered and defeated because our officers face an unfair fight. In the 1990s, our sense of morality extended to the relationships we developed overseas with people who could provide us insight and information. If their moral character was questioned by cubicle dwellers half a world away at HQS, we could not continue those relationships no matter how important or useful they were. White knights do not taint themselves with such associations, you see.

It isn't how local police departments stop crime. They work with moles and informants of poor moral character and sketchy backgrounds all the time. Same with the FBI. For whatever reason, the CIA is held to a higher standard in its actions overseas.

That may have made the people in Washington feel good. It may have helped with the relationship with the media. But it did not make Americans safer. Drawing those moral boundaries in the 1990s ended up being a great way to reduce our ability to detect the next attack against our people.

In forty years, I've learned another hard, unescapable truth: if we want to gain access into the inner workings of terrorist organizations, we have to do business with unsavory people. There are no terrorist white knights, only scum and associated scum who support their operations. If we want to gain visibility on what these groups are doing, what they are plotting, we have to use those people. There is no other way.

In the field, I learned to approach the dark realm and its actors as if we actually were cowboys, but the real ones like Wyatt Earp, who were skull-splitting bad-guy stompers. Justice and order do not come from playing nice. Guys like Earp knew that. It came from being the toughest, most dangerous badasses in town. Nobody fucks with people like that. When I worked the streets and jungles around the world, I made a point of letting every asset know that I would be their biggest friend as long as they played straight with me. But if they messed with me or my people, I would be their worst nightmare. In a place where there are no moral absolutes, that posture kept me and my people alive while laying the groundwork for success.

In the years to come, the United States will face a host of emerging threats. China is flexing its muscle on the international stage. They're not using the Soviet-era model of fomenting revolutions around the globe, but they are no less dangerous than our old Cold War adversary. They are more nuanced and subtler with the influence they've gained on every continent by using their financial resources to gain access to raw and strategic materials. Confronting the challenge of a rising China will be one of the Agency's primary missions in the decades to come. It will take courageous and daring leadership to succeed. Yet there will always be the competing tensions within the Agency between the meat eaters willing to confront those threats and the careerists mindful of the fallout any operation may cause. In truth, both are probably needed to keep the Agency balanced, but in wartime, as we have found ourselves in for the past twenty years, the CIA needs to be led by vigorous, aggressive, and fearless leaders willing to take the fight to the enemy on their turf, wherever that turf may be.

The torch Dewey passed to me on that warm California day will someday be handed off again. It is part of our cycle and tradition. The next generation coming of age will need to pick up this vocation with the same élan as every previous one. We need our best and brightest out there to be the nation's eyes and ears. Recruiting those incredible Americans will be as vital as the way we engage with our enemies and adversaries in the shadow world. This is the other main reason I chose to break my own vow of silence and put to page the lessons I've learned, the people I've met, and the successes I saw during my time with the Central Intelligence Agency.

To those reading my words and considering such a future: you will live a life few can imagine. The Agency is not a career, it is a calling, akin to devoting yourself to a monastic order. It becomes your entire identity. In its ranks, you'll be a very different kind of protector from our law enforcement agencies and military. We are the wraiths who operate where no one else dares to go. We find meaning in defending our people, even though those we guard will never know of our work. We are anonymous, invisible as shadows in the night.

If it is fame and fortune you seek, this is not the life for you. But if you want to work with some of the finest human beings you will ever meet, if you relish a challenge, seek a higher purpose, and want to live within a code of honor defined by loyalty and service, come join us. A world of adventures awaits.

# ACKNOWLEDGMENTS

I never had intentions of writing a book, and I never envisioned myself a published author. In fact, my only intention was to keep serving my country in any way possible and for as long as possible. My old boss and good friend Cofer Black was the first to harp at me regarding writing a book. At our frequent breakfast meets during our tenure at Blackwater, he would always end with "Ric, you are a good American; your story and career need to be told." A few years ago, when working on another of his literary masterpieces, Steve Coll called to interview me for his book *Directorate S*. Cofer brokered the introduction, as he knew I would not be favorably disposed to speak with any investigative reporter or even writer.

Steve spent a whole day asking me granular questions about post-9/11, about which Cofer assured him I had plenty of unclassified atmospherics. During our lunch, aspects of my personal life came up, and Steve further encouraged me to write a book about the CIA as seen through my eyes. Steve pushed back on my hesitation by saying that if I was really upset about how our Agency is portrayed in the media and especially in Hollywood, that I owed it to my family and colleagues to help clear the perception proliferated by the likes of Jason Bourne and

*American Made.* He even added, "I will help you find a publisher!" I was noncommittal, but my oldest son also encouraged me to write something for the family. "Pops," he said, "we don't have a clue what you did at the CIA. We don't want your story to disappear when you are gone." So I started a fleshed-out outline, but only for a family audience.

Fast-forward to 2018, when I got a call from my dear friend and mentor, Green Beret legend Sergeant Major Billy Waugh. Billy asked me to speak with Annie Jacobsen about a book she was researching, which had Billy as the main protagonist. Similar to what transpired with Steve also materialized with Annie, only that she immediately reached out to her literary agent, Jim Hornfischer. He, in turn, got me to New York City for a marathon interview with ten publishers, the most enthusiastic of which was Marc Resnick of St. Martin's Press. And as they say, the rest is history.

I want to thank Cofer, Steve, Annie, and Jim Hornfischer, without whom this book would have never left the family library. But they were not alone. Still fighting my hesitation, I consulted with two of my best Agency friends, Jose Rodriguez and Hank Crumpton. Both were very supportive and encouraged me to go for it. Marc Resnick for taking me under his wing after my literary agent became incapacitated. Last but not least, my writing coach, John Bruning, who so skillfully walked me through converting my "decent ops writing" skills into words that captured atmosphere, feelings, impressions, love, and other subtleties absent in CIA writing.

The true impetus for my writing is that I am deeply hurt when I see and read about how the CIA is depicted to the masses. At best, we are that pit bull chained in the backyard who is supposed to protect the homeowner from any and all harm. However, that loyal pit bull is never petted, thanked, or much less loved. In the worst light, we are a bunch of immoral—often rogue—mercenaries bent on carrying out illegal operations without presidential or congressional approvals. Bollocks!

The men and women of the CIA are the bravest, brightest, most dedicated, and most selfless I have ever been associated with. It is to them and their families that I dedicate this humble effort to clear our "Company's" name.

Of course, none of this happened in a vacuum. My life is rife with people, events, and circumstances that pushed me toward my God-intended path. In true form of Paulo Coelho's teachings, I was walking the path of the "Warrior of the Light." So I must start with Pararescue legend Chief Master Sergeant Wayne Fisk, who saw something in me during PJ training that I did not discover for myself for decades to come. To this day, he remains a close friend and mentor.

The list is endless, and there are many I cannot even name for security reasons. However, I must honor them in some form, even if it is in alias: Colonel Ray, my first CIA boss. Dewey Clarridge, a lifelong mentor of mine. "Cape Crusader," who was my last deputy and one of the smartest, bravest ops officers I ever worked with. "King Ralph," who gave me my shot at "Senior Grade" and who remains a trusted and admired friend.

Unfortunately, there is a plethora of colleagues who are no longer with us: Ben B., Les W., SF, and classmates Tim M. and Pat T., Jennifer Mathews, Mike Spann, Leon K., Glenn E., dear friend George B., dear friend Roy P., Frank A., mentor Jim D., former SFer Tom B., among too many others. And to my beloved Nicaraguan Contras who paid the ultimate price for the success of that mission.

Last but certainly not least, my family. I was blessed with the best parents possible. I am my pops's shadow, the fruit of his moral character, courage, conviction, and quick decision-making. From my mom, I inherited my thirst for reading and learning and her natural flair for always dressing the part. To my abuelo Emilin, who gave me his gift of cool under pressure. My beautiful and loyal wife, Carmen, the second love of my life, only after my daughter. Our three wonderful kids, all in dedicated service to God and country in their own very special way. I give no further details on them to afford them their own privacy, but I could not be prouder of them if my chest were twice the size. My cousin Manny—closest thing I have to a brother. And to my inner-circle "veterans of many adventures": Steve B., Mike B., BullDog, G. T. Robles, Michael F., Max V., S. M. O., and Godson Mike.

I also say thanks, one more time, to Monsignor Bryan O. Walsh for creating the Pedro Pan Program (Peter Pan), the venue that facilitated my legal journey to this wonderful country I call my home.

# INDEX